THE DEBATABASE BOOK
A Must-Have Guide for Successful Debate
THE EDITORS OF IDEA

Published by

international debate education association

400 West 59th Street / New York, NY 10019

The topics and arguments included in The Debatabase Book
represent the work of an international group of contributors with
diverse points of view. We would like to thank the following
for their contributions: James Action (UK), Heather, Begg (UK),
Kumar Bekbolotov (Kyrgystan), Matt But (UK), Joe Devanny
(UK), Thomas Dixon (UK), William J. Driscoll (US), Alastair
Endersby (UK), Alexis Hearndon (UK), Sebastian Isaac (UK),
Maryia Lahutsina (Belarus), Richard Mott (UK), Vikram Nair (UK),
Jacquleine Rose (UK), Jonathan Simons (UK), Andrea Stone
(US), Jason Stone (US), Richard Stupart (South Africa), Wu-
Meng Tan (Singapore), Hayden Taylor (UK), Bobby Webster (UK),
Robert Weekes (UK), Marc Whitmore (UK), and especially Wil-
liam J. Driscoll (US).

Library of Congress Cataloging-in-Publication Data
ISBN: 0-9702130-9-3

Debatabase book : a must have guide for successful
debate / the editors of IDEA.
        p. cm.
Summary: Presents background, arguments, and
resources on approximately 150 debate topics in
diverse areas. Includes the resolution, context,
pro and con, sample motions, and web links and
print resources.
Includes bibliographical references and index.
  ISBN 0-9702130-8-5
  1. Debates and debating. [1. Debates and debating.] I. International Debate Education Association.
  PN4181.D3945 2003
  808.53--dc21

2002153853

Design by Hernán Bonomo
Printed in the USA

▼ **IDEA Press Books**

• Table of **Contents**

Introduction

INTRODUCTION

Debatabase is a starting point on the road to participating in debates. The volume provides a beginning for those debaters who would like to learn about important topics being argued in the public sphere. Debaters can use this volume as a method of discovering the basic issues relevant to some of the more important topics being discussed in various public forums. It will provide debaters a brief look at some of the claims that can be used to support or to oppose many of the issues argued about by persons in democratic societies; it will also provide some sketches of evidence that can be used to support these claims. This volume is, however, only a starting point. Debaters interested in becoming very good debaters or excellent debaters will need to go beyond this volume if they intend to be able to intelligently discuss these issues in depth.

This introduction is intended to provide a theoretical framework within which information about argumentation and debate can be viewed; no attempt has been made to provide a general theory of argumentation. I begin with some basic distinctions among the terms communication, rhetoric, argumentation, and debate, progress to a description of the elements of argument that are most central to debate, and then to a discussion of how these elements can be structured into claims to support debate propositions. Following the discussion of argument structures, I move to a more detailed discussion of claims and propositions and finally discuss the kinds of evidence needed to support claims and propositions.

A caveat is needed before proceeding to the theoretical portion of this introduction. This introduction does not intend to be a practical, how-to guide to the creation of arguments. It does intend to provide the conceptual groundwork needed for debaters to learn how to create arguments according to a variety of methods.

Communication, rhetoric, argumentation, and debate

Communication, rhetoric, argumentation, and debate are related concepts. Starting with communication and proceeding to debate, the concepts become progressively narrowed. By beginning with the broadest concept—communication—and ending at the narrowest-debate, I intend to show how all these terms are interrelated.

Communication may be defined as the process whereby signs are used to convey information. Following this definition, communication is a very broad concept ranging from human, symbolic processes to the means that animals use to relate to one another. Some of these means are a part of the complex biology of both human and nonhuman animals. For instance, the behaviors of certain species of birds when strangers approach a nest of their young are a part of the biology of those species. The reason we know these are biological traits is that all members of the species use the same signs to indicate intrusion. Although all of our communication abilities—including rhetorical communication—are somehow built into our species biologically, all communication is not rhetorical.

The feature that most clearly distinguishes rhetoric from other forms of communication is the symbol. Although the ability to use symbolic forms of communication is certainly a biological trait of human beings, our ability to use symbols also allows us to use culturally and individually specific types of symbols. The clearest evidence that different cultures developed different symbols is the presence of different languages among human beings separated geographically. Even though all humans are born with the ability to use language, some of us learn Russian, others French,

and others English. The clearest example of symbolic communication is language. Language is an abstract method of using signs to refer to objects. The concept of a symbol differentiates rhetoric from other forms of communication. Symbols, hence rhetoric, are abstract methods of communication.

Still, all rhetoric is not argumentation. Rhetorical communication can be divided into various categories, two of which are narrative and metaphor.[1] Just to give a couple of examples, the narrative mode of rhetoric focuses on sequential time, the metaphoric mode of rhetoric focuses on comparing one thing to another, and the argumentative mode of rhetoric focuses on giving reasons. All of these modes of rhetoric are useful in debate, but the mode of rhetoric that is most central to debate is argumentation.

Argumentation is the process whereby humans use reason to communicate claims to one another. According to this definition, the focus on reason becomes the feature that distinguishes argumentation from other modes of rhetoric.[2] When people argue with one another, not only do they assert claims but they also assert reasons they believe the claims to be plausible or probable. Argumentation is a primary tool of debate, but it serves other activities as well. Argumentation is, for instance, an important tool in negotiation, conflict resolution, and persuasion. Debate is an activity that could hardly exist without argumentation.

Argumentation is useful in activities like negotiation and conflict resolution because it can be used to help people find ways to resolve their differences. But in some of these situations, differences cannot be resolved internally and an outside adjudicator must be called. These are the situations that we call debate. Thus, according to this view, debate is defined as the process of arguing about claims in situations where the outcome must be decided by an adjudicator. The focus of this introduction is on those elements of argumentation that are most often used in debate.

In some regards this focus is incomplete because some non-argumentative elements of communication and rhetoric often are used in debate even though they are not the most central features of debate. Some elements of rhetoric, namely metaphor and narrative, are very useful to debaters, but they are not included in this introduction because they are less central to debate than is argumentation. Beyond not including several rhetorical elements that sometimes are useful in debate, this introduction also excludes many elements of argumentation, choosing just the ones that are most central. Those central elements are evidence, reasoning, claims, and reservations. These elements are those that philosopher Stephen Toulmin introduced in 1958[3] and revised 30 years later.[4]

The Elements of Argument

Although in this introduction, some of Toulmin's terminology has been modified, because of its popular usage the model will still be referred to as the Toulmin model. Because it is only a model, the Toulmin model is only a rough approximation of the elements and their relationships to one another. The model is not intended as a descriptive diagram of actual arguments for a variety of reasons. First, it describes only those elements of an argument related to reasoning. It does not describe other important elements such as expressions of feelings or emotions unless those expressions are directly related to reasoning. Second, the model describes only the linguistic elements of reasoning. To the extent that an argument includes significant nonverbal elements, they are not covered by the model.[5] Third, the model applies only to the simplest of arguments. If an argument is composed of a variety of warrants or a cluster of evidence related to the claim in different ways, the model may not apply well, if at all. Despite these shortcomings, this model has proven itself useful for describing some of the key elements of arguments and how they function together. The diagrams shown on the following pages, illustrate the Toulmin model of argument:

The basic Toulmin model identifies four basic elements of argument: claim, data (which we call evidence), warrant, and reservation. The model of argu-

[1]- As far as I know, no one has successfully organized modes of rhetoric into a coherent taxonomy because the various modes overlap so much with one another. For instance, narratives and metaphors are used in arguments as metaphors and arguments are frequently found in narratives.

[2]- This is not to say that other forms of rhetoric do not involve the use of reason, just that the form of rhetoric where the focus on reason is most clearly in the foreground is argumentation.

[3]- *The Uses of Argument* (Cambridge, UK: Cambridge University Press, 1958).

[4]- Albert R. Jonsen and Stephen Toulmin, *The Abuse of Casuistry: A History of Moral Reasoning* (Berkeley: University of California Press, 1988).

[5]- Charles Arthur Willard. "On the Utility of Descriptive Diagrams for the Analysis and Criticism of Arguments." *Communication Monographs*, 43 (November, 1976), 308-19.

ment is most easily explained by a travel analogy. The evidence is the argument's starting point. The claim is the arguer's destination. The warrant is the means of travel, and the reservation involves questions or concerns the arguer may have about arrival at the destination. Toulmin's model can be used to diagram the structure of relatively simple arguments.

Structure of an Argument

A simple argument, for instance, consists of a single claim supported by a single claim, a piece of evidence, a single warrant, and perhaps (but not always) a single reservation. The following diagram illustrates Toulmin's diagram of a simple argument:

Simple Argument

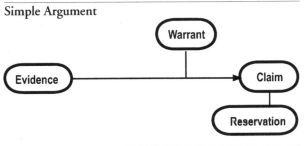

Toulmin illustrates this diagram using a simple argument claim that Harry is a British citizen because he was born in Bermuda. Here is how the structure of that argument was diagramed by Toulmin:

Simple Argument

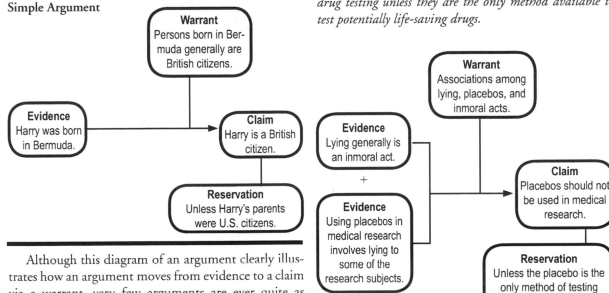

Although this diagram of an argument clearly illustrates how an argument moves from evidence to a claim via a warrant, very few arguments are ever quite as simple. For this reason, I have adapted Toulmin and Jonsen's model to illustrate a few different argument structures.

In addition to the simple argument suggested above, other argument structures include convergent and independent arguments. Although these do not even begin to exhaust all potential argument structures, they are some of the more common ones encountered in debate.

Convergent Arguments

A convergent argument is one where two or more bits of evidence converge with one another to support a claim. In other words, when a single piece of evidence is not sufficient, it must be combined with another piece of evidence in the effort to support the claim.

Convergent argument

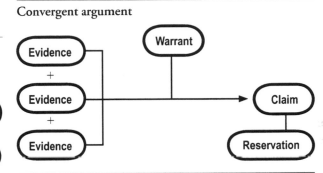

Consider as an illustration, the following convergent argument:

Lying is generally considered an immoral act. The use of placebos in drug testing research involves lying because some of the subjects are led falsely to believe they are being given real drugs. Therefore, placebos should not be used in drug testing unless they are the only method available to test potentially life-saving drugs.

This particular argument begins with two pieces of evidence. The first piece involves the value statement that "lying generally is considered an immoral act." This piece of evidence is a statement that is consistent with the audience's values regarding lying. The second piece of evidence is the factual statement that "the use of placebos in medical research involves a form of lying." The second piece of evidence involves the fact that when a researcher gives a placebo (e.g., a sugar pill) to a portion of the subjects in a study of a potentially life-saving drug, that researcher is lying to those subjects as they are led to believe that they are receiving a drug that may save their lives. The warrant then combines the evidence with a familiar pattern of reasoning—in this case, if an act in general is immoral then any particular instance of that act is likewise immoral. If lying is immoral in general, then using placebos in particular is also immoral.

The claim results from a convergence of the pieces of evidence and the warrant. In some instances, an arguer may not wish to hold to this claim in all circumstances. If the arguer wishes to define specific situations in which the claim does not hold, then the arguer adds a reservation to the argument. In this case, a reservation seems perfectly appropriate. Even though the arguer may generally object to lying and to the use of placebos, the arguer may wish to exempt situations where the use of a placebo is the "only method of testing a potentially life-saving drug."

The unique feature of the convergent structure of argument is that the arguer produces a collection of evidence that, if taken together, supports the claim. The structure of the argument is such that all of the evidence must be believed for the argument to be supported. If the audience does not accept any one piece of evidence, the entire argument structure falls. On the other hand, the independent argument structure is such that any single piece of evidence can provide sufficient support for the argument.

Independent Arguments

An arguer using an independent argument structure presents several pieces of evidence, any one of which provides sufficient support for the argument. In other words, a debater may present three pieces of evidence and claim that the members of the audience should accept the claim even if they are convinced only by a single piece of evidence. The following diagram illustrates the structure of an independent argument:

Independent Arguments

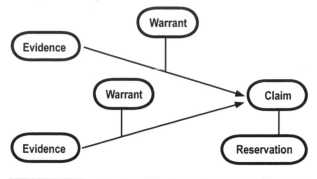

Take for instance the following argument against capital punishment:

On moral grounds, capital punishment ought to be abolished. If a society considers a murder immoral for taking a human life, how can that society then turn around and take the life of the murderer. Beyond moral grounds, capital punishment ought to be abolished because unlike other punishments, it alone is irreversible. If evidence is discovered after the execution, there is no way to bring the unjustly executed person back to life.

This argument about capital punishment can be represented in the following diagram:

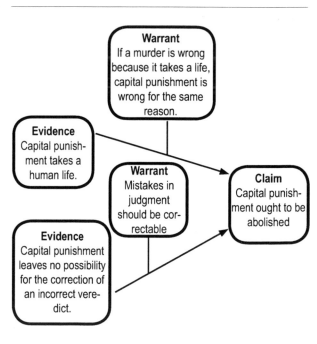

This example of an independent argument structure is based on two pieces of evidence, either of which is strong enough to support the claim that capital punishment ought to be abolished. The first piece of evidence involves the value of taking a human life, while the second involves the value of being able to correct a mistake. According to this argument, capital punishment ought to be abolished even if only one of the items of evidence is believed by the audience. The moral stricture against taking a life is, by itself, a sufficient reason to oppose capital punishment as is the danger of making an uncorrectable mistake. The strategic advantage of this form of argument structure is obvious. Whereas with convergent structures, the loss of one part of the argument endangers the entire argument, in the independent structure, the argument can prevail even if only a part of it survives.

The Toulmin diagram of an argument is useful because it illustrates the various parts of an argument and shows how they function together as a whole. The modifications with regard to argument structure make it even more useful. Still, the model has its shortcomings. One difficulty with the Toulmin diagram is that it does not provide any details regarding some of the elements. Some questions that the diagram leaves unanswered include:

- What are the different kinds of claims?
- How can different claims be combined to support various propositions?
- What are the different forms of evidence?
- What are the different kinds of argumentative warrants?
- What distinguishes good arguments from bad ones?

Claims and Propositions

Conceptually claims and propositions are the same kind of argumentative elements. Both are controversial statements that need reason for support. Both claims and propositions are created by a relationship between evidence and a warrant. Frequently, debaters combine several of these statements to support another statement. Each of the initial statements is a claim and the concluding statement is called a proposition.

Types of Claims and Propositions

Most authors divide claims and propositions into the traditional categories of fact, value, and policy. I have chosen not to use these traditional categories for two reasons. First, the traditional categories have no place for some important kinds of propositions that are not facts, or values, or policy. More specifically, the traditional categories have no place for propositions that seek to define concepts nor for propositions that seek to establish relationships between or among concepts. Second, the traditional categories separate evaluative and policy propositions while the system used here will consider propositions of policy as a specific kind of evaluative proposition. I use four main categories of propositions: definition, description, relationship, and evaluation. These categories, while they may not be exhaustive or mutually exclusive, provide a coherent system for the discussion of claims.

Definitions

Definitions answer the question, "Does it serve our purposes to say that Z is the proper definition of X?"[6] Arguing for a claim of definition involves two steps: positing the definition and making an argument for that definition. In carrying out the first step, one simply states that "X" is defined in this way. "Rhetoric is an action humans perform when they use symbols for the purpose of communicating with one another."[7] This sentence posits a definition of rhetoric.

Much of the time arguers perform the first step of positing a definition without constructing an argument to support it. They may do this because their audience does not require them to make an explicit argument in favor of the definition. The definition may, by itself, create a frame of mind in the audience that does not lead the audience to demand an argument in support of the definition. For instance, antiabortion forces in the United States succeeded in defining a procedure physicians called "intact dilation and extraction" as "partial-birth abortion."[8] Their definition was successful because it dominated the discourse on abortion and turned the controversy away from the issue of choice and toward a particular medical procedure that antiabortion forces could use more successfully. On the surface, the definition of "intact dilation and extraction" as "partial-birth abortion" may have seemed so sensible

[6]- Perhaps a more accurate way of stating the question is "Does it best serve our purposes to say that Z is the proper definition of X." This way of phrasing the question more clearly identifies the value dimensions of definitions–dimensions that will be discussed more fully later.

[7]- Sonja K. Foss, Karen A. Foss, & Robert Trapp. *Contemporary Perspectives on Rhetoric*. Prospect Heights, Illinois: Waveland, 1991, pp. 14

[8]- David Zarefsky, "Definitions." Keynote address to the Tenth NCA/AFA Summer Argumentation Conference, Alta, Utah, August 1997.

that no further argument was required.

An argument to support a claim of definition becomes necessary when the audience refuses to accept the definition that was posited without a supporting argument. An arguer's opponent will frequently encourage the audience to demand support for a definition. When antiabortion advocates defined their position as "pro-life," some in the "pro-choice" movement objected, claiming that "pro-choice" is also "pro-life." In cases like this one, the entire argument can turn on whether or not the arguer is able to successfully support a claim of definition.

In those instances when an arguer chooses to construct an argument to support a definition, the argument frequently revolves around the reasonableness of the scope and breadth of the definition. Is the definition so narrow that it excludes instances of the concept that ought to be included? Is the definition so broad that it fails to exclude instances that do not properly belong to the concept? Thus, in constructing an argument for a definition, an arguer might posit a definition, then argue that the definition is reasonable in terms of its scope and breadth. In fact, this is the criterion implicit in the objection to defining "antiabortion" as "pro-life." Choice advocates claimed that the definition of "pro-life" was so narrow in scope that it excluded pro-choice advocates. So in some cases, the arguments supporting a claim of definition are important. In other cases, the definition becomes evidence (sometimes implicit) for further arguments about whether a claim of definition was actually made.

Definitions themselves frequently are important, but they are also important to subsequent argumentative moves. Definitions are important because they often do the work of argument without opening the arguer's position to as much controversy as would otherwise be expected. Definitions may avoid controversy in two ways: by implying descriptions and by implying values.

Definitions imply descriptions by including elements in the definition that properly require evidentiary support. For instance, an arguer might claim that affirmative action is unfair and might define affirmative action as "racial preference quotas." Whether affirmative action programs require racial preference quotas is a matter of much controversy. But if the definition

is not contested by an audience or by an adversary, the definition shortcuts the argumentative process by avoiding controversy.

Definitions imply values by including terms that are value laden. For instance, when antiabortion advocates define the medical procedure of intact dilation and extraction as "partial-birth abortion" or even as "partial-birth infanticide," the values associated with birth and with infanticide are likely to be transferred to the medical procedure as well. In this case, antiabortion forces succeeded in shortcutting the argumentative process by avoiding the value controversy that is inherent in their definition.

So claims of definition are important. Ironically, they probably are less important when they are actually completed with supporting evidence than when they are implicitly used as descriptive and value evidence for further arguments.

Descriptions

Descriptions may characterize some feature of an object, concept, or event or may describe the object, concept, or event itself. Examples of descriptive claims include

- The rifle purported to have killed President Kennedy requires a minimum of 2.3 seconds between shots.
- Affirmative action programs must by their nature include hiring quotas.
- Jack Ruby was spotted in Parkland Hospital thirty minutes after President Kennedy was murdered.

Each of these statements are descriptive because they provide a verbal account or characterization of something. They are claims in the argumentative sense because they are controversial[9] and because they require reasons for support. Because some descriptions are not controversial, all descriptions are not descriptive arguments. Many or even most descriptions are not argumentative because they are not controversial. For instance, if a person simply describes observations of the colors of flowers—roses are red; violets blue—that person would not ordinarily give reasons to support these descriptions.

One kind of descriptive claim is a claim of historical fact. All statements about history are not histori-

---

[9]- With regard to the first example, some people claim that this action requires closer to four seconds when one takes into account the fact that a shooter must reacquire the subject in the scope. Regarding the second example, some supporters of affirmative action argue that hiring quotas are required only for a company with a past record of discrimination. In the third example, the primary source of the claim regarding Jack Ruby was A.P. reporter Seth Kantor; the Warren Commission claimed that Kantor was mistaken in his report.

cal claims. To be a historical claim a statement must be controversial and must require reason for its support. The statement, "O. J. Simpson won the Heisman Trophy," is not controversial and therefore not an argumentative claim. On the other hand, the statement, "O. J. Simpson killed Nicole Brown Simpson," not only is controversial, but also requires an arguer to present to reasons supporting or denying it.

Another kind of description is a claim of scientific fact. Scientific facts are statements that command the belief of the scientific community: "The Earth is the third planet from the sun." A claim of scientific fact is a controversial scientific statement believed by a scientist or a group of scientists, but not yet accepted by the entire scientific community: "Cold fusion can be produced in the laboratory." Like other factual statements, all scientific statements are not claims of scientific fact either because they are not controversial or because they do not require reasons to be given in their support. To say, "The Earth is the third planet from the sun," is not a claim because it is not controversial and because a person making that statement would not be expected to give reasons to support it. But the statement, "Cold fusion can be produced in a laboratory," is a controversial statement, and the scientific community would challenge anyone making that statement to support it with reason and evidence.

Illustrating different examples of descriptive claims is important in and of itself because people frequently argue about descriptive claims with no goal other than to try to settle a controversy regarding an account of science or history. As just one example, several hundred books and articles have been written presenting many different accounts of the assassinations of John Kennedy, Robert Kennedy, and Martin Luther King. But beyond being important for their own sake, descriptive claims also are important because they are needed when arguing about subsequent kinds of claims as well.

Descriptive claims frequently are used as evidence in relational and evaluative arguments. A claim describing the nature of an object frequently is needed before arguing that one object is related to another object. People might need to argue, for instance, that hiring quotas are essential features of affirmative action (a descriptive claim) before they can argue that affirmative action leads to differential treatment of persons in hiring pools (relational claim). Similarly, people may need to describe an object or phenomenon prior to evaluating that object. In this example, they would need to describe affirmative action before they argue that it is either good or bad.

A scientific description can be the final product of an argument or can be used as evidence for the further development of another kind of argument. Whether the primary determinant of homosexuality is genetic or cultural is an interesting claim from a purely scientific perspective. People can argue the facts that support the genetic explanation or the cultural one. However, this claim frequently has been used in the debate about the morality of homosexuality.[10] So in the case of the determinants of homosexuality, the descriptive claim is both important for its own sake and for the sake of other potential claims as well.

Descriptive historical claims are interesting both because they make statements about whether or not an event occurred as asserted and because they can be used as evidence in making further arguments.

• Lee Harvey Oswald killed President John Kennedy.
• O. J. Simpson murdered Nicole Brown Simpson and Ronald Goldman.
• U. S. ships *Maddox* and *Turner Joy* were attacked by the North Vietnamese in the Gulf of Tonkin.

Each of these are interesting and controversial claims of historical fact. These and other claims of historical fact also can be used as evidence for relational and evaluative arguments. For instance, the argument that the *Maddox* and *Turner Joy* were attacked by the North Vietnamese was used by President Johnson to persuade the Senate and the House of Representatives to pass the Tonkin Gulf Resolution giving Johnson a blank check to pursue the war in Vietnam. Subsequently arguments that the attack was at best provoked and at worse —faked were used by opponents of the Vietnam War to show that Johnson's actions were improper and even immoral.

Relationship Statements

Descriptive claims are about the nature of reality-- what is the essence of X or Y. Claims of relationship depend on, but go beyond, the essence of X or Y to the relationship between X and Y. Claims of relationship assert a connection between two or more objects, events, or phenomena. Like descriptive claims, claims of relationship can be important in their own right or

---

[10]- Some argue, for instance, that because the tendency for homosexuality is genetic, it is not a "choice" and therefore cannot be considered moral or immoral.

they can serve as evidence for the development of evaluative claims. Consider these claims:

- Secondhand smoke contributes significantly to health problems.
- The scandals of the Clinton administration are like those of the Nixon administration.
- Advertising has changed the role of women in the U.S.

All of these are claims of relationship because they assert a relationship between two objects or concepts (secondhand smoke and health, Clinton and Nixon, advertising and women). The relationships asserted in these examples are of two kinds: of contingency and of similarity.

Contingency

Some claims of relationship assert a relationship of contingency. The secondhand smoking example and the advertising example are of this kind. In each case, these claims assert that one object or phenomenon is dependent on another in one way or another. Sign and cause are two ways objects can be dependent on one another via some form of contingency.

Relationships of sign are one way to show that one thing is dependent on another thing.

Consider these:

- The pain in your child's abdomen probably means she has appendicitis.
- The palm print on the Mannlicher-Carcano rifle proves that Oswald handled the rifle supposedly used to shoot President Kennedy.

Both of the previous statements are claims about relationships of sign. The pain in the abdomen as a sign of appendicitis is dependent on the belief that the child actually has abdominal pain and a belief in the relationship between that pain and her appendix. The belief that Oswald handled the rifle that supposedly was used to shoot President Kennedy is dependent on the belief that he actually left his palm print on the murder weapon.

Arguments of sign played a very important—perhaps crucial—role in the criminal trial of O. J. Simpson for the murder of Ron Goldman and Nicole Brown-Simpson. The prosecution claimed that the presence of a bloody glove near Simpson's home was a sign that he was the murderer. In a dramatic turn of events, Simpson tried on the glove in the presence of the jury; it appeared to be too small to fit on his hand. This evidence allowed the defense to support its own claim in quite poetic language: "If the glove doesn't fit, you must acquit." According to the prosecution's claim, the glove was a sign of Simpson's guilt. According to the defense's claim, the glove signaled his innocence. This was a clear case where the argument centered around the relationship between the bloody glove and Simpson's guilt or innocence.

In the Simpson example, the claim of sign is important because if it were believed, the claim alone is sufficient to establish guilt (or innocence, depending on the nature of the argument). But like other claims, a claim of sign also can be used as evidence to establish a different claim. Say, for instance, that a person claims that "Photographs from the yacht, 'Monkey Business,' showed that Presidential candidate Gary Hart was an adulterer." The photographs are not direct evidence of adultery, but given their nature, they are strong signs of infidelity. One could then use this claim of sign to support an evaluative argument: "Gary Hart is not worthy of being President since he is an adulterer." In this case, the claim of sign becomes evidence to support an evaluative claim.

Relationships of sign may or may not involve relationships of cause. The relationship between pain and appendicitis is one of both sign and cause. The pain is a sign of the appendicitis and the appendicitis is a cause of the pain. A causal relationship is not directly involved in the example of the double murder of Goldman and Brown-Simpson or in the example about Oswald's palm print on the rifle. Although the palm print and the bloody glove were signs of murder, they were not causes of the murder.[11] Thus, relationships of sign are different from relationships of cause at least in terms of their focus.

Causal relationships are important in many forms of argument. The kind of causal claim varies from one instance to the next. A few examples include contributory causes, necessary and sufficient causes, blocking causes, and motive or responsibility.

Contributory causes are special kinds of causal statements. In many or most cases, a single event is not the cause of an effect. Certain conditions predispose certain effects; other conditions influence the occur-

---

[11]- One can make a case for a causal relationship between the murder and the bloody glove in that the act of committing the murder caused blood to get on the glove. The causal relationship between the palm print and the Kennedy murder is less direct, although one could say that the act of murdering President Kennedy caused Oswald's palm print to be on the murder weapon. This last claim is a weak one since the palm print could have been on the rifle long before the assassination.

rence of those effects. Finally, some condition precipitates that effect. For example, consider these three possible claims about the causes of heart attacks:

• Genetics are the cause of heart attacks.
• A high cholesterol diet can cause heart attack.
• Vigorous exercise causes heart attacks.

We know that some people are genetically more predisposed to heart attacks than others. If a person who already is predisposed to heart attacks regularly consumes a diet high in cholesterol, that diet contributes to the likelihood of heart attack. Suppose a person dies of a heart attack while on a morning jog. What was the cause? Genetics? Diet? Exercise? The answer is that all three factors may have been contributory causes. No single cause may have caused the heart attack, but all three conditions in combination may have resulted in a heart attack.

Necessary and sufficient causes frequently deal with singular causes rather than contributory causes. "Money is essential to happiness" is an example of a claim of necessary causation. To say that money is a necessary cause of happiness is not to say that the presence of money automatically leads to happiness. The claim does, however, imply that without money happiness is impossible. If one wanted to make a claim of sufficient causation using the same example, one might claim that "money is the key to happiness." Depending on how one interpreted that claim, it might mean that money brings happiness regardless of other conditions. In that case, one would have made a claim about a sufficient cause.

Necessary and sufficient causes are useful when arguing about relationships between and among various phenomena. They are also useful as evidence from which to construct other kinds of claims, particularly claims that evaluate a course of action. When an arguer proposes a strategy to eliminate an undesirable effect, evidence derived from a claim about a necessary condition of that effect is useful. Having made a claim about a necessary cause, one can forward a proposal to eliminate that necessary cause and thus eliminate the effect. For instance, if people believe that overeating is a necessary condition of obesity, they could use this causal claim as evidence to convince others that they need to quit overeating. Thus, making a claim about a necessary cause is a good way to support a plan for eliminating an effect.

Similarly, evidence derived from a claim about a sufficient cause is a good way to support a plan for producing an effect. If one can present a proposal that adds a sufficient cause, one can then claim that the proposal will produce some good effect. For instance, some diet commercials claim that their products are sufficient to cause one to lose weight. This claim of a sufficient causal condition can then be used as evidence to convince buyers to try their diet programs. Implied in such a claim is that regardless of what else one does, following the proposed diet will lead to weight loss.

Statements about motive are causal claims about the effects of human agents. Many causal claims, like those already discussed, are related to physical or biological phenomena. The relationships among genetics, diet, exercise, and heart disease are biological relationships. Various elements in a biological system affect other elements in that same system. In a similar manner, motives are a kind of causal explanation when human choice is involved in creating effects. Why, for instance, do senators and representatives stall legislation for campaign finance reform? Why do corporations knowingly produce dangerous products? The answers to these questions involve causal claims, but causal claims of a different order than those discussed earlier.

In an earlier example, genetics, diet, and exercise did not "choose" to cause heart disease. But in human systems choice is frequently an important element in determining what actions lead to what effects. One might claim that "representatives' and senators' self-interest motivate them to stall campaign finance reform" or that the "profit motive induces corporations knowingly to produce dangerous products." The kinds of causal questions that deal with motives are very useful when arguing about the effects of human actions.

Like other causal claims, claims about motive are useful as evidence in the construction of evaluative claims. A claim based on a senator's motive for stalling campaign finance reform might, for instance, be used as evidence to construct a further claim relevant to the wisdom of re-electing that senator. A claim that a particular corporation's desire for profits led to the production of unsafe products might be used as further evidence to support a claim asking for a boycott of that corporation.

The claims of relationship that have been discussed so far have involved relationships of contingency. In relationships of contingency, one phenomenon depends on or affects another. These claims of relationships have generally been divided into the categories of signs and cause. However, claims of contingency are not the only kind of claims of relationship. Claims of similarity are equally important kinds of relational claims.

Similarity

In addition to relationships based on contingency,

other statements of relationship assert a relationship of similarity. A claim of similarity asserts that two or more objects or concepts are similar in important ways. Claims of similarity are frequently found in what is called argument by analogy or argument by parallel case. Examples of claims of similarity include:

- Abortion is virtually the same as infanticide.
- The Clinton administration is like the Nixon administration.
- Capital punishment is state-sanctioned murder.

Each of these examples share certain characteristics. First, each example includes two objects or concepts (Clinton and Nixon, abortion and infanticide, and capital punishment and murder). Second, each example states that the two concepts or objects are similar in important regards.

Claims of similarity are useful when an arguer wants to do nothing more than support the idea that two or more objects and concepts are similar. Although the claim focuses on the similarity between the objects, it frequently carries another implied claim of evaluation. The claim that capital punishment is state-sanctioned murder is not a value-neutral statement. When confronted with such a claim, most audiences begin with the assumption that murder is a negatively valued concept. An arguer who succeeds in supporting the claim of similarity also succeeds in transferring the negative value associated with murder to the concept of capital punishment. In all of the above examples of claims of similarity, the arguer has two different purposes: to show that the two concepts or objects have similar characteristics, or to show that the two concepts or objects are evaluated in similar ways.

In some cases, the audience may not have enough familiarity with either of the two objects to understand the values associated with them. In such a case, a claim of similarity is sometimes the first step toward proving a claim of evaluation. Consider a hypothetical claim that states "Senator X's medical care plan is similar to one instituted in Canada." If the audience knew nothing about either Senator X's plan or the Canadian one, the arguer might establish this claim to be used as evidence in a later evaluative claim that "Senator X's plan should be accepted (or rejected)." In this case the arguer might present an evaluative claim regarding the success of the Canadian plan and then combine the two claims--one of similarity and one regarding acceptance or rejection.

Thus, claims of relationship fall into three broad categories: sign, causation, and similarity. In some cases, claims of relationship are supported by evidence built on claims of fact. Likewise, relational claims can be used to establish evaluative claims.

Claims of Evaluation

Evaluative claims go beyond descriptive claims and claims of relationship to the evaluation of an object, event, or concept. Evaluative claims are more complex kinds of claims because they ordinarily require some combination of other definitions, descriptions, and relational statements.

Evaluative claims bear a family resemblance to one another because they attach a value to one or more objects or events. Still, evaluative claims are so vast in number and in characteristics that they can be more easily viewed in these three categories: those that evaluate a single object, those that compare two objects with respect to some value, and those that suggest an action with respect to some object.

Claims that Evaluate a Single Object

Some evaluative claims simply argue that an object is attached in some way (positively or negatively) with some value. These kinds of claims involve both an object of evaluation and some value judgment to be applied to the object:

- Capital punishment is immoral.
- Private property is the root of all evil.
- Capitalism is good.

These examples of claims that attach a value to a single object all contain some object to be evaluated (capital punishment, private property, capitalism) and some value judgment that is applied to the objects (immoral, evil, good).

Some claims, like those mentioned above, imply rather broad value judgments. Others may contain more specific ones:

- Capital punishment is unfair in its application to minorities.
- Private property has led to an uncontrolled and immoral ruling class.
- Capitalism provides incentive for individual incentive.

These examples contain value judgments that are more specific than the broad ones cited earlier.

Claims that Compare Two Objects

Instead of evaluating a single object, some claims compare two objects with respect to some value to constitute a second category of evaluative claim. Unlike the previous category of evaluative claims, claims in this category include at least two objects of evaluation

and at least one value judgment to be applied to those objects. Consider these claims:
- Lying is more proper than hurting someone's feelings.
- Reagan was a better president than Clinton.

Each of these examples contains two objects (lying and hurting someone's feelings; Reagan and Clinton) and one value judgment to be applied to each object (more proper and better president).

Claims of Action

Claims of action, sometimes called claims of policy, are yet another category of evaluative claim:
- Capital punishment should be abolished.
- The United States should adopt a policy of free trade with Cuba.

These claims evaluate a concept by suggesting that action be taken with respect to that concept. Because an action can be evaluated only by comparison or contrast to other possible actions, claims of action by necessity compare at least two objects. The claim that capital punishment should be abolished compares the presence of capital punishment with its absence. The claim regarding free trade with Cuba implies a comparison of a policy of free trade with the present policy of trade embargo. In this regard, claims of action are similar to claims that compare two objects.

In a different regard, claims of action are different from the other categories of evaluative claims in that they rarely state the value judgment used to compare the two objects. The reason the value judgment is not ordinarily stated in the claim is that an action claim is frequently supported by a variety of other claims of evaluation each of which may be relying on a different value judgment. The claim about the abolition of capital punishment, for example, might be supported by other evaluative claims like
- Capital punishment is immoral.
- Capital punishment contributes to the brutalization of society.
- Capital punishment is racist.

To complicate matters even more, evaluative claims of action inherently are comparative claims. To argue in favor of a particular action is possible only in comparison to other actions. For instance, the previous claims imply that capital punishment is less moral, more brutal, and more racist than the alternatives. Because action claims usually require multiple, comparative claims as evidence to support them, action claims generally are more complicated than the other categories of action claims.

According to this category system, evaluative claims are generally divided into three types: claims that evaluate a single object, claims that evaluate two or more objects, and action claims. As indicated, one evaluative claim can sometimes be used as support for another evaluative claim, leading eventually to complicated claims built on a web of other claims.

In addition to the fact that evaluative claims are used both as the end product of an argument and as evidence for other evaluative claims, almost all evaluative claims are dependent on earlier descriptive claims and relational claims. Depending on whether or not the audience is familiar with and accepts the arguer's descriptive of the concept to be evaluated, the arguer making an evaluative claim may also want to explicitly make prior descriptive claims as well. In the previous examples, for instance, one can easily see how an arguer might need to describe certain features of capital punishment, private property, lying, Clinton, Reagan, free trade, or Cuba before launching into an evaluation of those concepts.

In many, but not all instances, an arguer also would need to use a claim of relationship as evidence to support the evaluative claim. To illustrate instances when a relational claim is and is not needed, consider the two examples of claims evaluating a single object. The claim that "capital punishment is immoral" can be supported by describing a feature of capital punishment (that it is the intentional taking of a human life) and evaluating that feature negatively (the intentional taking of a human life is an immoral act). A description and an evaluation are all that are necessary; relational evidence is not needed. The second claim that "private property is the root of all evil" is different. To make this claim, one first might describe the concept of private property then argue that private property leads to greed and selfishness (a relational claim), then argue that greed and selfishness are evil. A significant difference exists between the first argument and the second one: The first requires relational evidence and the second does not. In the first instance, the argument is evaluating an inherent feature of capital punishment; in the second, the argument evaluates an effect of private property. When arguing an inherent feature of a concept, relational evidence is unnecessary because the evaluation is of the feature rather than of an effect of the feature. But many times, by the nature of the claim, an arguer is forced to evaluate an effect of a concept. In those instances, the arguer is required to establish the effect by means of relational evidence.

In summary, four categories of evidence and claims include definitions, descriptions, relational statements (of contingency and of similarity), and evaluations. Sometimes claims are the end products of arguments; at other times they are used as evidence for the construction of further claims. This introduction has presented a category system and begun to explain how various types of claims are related to one another when one is used as evidence for another. This introduction has done little or nothing toward explaining how one constructs arguments for these various types of claims. The methods and processes of constructing these claims are the topics of later chapters.

Theory and Practice

This essay has provided some theoretical background relevant to argumentation in debating. Specifically, it has provided a discussion of the Toulmin model of argument and a more detailed description of two of Toulmin's elements: claims and evidence. The reason for focusing on these two elements is that the remainder of this volume provides information that can be transformed into evidence and claims to support propositions. Claims and evidence are the foundational elements of supporting propositions. Warrants and reservations, which are more likely to be individual creations than foundations, did not receive the same detailed discussion.

When using this volume, debaters need to remember that it is only a starting point. Good debaters, much less excellent debaters, will need to go beyond this volume. They will need to engage in individual and perhaps collective research into the details of other claims and evidence.

Then, of course, comes the actual practice of debating where debaters will be required to combine the evidence provided in this volume and from their own research with warrants and reservations to support claims and to combine those claims into arguments supporting or refuting propositions.

Robert Trapp
Professor of Rhetoric
Willamette University
Salem, Oregon, U.S.A.
January 2003

❧ DEBATE TOPICS

ABORTION ON DEMAND

Whether a woman has the right to terminate a pregnancy, and, if so, under what conditions, is one of the most contentious issues facing modern societies. For some, the question is even more fundamental: At what stage is the fetus to be regarded as a child? The battle lines are drawn between "pro-life" supporters, who argue that abortion is never permissible, and "pro-choice" adherents, who emphasize the mother's right to choose. In 1973 the US Supreme Court ruled that abortion was legal in its landmark decision Roe v. Wade. *Since then antiabortion groups have pressed to have the ruling overturned and have succeeded in having several states pass laws limiting the conditions under which abortion is permitted. Pro-choice groups have opposed these efforts and made support of* Roe *the litmus test for political and judicial candidates wanting their backing.*

PROS

Women should have control over their own bodies—they have to carry the child during pregnancy and undergo childbirth. No one else carries the child for her; it will be her responsibility alone, and thus she should have the sole right to decide. If a woman does not want to go through the full nine months and subsequent birth, then she should have the right to choose not to do so. There are few—if any—other cases where something with such profound consequences is forced upon a human being against her or his will. To appeal to the child's right to life is just circular—whether a fetus has rights or not, or can really be called a "child," is exactly what is at issue. Everyone agrees that children have rights and shouldn't be killed. Not everyone agrees that fetuses of two, four, eight, or even twenty weeks are children.

Not only is banning abortion a problem in theory, offending against a woman's right to choose, it is also a practical problem. A ban would not stop abortion but would drive it once again underground and into conditions where the health and safety of the woman are almost certainly at risk. Women would also circumvent the ban by traveling to countries where abortion is legal. Either the state would have to take the draconian measure of restricting freedom of movement, or it would have to admit that its law is unworkable in practice and abolish it.

Are we really taking about a "life?" At what point does a life begin? Is terminating a fetus, which can neither feel nor think and is not conscious of its own "existence,"

CONS

Of course, human rights should be respected, but no one has a right to make a decision with no reference to the rights and wishes of others. In this case, does the father have any rights in regard to the fate of the fetus? More important, though, pro-choice groups actively ignore the most important right—the child's right to life. What is more important than life? All other rights, including the mother's right to choice, surely stem from a prior right to life; if you have no right to any life, then how do you have a right to an autonomous one? A woman may ordinarily have a reasonable right to control her own body, but this does not confer on her the entirely separate (and insupportable) right to decide whether another human lives or dies.

Unborn children cannot articulate their right to life; they are vulnerable and must be protected. Many laws are difficult to implement, but degree of difficulty does not diminish the validity and underlying principle. People will kill other people, regardless of the law, but it does not follow that you shouldn't legislate against murder. Whether the state should restrain women from traveling for abortions is a separate question, but one that can be answered in the affirmative given what is at stake. Restricting someone's freedom is a small price to pay for protecting an innocent life.

The question of what life is can certainly be answered: It is sacred, inviolable, and absolute. The fetus, at whatever stage of development, will inevitably develop the

really commensurate with the killing of a person? If you affirm that human life is a quality independent of, and prior to, thought and feeling, you leave yourself the awkward task of explaining what truly "human" life is.

In cases where terminating a pregnancy is necessary to save a mother's life, surely abortion is permissible.

Not only medical emergencies present compelling grounds for termination. Women who have been raped should not have to suffer the additional torment of being pregnant with the product of that ordeal. To force a woman to produce a living, constant reminder of that act is unfair to both mother and child.

Finally, advances in medical technology have enabled us to determine during pregnancy whether the child will be disabled. In cases of severe disability, in which the child would have a very short, very painful and tragic life, it is surely right to allow parents to choose a termination. This avoids both the suffering of the parents and of the child.

human abilities to think, feel, and be aware of itself. The unborn child will have every ability and every opportunity that you yourself have, given the chance to be born.

While emergencies are tragic, it is by no means obvious that abortion is permissible. The "mother vs. child" dilemma is one that defies solution, and aborting to preserve one of the lives sets a dangerous precedent that killing one person to save another is acceptable. This is a clear, and unpalatable, case of treating a human being as a means to an end.

While rape is an appalling crime, is it the fault of the unborn child? The answer is no. Denying someone life because of the circumstances of conception is as unfair as anything else imaginable.

What right does anyone have to deprive another of life on the grounds that he deems that life not worth living? This arrogant and sinister presumption is impossible to justify, given that many people with disabilities lead fulfilling lives. What disabilities would be regarded as the watershed between life and termination? All civilized countries roundly condemn the practice of eugenics.

Sample Motions:
This House would forbid abortion on demand.
This House believes in a woman's right to choose.

Web Links:
• American Civil Liberties Union: Reproductive Freedom. <http://www.aclu.org/issues/reproduct/hmrr.html>
Provides information on the status of reproductive issues and reproductive rights from a pro-choice perspective.
• The National Right to Life Committee. <http://www.nrlc.org/>
Presents information on the status of issues like abortion, human cloning, euthanasia, and RU-486.
• ReligiousTolerance.Org: Abortion. <http://www.religioustolerance.org/abortion.htm>
Offers information on both the pro-life and pro-choice positions.

Further Reading:
Dworkin, Ronald. *Life's Dominion: An Argument About Abortion, Euthanasia, and Individual Freedom.* Vintage Books, 1994.

CRSO

AFFIRMATIVE ACTION

Affirmative action in the United States was born of the civil rights and women's movements of the 1960s and 1970s. It is designed to provide historically disadvantaged groups—minorities and women—special consideration in education, housing, and employment. Those institutions with affirmative action policies generally set goals for increased diversity, although the courts have ruled quotas unconstitutional. By the end of the twentieth century, Supreme Court decisions had limited affirmative action, and a vocal opposition movement was arguing that it was no longer necessary.

PROS

Women and minorities have frequently faced obstacles and difficulties in access to education and employment that white males did not. Affirmative action levels the playing field.

Affirmative action unlocks the unrealized potential of millions. Minority applicants are just as skilled as those from the majority but their talents are untapped because of lack of opportunity. The country gains enormously by using the talents of all our citizens.

Successful minority members are role models who will encourage the development of bright minority youngsters.

Bringing more minority applicants into the workplace will change racist and sexist attitudes because workers will begin to know each other as individuals rather than stereotypes.

The proportion of minorities in particular jobs should mirror that of the minority in the general population. The underrepresentation of minorities and women in certain fields leads to perceptions of institutional racism and sexism.

Getting minority candidates into top jobs will enable them to change the system "from the inside" to make it fairer for all.

CONS

All discrimination is negative. It is always wrong to select on any basis other than merit and ability. Affirmative action leads to able applicants being unfairly passed over.

Affirmative action results in less able applicants filling positions. Employers must have the flexibility to employ the best candidates to ensure efficiency and productivity.

Affirmative action undermines the achievements of minority members by creating the impression that success was unearned. Some members of minorities see affirmative action as patronizing and as tokenism on the part of the majority.

Affirmative action causes resentment among those who do not benefit from it and creates a backlash against minorities.

Granted, we should aim for improving minority representation in high-profile positions, but we should not sacrifice our emphasis on merit and ability. Instead we should give everyone better access to education so that we can choose on merit and without discrimination.

Educational institutions are becoming more diverse. This diversity ultimately will lead to increasing minority representation in senior positions in business, education, and government. Although the pace of change is not as fast as it might be, we have seen improvement. Continued implementation of affirmative action could lead to a backlash that stops progress.

Sample Motions:
    This House believes in affirmative action.
    This House believes race does matter.
    This House would act affirmatively.

Web Links:
    • Affirmative Action and Diversity Project. <http://aad.english.ucsb.edu/>
    Site maintained by the University of California, Santa Barbara, offering articles and theoretical analysis, public documents, current
    legislative initiatives, and resources on affirmative action.
    • Affirmative Action Special Report. <http://www.washingtonpost.com/wp-srv/politics/special/affirm/affirm.htm>
    Washington Post site offering overview of issue, key stories from the *Post*, and links to other resources.

Further Reading:
    Beckwith, Francis J., and Todd E. Jones. *Affirmative Action: Social Justice or Reverse Discrimination?* Prometheus, 1997.
    Curry, George E., and Cornel West, eds. *The Affirmative Action Debate.* Perseus, 1996.
    Mosley, Albert, and Nicholas Capaldi. *Affirmative Action: Social Justice or Unfair Preference?* Rowman and Littlefield, 1996.

CR80

AFGHANISTAN, INVASION OF

Even before the terrorist attack on the World Trade Center in New York on September 11, 2001, Afghanistan was probably the most isolated country in the world. Only three countries recognized its Taliban rulers, who in the mid-1990s had swept across that country to impose a very strict and distinctive form of Islamic law upon the Afghan people. The Taliban did end nearly 20 years of civil war in the 90% of the country that they controlled. Osama bin Laden, an exiled Saudi Arabian responsible for the World Trade Center attacks and for other terrorist attacks in the 1990s, had based his Al Qaeda organization in Afghanistan since 1996. The Taliban said that bin Laden was a "guest of the Afghan people" and refused to give him up, prompting military action against the regime.

PROS

After the September 11 attacks, the US was fully justified in waging war to punish those responsible and to prevent future attacks. The Taliban government was not a passive host of bin Laden but was closely associated with him ideologically and in his debt for the crucial support he gave it in the civil war. By sheltering him and his terrorist network and by refusing to give him up, the Taliban became his accomplice in terrorism and should be overthrown in the interests of justice and global peace.

The invasion of Afghanistan was aimed directly at capturing bin Laden and overthrowing the Taliban regime that harbored him. It was not a war against the Afghan people. The Afghan people, especially women and ethnic and religious minorities, suffered greatly under Taliban rule. They deserve a better government. In the

CONS

Even if bin Laden is guilty of masterminding the September 11 atrocities, this is no reason for a war on Afghanistan. Given the fragmentary nature of government, the Taliban was probably incapable of seizing him even had it wished to do so.

Even if the Taliban was judged to be equally guilty with bin Laden, the Afghan people were not. In the long run, the invasion of Afghanistan is likely to lead to a prolonged power struggle or civil war between different ethnic groups or local warlords, as has happened frequently in Afghan history. This will lead to the loss

past few years, the Taliban made delivering humanitarian relief very difficult for the UN and other aid agencies, so the invasion improved conditions in the country.

Invasion was the only way to capture bin Laden and destroy his terrorist organization. Bombing on its own can prepare the way for a ground invasion, guaranteeing air supremacy and disrupting the enemy's command and control systems, but without the eventual commitment of land forces the global coalition formed by the US could not hope to have achieved its objectives. In addition, because the Taliban regime was so isolated before September 2001, no meaningful diplomatic sanctions could have been applied in an attempt to achieve these aims peacefully.

Invasion was the only way to prevent future terrorists using Afghanistan as a base. The Taliban has provided a supportive base for a range of terrorist groups seeking to overthrow regimes in Central Asia, China, and Kashmir, as well as for the global terrorist campaign of Al Qaeda. The stability of the whole Central Asian region depends on the installation in Afghanistan of a new government dedicated to peaceful coexistence with its neighbors. This can be achieved only through an invasion.

Swift and decisive action against Afghanistan was necessary as a deterrent to other regimes thinking of supporting terrorism. If it is clear that allowing attacks upon other countries will result in massive retaliation and the swift overthrow of the sponsoring regime, then the world will have become a safer place and some good will have come out of the tragedy of September 11.

of many innocent lives, prevent the delivery of humanitarian aid to millions of starving Afghans, and create a terrible refugee crisis.

Invading Afghanistan could not guarantee the capture of bin Laden. His familiarity with the hostile terrain and proximity to sympathizers in lawless areas of Pakistan offered him plenty of hiding places.

An invasion using conventional military tactics will never be effective against a diffuse, highly secretive international network like Al Qaeda. If the organization is driven out of one country, it will find somewhere else to base its activities. To make the whole population of Afghanistan suffer in the vain hope of damaging such an elusive organization was and is unacceptable.

Ill-considered action against Afghanistan has made the US in particular, and the West in general, more widely feared and hated. The invasion has increased sympathy for the Afghan people and bin Laden, especially in Islamic countries. This in itself seriously increases the risk of future terrorist attacks, but it also threatens moderate and pro-Western Islamic nations.

Sample Motions:
This House supports the invasion of Afghanistan.
This House celebrates the toppling of the Taliban.
This House would overthrow regimes that support terrorism.

Web Links:
• "Across the Great Divide."
<http://newyorker.com/FROM_THE_ARCHIVE/ARCHIVES/?010924fr_archive05>
An article from the *New Yorker* magazine (May 2000) providing background on the Taliban.
• The Taliban: Afghan's Fundamentalist Leaders. <http://www.cbc.ca/news/indepth/background/taliban.html>
Canadian Broadcasting Company article on the Taliban, including a partial list of what was banned under its regime.

• Time.com Primer: Understand the Taliban and Afghanistan.
 <http://www.time.com/time/nation/article/0,8599,175372,00.html>
Article providing background on the Taliban, the problems bin Laden posed for it, and the politics of the area.
• United States Department of Defense. <http://www.defenselink.mil>
Provides up-to-date news on the military aspects of the campaign against terrorism, including the invasion of Afghanistan.

Further Reading:
Cooley, John K. *Unholy Wars.* Stylus, 2000.
Gohari, M. J. *The Taliban: Ascent to Power.* Oxford University Press Print on Demand, 2001.
Goodson, Larry. *Afghanistan's Endless War: State Failure, Regional Politics and the Rise of the Taliban.* University of Washington Press, 2001.
Margolis, Eric. *War at the Top of the World: The Struggle for Afghanistan, Kashmir and Tibet.* Routledge, 2001.
Marsden, Peter. *The Taliban: War and Religion in Afghanistan.* Zed Books, 2002.

CRSE

AFRICAN AFFAIRS, OUTSIDE INTERVENTION IN

Africa has had some of the bloodiest and most violent conflicts of recent decades. In Rwanda, for example, hundreds of thousands of people died during the 1990s in a genocidal war. In the United States and in Europe international organizations such as the United Nations have been criticized for their slowness in dealing with these conflicts. Others maintain, however, that non-African organizations and former colonial powers have no legitimate role to play in Africa's politics and African conflicts. African conflicts need African solutions, not artificial resolutions imposed by non-African nations and organizations.

PROS

Often, only neighboring countries are able to respond to crises in a timely manner. A case in point was the South African intervention in an uprising in Lesotho. It stabilized the country and restored the rightful ruler, thus preventing a potential civil war.

Regional intervention is often more effective in producing change. While international groups such as the UN may be successful in keeping the peace, their philosophy leaves once their soldiers go home. By having regional groups intervene, the changes they impose remain after the soldiers depart. Regional politics will ensure political progress.

The unique situations and power organizations present in many African conflicts are best understood by the countries involved and their immediate neighbors. A one-size-fits-all international response fails to take into

CONS

Is the involvement of African countries really without self-interest? For example, Zimbabwe's involvement in the war in the Democratic Republic of the Congo (DRC) was, at least in part, to enable it to gain access to the diamond mines and other resources in the war zones. Some neighboring countries have a greater vested interest in fueling wars than in stopping them.

The effect of regional blocs on many African despots has been nil. For example, Zimbabwe's President Robert Mugabe has consistently ignored condemnation from neighboring countries. The influence works both ways: Many corrupt but politically powerful countries force their neighbors to condone their acts. In the case of Zimbabwe, cronyism, especially in the Southern African Development Community (SADEC), has resulted in many African nations condoning human rights abuses in the country.

The "unique understanding" of African politics is often no more than cronyism or dictators ensuring each other's continued power. In these cases, an impartial international intervention is far preferable. In other cases this

account special circumstances and frequently results in the breakdown of negotiations or mediation. African leaders are also more likely to trust and cooperate with regional organizations, such as SADEC, than with international organizations.

African countries must be seen to be successfully pursuing democratic and economic development. Many African leaders still carry colonial resentments that make foreign intervention difficult or impossible. These leaders will be willing to listen to African approaches to a problem, while automatically distrusting foreign ones, however well intentioned.

Most of the powerful countries and international organizations are loathe to become involved in the sort of peacemaking (as opposed to peacekeeping) needed in African countries. Active and direct participation of infantry and other elements of armies is required to fight guerrilla wars such as that in the DRC. The current trend away from this sort of military intervention is ill suited to addressing African problems. African countries, by contrast, have already illustrated that they are willing and able to become involved in this capacity, as evidenced in the DRC.

unique understanding means the surrounding countries have aligned themselves with different sides in the war, escalating it, rather than contributing to peace.

We need to be sure that the intervention is justified. While many countries may be democratic in name only, it is generally the role of the international community to determine whether violating the sovereignty of another country is justified. Assuming that such decision could best be made by the countries closest to the "despots" would be a mistake because those countries would probably be the least impartial. Many ongoing conflicts have been started or sustained on the belief of neighbors that it was the moral thing to do.

Just because the intervening country uses infantry or tanks instead of negotiation or aerial bombardment doesn't make it any more likely to restore peace. Vietnam is the classic example of how using infantry to intervene in a guerrilla war is futile. On an African stage, infantry intervention by neighboring countries has increased only the death toll, not the success at ending the war.

Sample Motions:
   This House would keep its own peace.
   This House doesn't need the UN/US.
   This House would solve its own problems.

Web Links:
   • Amnesty International: Democratic Republic of Congo: War Against Unarmed Civilians. <http://www.web.amnesty.org/ai.nsf/index/AFR620361998>
   Overview of human rights issues in the Democratic Republic of Congo by leading human rights organization.
   • When All Else Fails, Mugabe Gets Rough. <http://www.lowell.edu/users/grundy/public/oped001.html>
   Short essay on Robert Mugabe's oppressive rule in Zimbabwe.

Further Reading:
   Du Plessis, L., and M. Hough. *Managing African Conflict: The Challenge of Military Intervention.* HSRC Publishers, 2000.
   Smock, David R., ed. *Making War and Waging Peace: Foreign Intervention in Africa.* United States Institute of Peace Press, 1993.
   West, Harry G., ed. *Conflict and Its Resolution in Contemporary Africa.* University Press of America, 1997.

CRSO

AFRICAN LANGUAGES IN AFRICAN SCHOOLS

Many African schools use French and English in the classroom, a legacy of Africa's colonial past. However, this may not altogether undermine the value of the practice. English is increasingly becoming an international language for both business and culture. Would African nations be putting themselves at a disadvantage if they taught their own distinctive linguistic and cultural heritages by using native languages in the classroom?

PROS

The use of non-African languages such as French and English in African schools is a throwback to colonialism. They were adopted more by the order of the rulers of the day than for any practical advantage they might give.

If the issue is one of understanding, then it is a weak argument. Many countries (e.g., Japan and Germany) have proved that they can be powerful both academically and economically by teaching pupils in their mother tongue while providing early and comprehensive instruction in English as a second language. Instruction in the language of the country serves to maintain cultural identity; translation is an easy option for turning English texts into the required language. This may not even be necessary if schools encourage proficiency in English as a second language.

Instead of looking at how indigenous languages can fit into the global society, we should look at how English fits into other societies. The vast majority of Africans have grown up speaking languages other than English as their first language; thus by adopting English as the standard language of your country, you are essentially disempowering most citizens in academic, commercial, and even social spheres.

Perhaps English may have a role in the future of developing countries—when they are powerful enough to compete globally. For the moment, however, many are divided internally—most often on ethnic lines. Only by respecting people's ethnicity (of which language is an important component) will Africans ever be able to achieve the sort of national strength to compete globally. Until then, the use of English will handicap, not help, African nations.

Making an indigenous language a first language does not exclude making English a second language. The standard of education for each language must remain

CONS

Fluency in English confers many academic advantages. English is the language of most academic publications, of world business, and of other modern resources such as those on the Internet. People who do not know English are handicapped.

Developing African countries are not in the same position as highly industrialized and computerized Japan and Germany. Developing countries do not have the resources to teach a second language to the level of high proficiency that is possible in developed nations. Translation is not only tedious but also delays the accessibility of important scientific and academic texts for experts in the country. Translation is also not an acceptable option in conversation, such as conferences and speeches.

The success of First World nations should not be used as evidence for the success of instruction in another language because it is based on highly developed educational systems that are lacking in most African nations.

The influences of the world on a country cannot be ignored. By adopting an indigenous language, you are isolating your country linguistically from the rest of the world. No matter how good that may be for cohesion within a country, your country will be held hostage in international relations by those few who are able to understand and negotiate in English.

Many African countries do not have one or even two indigenous languages. South Africa, for example, has 10 official languages that are not English. If you allow

high, but we are respecting pupils' rights to become more proficient in the language they commonly use in their society; this is far more beneficial to them than having it relegated to second-language status. English, by contrast, is spoken much less frequently in African countries, and making it a second language recognizes this.

people to opt for one of these as a first language, you are dividing your country. If you declare one language to be the norm, it would have to be English because it has the most practical use for your country Adopting a language other than English would leave a country with the same problem of global isolation raised earlier.

Sample Motions:
This House would place its own culture first.
This House would put itself first.
This House believes in a language barrier.
This House would put English last.

CRSO

AIDS DRUGS FOR DEVELOPING COUNTRIES

The vast majority of people infected with HIV/AIDS live in Africa, more specifically, sub-Saharan Africa. These typically poorer and developing countries are confronting the issue of the cost of drugs for treating the disease. Some nations say that they cannot afford the drugs and that drug companies are making an immoral profit; some nations have threatened to ignore the patents of pharmaceutical companies and to manufacture generic forms of HIV/AIDS drugs unless the companies agree to lower their prices for poorer markets.

PROS

Without a doubt many of the world's pharmaceutical companies are making large profits by selling drugs to poor nations that have a great portion of their population infected with HIV/AIDS. This is an immoral exploitation of those AIDS sufferers who can least afford to pay for treatment and who have the least power internationally to negotiate cheaper prices.

The countries with the biggest AIDS problems are a captive market and are forced to pay whatever the drug companies demand for their products. Poor nations are thus justified in using the threat of producing generic drugs to force drug companies to lower prices.

Generic drugs would be far cheaper to produce and would avoid the shipping costs from factories in Europe or America. Generic drugs have no research and development costs to recoup, so they could be sold for a

CONS

Just like any business, the pharmaceutical companies need to recoup significant financial investment in research and development. The development of AIDS drugs is highly technical, and a measurable return on initial financial investment is needed if companies are to have any reason to continue drug research and development.

Drug companies are as much subject to the forces of the free market as any other business. The threat of illegally producing generic drugs only further serves to discourage drug companies from creating new and more effective medicines because the developing nations have shown them that patent protections will be ignored.

Because most of the drug companies are based in richer, First World nations, they have both the technology to produce effective medicines and the funding to ensure that no corners are cut in the process. Poorer nations

price greatly reduced from current levels. The cost of keeping a person on AZT or other drug cocktails is exorbitant; such cost would be greatly reduced through the use of generic drugs.

would almost certainly cut chemical corners in manufacturing generic drugs should the technology for large-scale manufacture even be available. In addition, by contravening international treaties covering patents, they would not benefit from the next generation of AIDS drugs because companies would be reluctant to supply the newer drugs to a country that steals a drug formula to manufacture generic drugs.

Millions of people will continue to suffer while drug companies refuse to make AIDS medication available to poorer nations at a price they can afford. Are they trying to use the millions of HIV sufferers as hostages in their battle to get the prices they want?

Is it right that those infected with HIV in the Third World get huge discounts while those in the First World pay full price? Developed nations may even have to pay more if the drug companies decide to subsidize their "charity sales" to poor countries. Are not poor countries themselves using sufferers as hostages? Many developing nations could realize significant long-term savings by buying and using preventive medicines to stop mother-to-child transmission, etc.

Drug companies will not lose money by reducing prices; their market will expand. If prices are reduced, the drugs will become affordable to millions of sufferers, many of whom will be using products like AZT for the rest of their lives.

The majority of Third World countries would be unable to afford the drugs even at a breakeven price. One-off treatments to prevent mother-to-child transmission, for example, would be expensive enough. The cost for complex drug cocktails would still be completely out of reach of developing nations. Drug companies would have to sell their medications at a loss to make them affordable to most developing nations.

HIV/AIDS treatments are as cheap as they can be at present. By buying the medicines now, especially for preventative purposes, developing nations can reduce the chance of future HIV infection in their populations and thus not need to buy the next generation of (inevitably more expensive) drugs.

No matter how low the drug companies price HIV/AIDS treatments, they are unlikely to ever be cheap enough: As the number of HIV infected people in Africa grows, the strain on national health budgets will become unbearable. Developing countries are better off pursuing preventative measures and education. Governments will need to use their health care funds carefully—producing generic medicines offers significant savings.

Sample Motions:
    This House would insist on cheaper drugs.
    This House believes that capitalism lets the sick suffer.
    This House wants the First World to help.
    This House needs help with AIDS.
    This House would fight AIDS.

Web Links:
    • HEALTH: Cheaper AIDS Drugs a Myth, Says Medical Aid Agency. <http://www.aegis.com/news/ips/2000/IP000505.html> International Press Service article on the controversy surrounding pharmaceutical company agreements to supply inexpensive HIV/AIDS drugs to poor countries.

Further Reading:
  Hope, Kempe R. *AIDS and Development in Africa: A Social Science Perspective.* Haworth, 1999.
  Intensifying Action Against Hiv/AIDS in Africa: Responding to a Development Crisis. World Bank, 2000.
  Webb, Douglas. *HIV and AIDS in Africa.* Pluto Press, 1997.

CR80

ALCOHOL, BANNING OF

In almost all countries, adults can buy and consume alcohol with very little restriction (although there are often restrictions on the times and places alcohol can be sold). This is a marked contrast to the legal status of other mind-altering drugs, including marijuana, cocaine, Ecstasy (methamphetamine), and heroin. Alcohol abuse has a serious impact on society. In 2000 alcohol-related traffic accidents were responsible for almost 17,000 deaths and hundreds of thousands of injuries in the United States. In 1996 alcohol-related crimes cost the US $19.7 billion, while alcohol abuse resulted in $82 billion in lost productivity. Despite the far-reaching impact of alcohol abuse, the failure of Prohibition in the United States during the 1920s and 1930s makes most people very wary of trying a ban again.

PROS

Alcohol is just as potentially addictive as many illegal drugs. Those who become addicted often lose their marriages, jobs, families, and even their lives. A large proportion of homeless people were made so because of alcoholism. Any drug this addictive and destructive should be illegal.

In many countries alcohol is a contributory factor in 60–70% of violent crimes, including child abuse, domestic violence, sexual assault, and murder. In addition, alcohol is far and away the leading cause of public disorder, street fights, etc. In short, alcohol is one of the prime causes of violence and crime in modern society, and its banning would immediately reduce the incidence of these crimes.

Although organizations like Mothers Against Drunk Driving have successfully reduced the number of drunk-driving deaths in the United States, deaths and serious injuries caused by drunk drivers still run to the thousands each year. This is unacceptable. Alcohol should simply be banned.

CONS

The perfect society might prohibit the production and sale of alcohol. However, in most cultures, alcohol, unlike other drugs, is an integral part of social life and culture. To ban it is completely impractical. Doing so would make criminals of billions of people and create the biggest black market the world has ever seen.

Human beings are naturally inclined to violence and conflict. Sex and violence are primal parts of our genetic make-up, and we do not need alcohol to bring them to the surface. At worst, alcohol may slightly exaggerate these tendencies—but that makes it the occasion, not the underlying cause, of violent crimes. The underlying causes are biological and social. Making rape and murder illegal does not eradicate rape and murder, so it is unlikely that making alcohol consumption illegal will do so either.

The progress made against drunk driving in recent decades has been very encouraging. We should continue to campaign against it and have every reason to hope that campaigns to restrict drinking and driving will eventually eradicate the problem. Injuries and deaths, while tragic, are not a good enough reason to take away the civil liberties of the vast majority of law-abiding citizens by depriving them of the pleasure of drinking alcohol.

We need consistency in our drug laws. If marijuana, which is not very addictive and which results in virtually no violent crime or public disorder, needs to be banned because of its mind-altering effects, then how much more so should alcohol be banned?

Currently thousands of people are employed by the alcohol industry. However, the fact that an immoral industry employs a lot of people is never a good argument to keep that immoral industry going. Instead, the government should fund programs to retrain workers.

Tax revenues would be lost if alcohol were banned. Again, however, this is not a principled reason to reject the proposition, simply a practical problem. Governments could significantly reduce spending on police and health through the reduction in crime and alcohol-related illness resulting from an alcohol ban.

Yes, we should have consistent drug laws, which is why it is absurd for marijuana to be illegal. Marijuana and alcohol should both be legal drugs because the vast majority of people know how to use them safely and responsibly.

The alcohol industry is an enormous global industry. Thus, not only would banning alcohol infringe on people's civil liberties to a unacceptable degree, it would also put thousands of people out of work.

Currently governments raise large amounts of revenue from taxes and duties payable on alcohol. To ban alcohol would take away a major source of funding for public services. In addition, enforcing the ban would call for much additional policing. It would also create a new class of illegal drug users, traffickers, and dealers that would be unprecedented in size.

Sample Motions:
   This House would ban alcohol.
   This House would hit the bottle.
   This House believes that alcohol is the root of all evil.

Web Links:
   • Alcoholics Anonymous. < http://www.alcoholics-anonymous.org/>
   Offers information on the organization's program and services.
   • Mothers Against Drunk Driving (MADD). < http://www.madd.org/>
   Good source for statistics, laws, and initiatives on drunk driving and underage drinking.
   • The National Clearing House for Alcohol and Drug Information. <http://www.health.org/catalog/index.htm>
   Excellent source for links to a large number of articles on alcohol, alcoholism, and the social and economic impact of problem drinking.

Further Reading:
   Plant, Martin, and Douglas Cameron, eds. *The Alcohol Report*. Free Assn. Books, 2000.

CR£O

AMERICAN CULTURE: SHOULD IT BE FEARED?

The United States has the strongest economy in the world—and through that economy has exported its culture around the globe: American manufactured goods are ubiquitous; American television shows are familiar fare as far away as eastern Europe and India; American fast food chains have planted restaurants in cities from Dublin to Tokyo. In addition, American films dominate the movie screens of every continent. The Internet itself is an American invention, populated largely by American sites. In short, people around the world are constantly exposed to the American way of life—and have, to varying degrees, adopted American customs and values. The world's peoples, however, have shown some resistance and resentment. One striking example came in 1999 when French farmers vandalized a McDonald's franchise. They are not alone: Political and cultural leaders in many countries have denounced the insidious influence of American culture, which may weaken traditional and indigenous cultures.

PROS

American culture is materialistic and individualistic. Americans are concerned primarily with their own personal wealth and well-being, and give insufficient regard to the good of society as a whole.

American culture has a strong component of violence—evidenced by widespread gun ownership, the death penalty, and the focus on crime and violence in American entertainment. European cultures, in particular, are more peaceful and humane.

American society is driven by consumption—not just of goods and services, but also of food. The American diet, fast food for the most part, is unhealthy and accounts for the epidemic of obesity in America. By copying America, other countries are jeopardizing the health of their citizens.

American culture is ignorant and arrogant. Americans have little understanding of other parts of the world, but reflexively assume that American culture is superior to everything else. Americans are intent upon imposing their culture on the world.

America seeks to dominate the world, but it does not recognize its responsibilities to the world; America has not done enough to protect the environment or to eliminate disease and poverty in other countries.

CONS

Democracy has functioned in America longer than anywhere else in the world. American society is founded on the importance of individual liberty and is devoted to protecting individual rights and freedoms.

The United States offers real opportunities for its citizens to improve their lives. Americans are not bound to stay in the same social and economic class as their parents or grandparents. With universal public education, and a system of higher education that accommodates millions of students, many of them from foreign lands, America helps hard workers to get ahead.

America prizes and rewards creativity and leads the world in innovation. America continually develops new products and new technologies; American advances in medicine and pharmaceuticals have improved health and lengthened lives the world over.

The United States is one of the world's most diverse and tolerant societies. The nation was founded by people who came from different countries and practiced different religions; throughout its history, America has welcomed immigrants from all over the world. American identity is not based on ethnicity.

The American commitment to improving the world began with the Marshall Plan, which rebuilt Europe after World War II. The United States has been a leader in helping to develop the economies of poorer nations.

Sample Motions:
  This House supports the restriction of foreign programs on national television.
  This House would forbid further construction of golden arches.

Web Links:
- Anti-Americanism Has Taken the World by Storm.
<http://www.guardian.co.uk/comment/story/0%2C3604%2C645562%2C00.html>
An essay by author Salman Rushdie about reasons for anti-American sentiment.
- Canadian Nationalism and Anti-Americanism. <http://www.unitednorthamerica.org/index.shtml>
A Web site that examines the possibility of the political amalgamation of the US and Canada; also discusses questions of Canadian identity and American cultural influence.
- Why Anti-Americanism? <http://www.empower.org/patriotism/podhoretz.pdf>
An essay by conservative writer Norman Podhoretz that offers a defense of American values.

Further Reading:
Barber, Benjamin. *Jihad vs. McWorld: How Globalism and Tribalism Are Reshaping the World.* Ballantine, 1996.
Hardt, Michael, and Antonio Negri. *Empire.* Harvard University Press, 2001.
Huntington, Samuel P. *The Clash of Civilizations and the Remaking of the World Order.* Touchstone, 1998.

ભ્ઠ

ANARCHISM

Anarchism is a political philosophy that supports the elimination of all forms of government. Anarchists believe that any government, even a democracy, ultimately serves the interests of a small elite while exploiting the working class. It was prominent in the nineteenth and early twentieth centuries but waned after the 1930s. Recent large-scale anticapitalism protests such as in London in 2000 and at the World Trade Organization meeting in Seattle in 2001 have led people to question the rhetoric and claims of the anarchists.

PROS

Anarchism is essentially a fight for human freedom. Modern nations, even those that claim to be democracies, stifle their citizens with oppressive and artificial machinery imposed by the elites, the governing classes. It is better to live without such controls. This does not mean anarchists stand for complete chaos; they support cooperation and barter between individuals as profitable. Only without controls can humans truly live naturally and freely.

Anarchists believe in a classless society. Modern democracies are divided into social classes that continually vie with each other. Nations have created barriers between people that cause hatred and misery. Anarchy removes these barriers by removing the apparatus that makes economic subjection of others possible.

Nations repress their citizens by removing their ability to govern themselves. Most "democracies" are in fact nothing of the sort. Are elections every two, four, or

CONS

Anarchism is marked by exactly this sort of utopian, unrealistic argument. Far from freeing humans, anarchy allows them to be dominated by primitive forces that a government has eliminated; for example, laws and the police prevent the use of physical force by the strong to oppress the weak. In addition, a nation's government allows industries to be organized and function and agriculture to harvest crops and feed the populace. All advances in art and science have been made possible by governments that peaceably bring people and resources together. Anarchism is merely a backward and dreamy approach to the serious matters of human governance.

Anarchism would not make everyone equal. A truly "classless" society is not achievable. Some men and women become dominant over others because of natural intelligence, skill, cunning, attractiveness, or any other advantage.

Democracy indeed has many problems. These can, however, be solved by devolving power to state and local governments and by holding more frequent elec-

six years really fully representative of individual opinions? The existence of "spin doctors" and attempts to manipulate the media show how governments are misleading the people, not being controlled by them.

Anarchism has nothing to do with violent groups and individuals that hijack anarchist events for their own reasons. The vast majority of anarchists are peaceable protesters who would never use violence. Anarchism is a viable and fair way of life that allows humans to live and interact naturally.

tions and referenda. There is no need to do away with nations entirely.

As can clearly be seen from recent violent acts, anarchy is largely a front for organized terrorist gangs, violent individuals and groups, and other troublemakers. Their calls for pacifism belie their true nature, and their arguments smack of dangerous utopianism. Anarchists seek to subvert all the advances made by humankind over the last millennium.

Sample Motions:
    This House believes that anarchy rules.
    This House would bring down the state.

Web Links:
    • The Anarchist FAQ Webpage. < http://www.geocities.com/CapitolHill/1931/>
    Presents an overview of anarchism in a Q & A format.
    • Movement for Anarchy. <http://www.anarchy-movement.com/>
    Contains information on political theories and topics as well as biographical information on important anarchists.

Further Reading:
    Goldman, Emma. *Anarchism and Other Essays.* Dover, 1970.
    Kropotkin, Peter. *Anarchism and Anarchist Communism: Its Basics and Principles.* Left Bank Books, 1987.
    Meltzer, Albert. *Anarchism: Arguments For and Against.* A.K. Pr. Distribution, 1966.

CRSO

ANIMAL RIGHTS

In the nineteenth century reformers began urging the more humane treatment of animals and founded groups like the American Society for the Prevention of Cruelty to Animals to improve the conditions first of working animals and then of domestic and farm animals as well. In the 1970s Australian philosopher Peter Singer became one of the first to argue that animals have rights. While most people agree that humans have an obligation to care for animals and treat them humanely, the idea that they have rights remains contentious.

PROS

Human beings are accorded rights on the basis that they are able to think and to feel pain. Many other animals are also able to think (to some extent) and are certainly able to feel pain. Therefore nonhuman animals should also be accorded rights, e.g., to a free and healthy life.

CONS

Human beings are infinitely more complex than any other living creatures. Their abilities to think and talk, to form social systems with rights and responsibilities, and to feel emotions are developed well beyond any other animals. Trying to prevent the most obvious cases of unnecessary suffering or torture of animals is reasonable, but beyond that, nonhuman animals do not deserve to be given "rights."

Ever since the publication of Charles Darwin's *Origin of Species* in 1859 we have known that human beings are related by common ancestry to all other animals. We owe a duty of care to our animal cousins.

That we are (incredibly distantly) related to other animals does not mean that they have "rights." This sort of thinking would lead to absurdities. Should we respect the "right" to life of bacteria? We might wish to reduce unnecessary animal suffering, but not because all creatures to which we are distantly related have rights.

We should err on the side of caution in ascribing rights to human or nonhuman creatures. If we place high standards (such as the ability to think, speak, or even to enter into a social contract) on the ascription of rights, there is a danger that not only animals but also human infants and mentally handicapped adults will be considered to have no rights.

Only human beings who are members of society have rights. Rights are privileges that come with certain social duties and moral responsibilities. Animals are not capable of entering into this sort of "social contract"—they are neither moral nor immoral, they are amoral. They do not respect our "rights," and they are irrational and entirely instinctual. Amoral and irrational creatures have neither rights nor duties—they are more like robots than people. All human beings or potential human beings (e.g., unborn children) can potentially be given rights, but nonhuman animals do not fall into that category.

Cruelty to animals is the sign of an uncivilized society; it encourages violence and barbarism in society more generally. A society that respects animals and restrains base and violent instincts is a more civilized one.

Using animals for our own nutrition and pleasure is completely natural. In the wild animals struggle to survive, are hunted by predators, and compete for food and resources. Human beings have been successful in this struggle for existence and do not need to feel ashamed of exploiting their position as a successful species in the evolutionary process.

That a small number of extremists and criminals have attached themselves to the animal rights movement does not invalidate the cause. Why shouldn't animal rights supporters and activists take medicine? They are morally obligated to take care of themselves in the best way they can until more humane research methods are developed and implemented.

Animal rights activists are hypocrites, extremists, and terrorists who don't care about human life. Organizations like the Animal Liberation Front use terrorist tactics and death threats; People for the Ethical Treatment of Animals is also an extremist organization. These extremists still avail themselves of modern medicine, however, which could not have been developed without experiments and tests on animals. Animal welfare is a reasonable concern, but talking of animal "rights" is a sign of extremism and irrationality.

Sample Motions:
 This House believes that animals have rights too.
 This House would respect animals' rights.
 This House condemns the exploitation of animals.

Web Links:
 • Animal Rights FAQ. http://www.animal-rights.com/arpage.htm>
 Includes about 100 FAQs, biographies of animal rights activists, lists of US and UK organizations, bibliography, and links to other animal rights groups.
 • EthicsUpdates.Edu: The Moral Status of Animals. <http://ethics.acusd.edu/animal.html>
 Includes essays on the moral status of animals as well as links to Supreme Court decisions on animals and sites relating to animal rights.

• People for the Ethical Treatment of Animals. <http://www.peta-online.org/>
Home page for radical animal rights organization includes news stories on animals and animal rights.

Further Reading:
Singer, Peter. *Animal Liberation*. Avon, 1991.
Wise, Steven M., and Jane Goodall. *Rattling the Cage: Toward Legal Rights for Animals*. Perseus, 2000.

CREO

ARTS SUBSIDIES, ABOLITION OF

Government support for the arts has a long history, with members of the aristocracy having acted as patrons for artists, including Beethoven, Mozart, and Shakespeare. Now, artists, including poets, playwrights, painters and sculptors, and performance artists, receive subsidies or grants from governmental and non-governmental organizations. Much of the funding these organizations receive is provided by the National Endowment for the Arts (NEA), which was founded in 1965. In the mid-1990s, the NEA came under fire for supporting artists who produced and exhibited what many considered objectionable, even pornographic, work masquerading under the rubric of "art." Since then, the NEA has focused more on supporting mainstream efforts like community theater and arts education. The cry to abolish the NEA has subsided and Congress has expressed its approval of the NEA. Although the NEA is again on firm footing, the legitimacy of government subsidies for artists is still in question.

PROS

The financial struggle that artists experience is one way to weed the good artists from the bad. Only those who are truly dedicated will make the sacrifices needed to succeed. Others will enter other occupations where their creativity and talents can be rewarded. Artists could also find paid employment that will enable them to continue working on their art. If an artist's work is worthy of financial support, that artist will find a patron from the private sector who will support him or her.

Government subsidies for art simply take money away from middle-class and low-income people to subsidize a self-indulgent hobby for the rich. The kind of art that the majority of Americans are interested in, popular movies and music, for example, is not subsidized. Just as a rock band should not receive government funds to make ticket prices lower, neither should operas or ballets. Let the rich who want to attend these kinds of performances pay full price; why should taxpayers underwrite bargain prices for entertainment for the wealthy?

Subsidies could function as a way to reward artists who are creating what the government prefers. In this way, subsidies could lead to government censorship of art to silence critics. Communist dictatorships subsi-

CONS

The creative process needs time. If artists must work to make ends meet, when will they have the time and the creative energy to complete their projects? Without federal funding for grants, few artists will be able to continue their work and maintain a reasonable standard of living. Artists will be forced to enter the workforce and abandon art.

The NEA costs each American only 36 cents a year. Although some NEA money is used to support arts that are traditionally supported by individuals with higher incomes, much of the NEA budget supports artists who work with programs like art education in schools and community theater. Projects like these benefit all children and give people across the country ways to contribute to making their community a better place.

Arts in America are a unifying experience. People from different backgrounds can communicate through art and share experiences and talents. Artistic expression is central to who we are as Americans and as human

dized "patriotic art" but squelched independent artists. Having artists rely on the government for their "daily bread" risks their artistic integrity; how could they be social critics and advocate for change in the system, when it is the system that is putting food on the table? The strings attached to subsidies make them potential weapons against democracy.

Historically, patrons did not support unknown and unproven talent. Artists gained patronage only after proving their worth. In the current system of subsidies, new, unproven, and often substandard artists receive grants. Artists who are already successful generally do not need the grants to meet their living expenses. Mozart and Beethoven, if they were living today, would find many opportunities in the private sector and would not need to rely on government subsidies.

Subsidies usually support artists who have created art that most people object to. Robert Mapplethorpe with his homoerotic photographs and Andres Serrano with his photograph of a crucifix submerged in his own urine are specific examples of artists who taxpayers have supported. Artists should have the freedom to create any type of art they want, but taxpayer money should not be used to fund projects that are indecent. If private funds are used, then the American people cannot claim they have involuntarily supported the creation of perverse and vile works.

beings. Supporting artists is crucial to preserving our values and transmitting our American heritage to future generations. In addition, federal support of artists is patriotic because art builds and preserves American traditions. The grant process, because it is run by artists, ensures the independence of the NEA and reduces the danger of censorship.

Tradition is on the side of those in power supporting the arts. Since the Renaissance, composers and artists have been supported by popes, kings, and other patrons. In our democracy, this burden falls to government to ensure that the next Mozart or Beethoven will not forgo his or her artistic vision for lack of funds.

The Mapplethorpe and Serrano cases are isolated incidents. The vast majority of art that is produced through subsidies is art that most taxpayers would support. The NEA has made many changes in the way it awards grants since those incidents. In fact, many of the same members of Congress who called for an abolition of the NEA over this issue voted for an increase in funding in July of 2002. Congress mandates that the criteria of decency and respect be used in evaluating grant proposals. Overall, the artwork supported by subsidies would make most Americans proud.

Sample Motions:
This House would tell Congress to stop funding the NEA's artist subsidy programs.
This House believes that subsidizing artists is detrimental to democracy.
This House would increase subsidies for artists.
This House believes that stopping subsidies would harm art in America.

Web Links:
• Libertarian Party Position on Subsidies. <http://www.lp.org/press/archive.php?function=view&record=376>
Libertarian Party argues against government funding of the arts.
• National Endowment for the Arts. <http://arts.endow.gov>
Site maintained by the agency in charge of distributing federal grants to the arts contains useful information about how the process works and about the benefits of art in America.
• NPR's Talk of the Nation Archive. <http://www.npr.org/ramarchives/ne091901-2.ram>
Audio recording of a debate on NPR's *Talk of the Nation* offers multiple arguments on both sides of the funding debate.

Further Reading:
Bolton, Richard, ed. *Culture Wars: Documents from the Recent Controversies in the Arts.* New Press, 1992.
Netzer, Dick, and Dick Mietzer. *The Subsidized Muse: Public Support for the Arts in the United States.* Ashgate, 1993.
Zeigler, Joseph Wesley, et al. *Arts in Crisis: The National Endowment for the Arts Versus America.* A Cappella Books, 1994.

ASSASSINATION OF A DICTATOR

Often considered in the context of Adolph Hitler and Joseph Stalin, the issue regained topicality in the 1990s as leaders such as Saddam Hussein in Iraq and Slobodan Milosovic in Yugoslavia pursued bloody policies that led to war, ethnic cleansing, and genocide.

PROS

Deaths and much suffering could be prevented if one man is killed. The greater good demands a single evil act, especially if it would avert the immediate and certain danger of much worse evil.

Dictatorial systems are highly personal, so removing the driving force behind such a regime will result in its collapse, allowing a more popular and liberal government to replace it.

Assassination of a dictator may be the only way to effect change in a country where a repressive police state prevents any possibility of internal opposition. Cowed populaces need a signal in order to find the courage to campaign for change.

Dictators are a threat to international peace, not just to their own people. They tend to attack other countries to divert attention from their unpopular actions at home, thus assassination is justified as a means of preventing a war that might rapidly become regional or global.

If scruples over the morality of our actions prevent us from pursuing a greater good, effectively opposing evil will never be possible. Dictators themselves ignore most ethical standards and international conventions, thereby effectively placing themselves beyond the protection of the law.

The alternatives to assassination would all leave a dictator in power for many years. In that time not only will many more people suffer under a repressive system, but also the policies pursued by an out-of-touch and unrepresentative regime are likely to do serious harm

CONS

Murder can never be justified. If we assume the role of executioner without the backing of law, we are sinking to the level of the dictators. Any new government founded upon such an arbitrary act will lack moral legitimacy, undermining its popular support and making its failure likely.

Killing the individual will achieve nothing. Dictators are part of a wider ruling elite from which someone sharing the same autocratic values will emerge to take the assassinated leader's place. This successor is likely to use the assassination as the excuse for further repression.

Assassination is likely to be counterproductive, rallying popular feeling around a repressive regime as external enemies or internal minorities are blamed, rightly or wrongly, for the act. An unsuccessful assassination attempt is even more likely to bring about such a result.

Sometimes dictatorship is preferable to the alternatives, especially for those outside the country itself. Great powers have often supported autocrats who promote such powers' geopolitical interests in a way that a democratic regime would not. Sometimes dictators have successfully held together countries that otherwise might have descended into civil war and ethnic strife.

By assuming the power to take life arbitrarily, even in an apparently good cause, we cheapen the value of life itself. Many terrorists, criminals, and dictators could and have claimed similar legitimacy for their violent actions. Only if we respect human rights absolutely will our promotion of these values seem valid to others.

Alternatives such as constructive engagement or economic sanctions are preferable and much more likely to result in eventual liberalization of the regime, albeit slowly. The examples of Eastern Europe in 1989 and Yugoslavia in 2000 show that even in apparently hope-

to the whole nation and its economy, making eventual rebuilding much more costly in both human and economic terms.

less cases, change can come through popular action, often quickly and without great violence.

Sample Motions:
This House would assassinate a dictator.
This House would assassinate. . . (supply name of current dictator).
This House believes that murder isn't always wrong.
This House believes that violence is sometimes the answer.

Further Reading:
Boesche, Robert. *Theories of Tyranny: From Plato to Arendt.* Pennsylvania State University Press, 1995.
Brooker, Paul. *Non-Democratic Regimes: Theory, Government & Politics.* St. Martin's Press, 2000.
Lee, Stephen. *European Dictatorships, 1918–1945.* Routledge, 2000.

ASSISTED SUICIDE

Assisted suicide is currently being discussed and debated in many countries. The central question is: If a terminally ill person decides that he or she wishes to end his or her life, is it acceptable for others, primarily physicians, to assist them? For many years assisted suicide was illegal in all US states, but in the past decades organizations like the Hemlock Society and individuals, most notably Dr Jack Kevorkian, have campaigned for a change in the law. They argue that terminally ill patients should not have to suffer needlessly and should be able to die with dignity. In 1997 Oregon became the first state to legalize physician-assisted suicide. Four years later conservative attorney general John Ashcroft ordered federal drug agents to punish doctors who used federally controlled drugs to help the terminally ill die. In April 2002 a district judge ruled that Ashcroft had overstepped his authority. In 2001 the Netherlands became the first country to legalize euthanasia and physician-assisted suicide.

PROS

Every human being has a right to life, perhaps the most basic and fundamental of all our rights. However, with every right comes a choice. The right to speech does not remove the option to remain silent; the right to vote brings with it the right to abstain. In the same way, the right to choose to die is implicit in the right to life.

Those in the late stages of a terminal disease have a horrific future: the gradual decline of the body, the failure of organs, and the need for artificial life support. In some cases, the illness will slowly destroy their minds, the essence of themselves. Even when this is not the case, the huge amounts of medication required to "control" pain will often leave them in a delirious and incapable state. Faced with this, it is surely more humane that these individuals be allowed to choose the manner

CONS

There is no comparison between the right to life and other rights. When you choose to remain silent, you may change your mind at a later date; when you choose to die, you have no such second chance. Participating in someone's death is to participate in depriving them of all choices they might make in the future and is therefore immoral.

It is always wrong to give up on life. Modern palliative care is immensely flexible and effective, and helps to preserve quality of life as far as possible. Terminally ill patients need never be in pain, even at the very end. Society's role is to help them live their lives as well as they can. Counseling, which helps patients come to terms with their condition, can help.

of their own end and die with dignity.

Society recognizes that suicide is unfortunate but acceptable in some circumstances. Those who end their own lives are not seen as evil. The illegality of assisted suicide is therefore particularly cruel for those who are disabled by disease and are unable to die without assistance.

Those who commit suicide are not evil, and those who attempt to take their own lives are not prosecuted. However, if someone is threatening to kill himself or herself, your moral duty is to try to stop them. You would not, for example, simply ignore a man standing on a ledge and threatening to jump simply because it is his choice; and you would definitely not assist in his suicide by pushing him. In the same way, you should try to help a person with a terminal illness, not help him to die.

Suicide is a lonely, desperate act, carried out in secrecy and often is a cry for help. The impact on the family can be catastrophic. By legalizing assisted suicide, the process can be brought out into the open. In some cases, families might have been unaware of the true feelings of their loved one. Being forced to confront the issue of a family member's illness may do great good, perhaps even allowing the family to persuade the patient not to end his life. In other cases, it makes the family part of the process. They can understand the reasons behind a patient's decision without feelings of guilt and recrimination, and the terminally ill patient can speak openly to them about her feelings before her death.

Demanding that family members take part in such a decision can be an unbearable burden. Many may resent a loved one's decision to die and would be either emotionally scarred or estranged by the prospect of being in any way involved with the death. Assisted suicide also introduces a new danger, that the terminally ill may be pressured into ending their lives by others who are not prepared to support them through their illness. Even the most well regulated system would have no way to ensure that this did not happen.

At the moment, doctors are often put into an impossible position. A good doctor will form close bonds with patients and will want to give them the best quality of life possible. However, when a patient has lost or is losing his ability to live with dignity and expresses a strong desire to die, doctors are legally unable to help. To say that modern medicine can totally eradicate pain is a tragic oversimplification of suffering. While physical pain may be alleviated, the emotional pain of a slow and lingering death, of the loss of the ability to live a meaningful life, can be horrific. A doctor's duty is to address his or her patient's suffering, be it physical or emotional. As a result, doctors are already helping their patients to die—although it is not legal, assisted suicide does happen. It would be far better to recognize this and bring the process into the open, where it can be regulated. True abuses of the doctor-patient relationship and incidents of involuntary euthanasia would then be far easier to limit.

A doctor's role must remain clear. The guiding principle of medical ethics is to do no harm: A physician must not be involved in deliberately harming her patient. Without this principle, the medical profession would lose a great deal of trust; admitting that killing is an acceptable part of a doctor's role would likely increase the danger of involuntary euthanasia, not reduce it. Legalizing assisted suicide also places an unreasonable burden on doctors. The daily decisions made to preserve life can be difficult enough. To require them to also carry the immense moral responsibility of deciding who can and cannot die, and the further responsibility of actually killing patients, is unacceptable. This is why the vast majority of medical professionals oppose the legalization of assisted suicide: Ending the life of a patient goes against all they stand for.

Sample Motions:
This House would legalize assisted suicide.
This House would die with dignity.

Web Links:
- Doctor-Assisted Suicide: A Guide to Websites and the Literature. <http://web.lwc.edu/administrative/library/suic.htm>
Links to general information and sites, pro and con, on physician-assisted suicide. Contains an excellent chronology.
- Euthanasia.Com. <http://www.euthanasia.com/>
Provides medical and legal information from those opposed to assisted suicide.
- FinalExit.Org. <http://www.finalexit.org/>
General site containing information on legislation, euthanasia in practice, and individuals prominent in the campaign to legalize assisted suicide.
- The Hemlock Society. <http://www.hemlock.org/>
Right-to-die group provides information on organization services and the progress of legislation legalizing assisted suicide.

Further Reading:
Dworkin, Gerald, R. G. Fry, and Sissela Bok. *Euthanasia and Physician-Assisted Suicide.* Cambridge University Press, 1998.
Humphrey, Derek. *Final Exit: The Practicalities of Self-Deliverance and Assisted Suicide for the Dying.* DTP, 1997.
Shavelson, Lonny. *A Chosen Death: The Dying Confront Assisted Suicide.* University of California Press, 1998.

CRSO

BIODIVERSITY AND ENDANGERED SPECIES

"Biodiversity" refers to the variety of bacteria, plants, and animals that live on our planet and the unique behavioral patterns and activities of each species. Scientists believe that biodiversity is essential to human life on Earth. In recent years environmentalists have become concerned about the decline in the number of species. International agreements such as the Convention on International Trade in Endangered Species of Wild Fauna and Flora (CITES) aim to protect biodiversity. Nevertheless, current research suggests that species are disappearing at an alarming rate and that approximately one-quarter of all species will be extinct within the next few decades. Environmentalists are particularly concerned about endangered species in developing nations, where the economic needs of a poor population may threaten the existence of other life.

PROS

The species Homo sapiens is unprecedented and unique among all life on Earth. Human sentience and intelligence far surpass those of other creatures. These gifts have allowed human beings to populate the Earth, construct civilizations and build industry, and affect the environment in a way that no other species can. This great power comes with great responsibility, and we should avoid abusing our planet, lest we cause irreparable damage—damage like the extinction of species and the consequent reduction in biodiversity caused by deforestation, over-fishing, hunting, and the illegal trade in animal products and exotic animals themselves.

Protecting endangered species is an extension of our existing system of ethics. Just as modern civilization

CONS

The idea that extinctions will lead to ecological disaster is an exaggeration. Fossil evidence shows that mass extinctions have occurred many times throughout the history of life on Earth, one of the most recent being the die-out of the dinosaurs. After every collapse of biodiversity, it has rebounded, with Earth coming to no lasting harm. Extinctions are simply part of the natural evolutionary process.

No species on Earth would put the interest of another species above its own, so why should human beings?

protects its weaker and less able members, so humanity should safeguard the welfare of other, less-privileged species. Animals are sentient creatures whose welfare we should protect (even if they may not have the same full "rights" that we accord to human beings).

Furthermore, since the very beginnings of life, nature has operated by the Darwinian principle of "survival of the fittest." Life forms will always risk extinction unless they adapt to new challenges. Humans have no obligation to save the weaker species; if they cannot match our pace, they deserve to die out and be supplanted by others.

The most successful pharmaceuticals have often used nature as a starting point. Antibiotics were first discovered through the study of fungi, and many anti-cancer drugs are derived from the bark of Amazon trees. Every time a species becomes extinct, scientists forever lose an opportunity to make a new discovery.

Modern science has advanced to the point where inspiration from nature is no longer required. Today, medicines derived from natural products are in the minority. In any case, the upcoming era of genetic engineering will allow humankind to rid itself of disease without resorting to medicines.

As occupants of this planet, we must have respect for other life forms, especially since life on Earth may be the only life in the universe. We can show this respect by making every effort to prevent the extinction of existing species, thereby preserving biodiversity.

Even if this respect was justified, its expression comes at a significant cost. Biodiversity policies are costly and spend taxpayers' money that could better be used on health care and social services. It does not make sense for us to concentrate on other species when humanity has not yet sorted out its own welfare.

Maintaining biodiversity is a global problem and demands a global solution. The developed world should apply pressure on the developing world to adopt more environmentally friendly policies.

Environmental protection and the protection of biodiversity are very much a luxury of developed nations (First World). Many of these policies are beyond the financial means of developing nations, and implementing them would stunt economic growth and disenfranchise their citizens. It is hypocritical for developed nations to criticize the lack of environmental protection in the developing world, considering that the First World got to its current position through an Industrial Revolution that paid no heed to biodiversity, pollution, and other such concerns.

Sample Motions:
This House believes in biodiversity.
This House fears the way of the dodo.

Web Links:
- Bagheera. <http://www.bagheera.com/inthewild/vanishing.htm>
Presents information on approximately 30 endangered animals, the problems they face and what can be done to save them from extinction.
- The Born Free Foundation. <http://www.bornfree.org.uk/>
Site dedicated to the conservation of rare species in their natural habitat and the phasing out of traditional zoos.
- EELink.Net: Endangered Species. <http://eelink.net/EndSpp>
Offers information on endangered and extinct species, laws and policies on endangered species, and organizations involved in supporting biodiversity.
- The Natural History Museum, London: Biodiversity and World Map. <http://www.nhm.ac.uk/science/projects/worldmap/>
Contains map of global biodiversity as well as information on biogeography and conservation priorities.
- San Diego Zoo: Endangered Species Report. <http://www.sandiegozoo.org/special/abcnews/index.html>
Offers information on what scientists are doing to understand and alleviate the plight of endangered species.
- Tom Lovejoy's Reith Lecture on Biodiversity. <http://news.bbc.co.uk/hi/english/static/events/reith_2000/lecture2.stm>

Lecture supporting ecosystem management to sustain biodiversity.
• The Virtual Library of Ecology & Biodiversity. <http://conbio.net/vl/>
Provides links to hundreds of sites on ecology and biodiversity.
• World Conservation Monitoring Centre: Biodiversity. <http://www.wcmc.org.uk/species/index.html>
Presents information on the status, trends, and distribution of species in support of conservation and the sustainable management of biodiversity.
• World Conservation Monitoring Centre: CITES. <http://www.wcmc.org.uk/CITES/eng/index.shtml>
A clearinghouse for data and resources on biodiversity.

Further Reading:
Dobson, Andrew. *Conservation and Biodiversity.* H. W Freeman, 1998.
Eldredge, Niles. *Life in the Balance: Humanity and the Biodiversity Crisis.* Princeton University Press, 2000.
Jeffries, Mike. *Biodiversity and Conservation.* Routledge, 1997.

ᐊᔕᐁ

CALENDAR REFORM

This is an interesting proposition, if one that is not taken particularly seriously. Past suggestions to reform the Gregorian calendar have all failed in the face of tradition, convenience, and apathy. Three of the most common proposals for reform are:

*• The **World Calendar** is based on a 52-week, 364-day year, starting on Sunday, January 1. The 365th day has no day of the week and is called "Year-End Day." In leap years a Leap-Year Day is inserted between June and July. January, April, July, and October all have 31 days; the other months have 30.*

*• The **International Fixed Calendar** divides the year into 13 months of 28 days each, with the 365th day ("Year Day") outside the months, and a Leap Day after June 28th in leap years. All months begin on Sundays. The new month, which would come between June and July, is called Sol.*

*• The **Perpetual Calendar** has four three-month quarters, each beginning on a Monday. Like the previous two calendars, an extra Year-End Day and Leap-Year Day are inserted.*

PROS

The Gregorian calendar has 12 months of different lengths (with no month being one-twelfth of the year), uneven half- and quarter-years, and no standard first day of the year or of any month. This makes financial planning in particular difficult, and public holidays are irregular. Some companies use the International Fixed Calendar to pay their employees; others work on the basis of 13 months and give the last month's pay as a Christmas bonus.

The Gregorian calendar is fixed on the starting date of 1 C.E., which has significance only for Christians as the supposed year of Christ's birth. A standard calendar for all religions and countries makes much more sense, fixed on a starting point in history with significance for all people.

History and the increasing globalization of modern

CONS

Under all of the proposed calendars, national holidays would have to be changed and regular religious observances disturbed. The Y2K computer programming problem at the end of 1999 showed us how costly readjusting the calendar can be in the workplace. The administrative and financial burden caused by introducing a new calendar is so immense as to make the idea unthinkable.

Any choice of a starting point for a calendar is arbitrary, and although the Gregorian calendar had its origins in Christian history, it has its own significance by now. A standard calendar for all races and religions is utterly inappropriate: Different cultures have different holidays, and their calendars should be appropriate to their traditions.

Reform is not remotely inevitable, given the total lack

society have shown us that standardization is inevitable. Just as the metric system is increasingly commonplace, calendar reform is sure to come.

The calendar has been successfully reformed in the past; the Gregorian calendar was devised only in 1582 (by Pope Gregory XIII). There would be a cost in reforming again, but this would be offset in the long term by savings resulting from simplification.

of support for change other than by radical fringe groups. If accounting departments want to follow calendars different from those used by the rest of society, they can; calendar years, tax years, and academic years are frequently different anyway.

Calendar reform has also failed in the past, e.g., the French revolutionaries introduced a new calendar in 1793 and abandoned it in 1806, and in the Soviet Union five-day weeks (without Saturday or Sunday) were temporarily implemented.

Sample Motions:
This House would reform the calendar.
This House believes that the Gregorian calendar makes no sense.

Web Links:
- Calendars. <http://astro.nmsu.edu/~lhuber/leaphist.html>
Offers information on the history and principles behind various calendars, including the Indian, Hebrew, and Islamic calendars.
- Calendar Reform. <http://personal.ecu.edu/mccartyr/calendar-reform.html>
Offers articles on historical calendar reforms as well as current proposals for change.
- The Calendar Zone. <http://www.calendarzone.com>
Provides links to information on calendar reform and a wide range of calendars.

Further Reading:
Travis, Timothy. 4000, *The Fifth Milenium, Six Revolooshunairy Ideas*. Astcr Esprit Press, 1994.

ᘓᔈᘎ❶

CAMPAIGN FINANCE REFORM

Political campaigns have changed in nature in the modern era. Two centuries ago, political campaigning was thought to be "ungentlemanly"; today, cross-country trips and expensive television advertisements have become both necessary and the norm. The need for ever-larger sums of money has created a crisis in the political system because donors of large sums can attain positions of tremendous influence. Recognizing the natural link between money and political corruption, Congress took steps to limit personal donations to candidates during the 1970s. The huge sums, however, continued to flow: Major donors made contributions to the political parties, rather than to the candidates directly—and the parties offered indirect support to the candidates (e.g., through issue ads that supported a candidate's position, but not the candidate by name). Many politicians argued that the system was being corrupted by money and by the need to raise it, and pushed for radical reforms. Others defended the system as it stood, arguing that citizens should be free to use their money to advance their political ideas.

PROS

With contributions to a candidate, donors effectively buy influence (or at least access, which may be the same thing), so that their interests are represented when laws are made. The result is inequality: The wealthy have more influence than the poor.

CONS

Donors give money to a candidate because they agree with the candidate's positions. The donation is, in effect, a form of speech and should be protected by the First Amendment.

More often than not, television campaigns are superficial and distorted. Advertisements should be replaced by publicly financed forums that would allow candidates to discuss political issues in a substantive way.

Candidates cannot convey their ideas to the voting populace without expensive advertising campaigns in the electronic and print media. Finance reform impedes their ability to communicate with voters.

The cost of running political campaigns has gotten so high that ordinary citizens cannot run for office; candidates need to be personally wealthy or well connected to sources of funds. Finance reform would level the playing field.

As no limit is placed on how much can be spent by wealthy candidates to finance their own campaigns, finance reform will put poorer candidates, who depend on contributions, at a disadvantage.

The cost of political campaigns has forced legislators to spend much of their time raising money for their reelection campaigns. Limiting campaign expenses would eliminate this distraction.

Experience has shown that incumbents usually have an advantage in elections, largely because they are well known. Finance reform will hurt the ability of challengers to overcome that advantage.

Large contributions are made by large organizations: corporations, unions, trade associations and the like. The size of these contributions means that legislators pay more attention to the organizations and less attention to individual voters.

Legislators pass laws that have direct and immediate effects on organizations. These organizations should be free to support candidates who are sympathetic to their interests.

Although Congress passed laws limiting campaign contributions almost 30 years ago, the emergence of political action committees and "soft money" (given to parties, rather than candidates) has made the original restrictions useless. Reform is needed to close loopholes.

Any restrictions are doomed to fail because individuals and organizations will never surrender their right to express themselves politically. No restrictions should be placed on contributions, which should, however, be fully disclosed to the public.

Sample Motions:

This House would make all political campaigns publicly financed.

This House would ban paid political advertising on television.

Web Links:

• The Cato Institute: Money and Politics. <http://www.cato.org/campaignfinance/>

Members of the institute offer arguments on why campaign finance reform is unconstitutional.

• Hoover Institution, Public Policy Inquiry: Campaign Finance. <http://www.campaignfinancesite.org/>

The Hoover Institution at Stanford University offers history, Supreme Court rulings, proposals, and current legislation.

• Public Campaign: Clean Money, Clean Elections. <http://www.publicampaign.org>

Web site of an advocacy group that supports sweeping reforms.

Further Reading:

Corrado, Anthony, et al. *Campaign Finance Reform: A Sourcebook*. Brookings Institution, 1997.

Donnelly, David, et al. *Money and Politics: Financing Our Elections Democratically*. Beacon Press, 1999.

Smith, Bradley A. *Unfree Speech: The Folly of Campaign Finance Reform*. Princeton University Press, 2001.

CR℘

CAPITAL PUNISHMENT

Before Ryan left office in early 2003, he pardoned four death row inmates and commuted the death sentences of all other inmates to life in prison without parole. In a speech justifying his action he said that the state's death penalty system was "arbitrary and capricious-and, therefore, immoral."

PROS

The principle of capital punishment is that certain crimes deserve nothing less than death as a just, proportionate, and effective response. The problems associated with the death penalty are concerned with its implementation rather than its principle. Murderers forgo their rights as humans the moment they take away the rights of another human. By wielding such a powerful punishment as the response to murder, society is affirming the value that is placed on the right to life of the innocent person. Many more innocent people have been killed by released, paroled, or escaped murderers than innocent people executed.

Capital punishment is 100% effective as a deterrent to the criminal being executed; that killer cannot commit any more crimes. As a deterrent to others, it depends on how often the death penalty is applied. In the US, where less than 1% of murderers are executed, it is difficult to assess the true effect of deterrence. But a 1985 study (Stephen K. Layson, University of North Carolina) showed that one execution deterred 18 murders.

If and when discrimination occurs, it should be corrected. Consistent application of the death penalty against murderers of all races would abolish the idea that it can be a racist tool. Make the death penalty mandatory in all capital cases.

Opponents of the death penalty prefer to ignore the fact that they themselves are responsible for its high costs by filing a neverending succession of appeals. Prisons in many countries are overcrowded and underfunded. This problem is made worse by life sentences or delayed death sentences for murderers. Why should the taxpayer bear the cost of supporting a murderer for an entire lifetime?

Different countries and societies can have different attitudes toward the justifiability of executing mentally incompetent or teenaged murderers. If society opposes such executions, then implementation of the death

CONS

Execution is, in simplest terms, state-sanctioned killing. It devalues the respect we place on human life. How can we say that killing is wrong if we sanction killing criminals? More important is the proven risk of executing innocent people. At least 23 innocent people were executed in the US in the twentieth century. The execution of an innocent person can never be justified.

Higher execution rates can actually increase violent crime rates. California averaged six executions annually from 1952 to 1967 and had twice the murder rate of the period from 1968 until 1991, when there were no executions. In New York, from 1907 to 1964, the months immediately following an execution saw murders increase by an average of two.

Implementation of the death penalty, particularly in America, can suffer from social or racial bias and can be used as a weapon against a certain section of society. In the US nearly 90% of those executed were convicted of killing whites, despite the fact that non-whites make up more than 50% of all murder victims.

Capital punishment costs more than life without parole. Studies in the US show that capital cases, from arrest to execution, cost between $1 million and $7 million. A case resulting in life imprisonment costs around $500,000.

Defendants who are mentally incompetent will often answer "Yes" to questions in the desire to please others. This can lead to false confessions. Over 30 mentally retarded people have been executed in the US since

PROS	CONS
penalty in these cases is a problem. For opponents to seize on such cases is to cloud the issue; this is not an argument against the principle.	1976.
Some criminals are beyond rehabilitation. Perhaps capital punishment should be reserved for serial killers, terrorists, murderers of policemen, and so on.	By executing criminals you are ruling out the possibility of rehabilitation. You have to consider that they may repent of their crime, serve a sentence as punishment, and emerge as a reformed and useful member of society.

Sample Motions:

This House supports the death penalty.

This House would take an eye for an eye, a tooth for a tooth, and a life for a life.

Web Links:

- Amnesty International and the Death Penalty. <http://www.web.amnesty.org/rmp/dplibrary.nsf/index?openview>
Presents facts and figures on the death penalty as well as current developments on the issue.
- Derechos Human Rights: Death Penalty Links. <http://www.derechos.org/dp/>
Links to hundreds of sites on all aspects of the death penalty, both pro and con.
- Issues and Controversies: The Death Penalty. <http://www.facts.com/cd/i00015.htm>
Provides a good overview of the issue in the US to 1997.
- Pro-Death Penalty.Com. <http://www.prodeathpenalty.com>
Offers information from a pro-death penalty point of view; also contains good statistical information.

Further Reading:

Costanzo, Mark. *Just Revenge: Costs and Consequences of the Death Penalty.* St. Martin's Press, 1997.

Hanks, Gardner. *Against the Death Penalty: Christian and Secular Arguments Against Capital Punishment.* Herald Press, 1997.

Pojman, Louis, and Jeffrey Reiman. *The Death Penalty: For and Against.* Rowman and Littlefield, 1998.

CREO

CELL PHONES, BANNING OF USE IN CARS

The use of cell phones while driving has been blamed for causing a considerable number of traffic accidents. As a result, a number of countries are seriously considering prohibiting drivers from using them, following the lead of Ireland and New York State. Although the ban seems logical to some, others contend that it will not solve the problem of distracted drivers.

PROS

Using a cell phone while driving is very dangerous. Physically holding a handset removes one hand from the controls, making accidents more likely, while dialing is even worse, as it also requires users to divert attention from the road. Research shows that drivers speaking on a cell phone have much slower reactions in braking tests than nonusers; such drivers have reaction times that are worse even than the reaction times of drunk drivers.

CONS

Clearly, using a cell phone while driving can be dangerous in some circumstances, but such use is not dangerous in many situations, for example while the car is at a standstill in gridlocked traffic, while waiting at traffic lights, or while driving on a quiet road with good visibility. Other actions in a car can be at least as distracting—eating, changing tapes, retuning the radio, arguing with passengers about directions, trying to stop children squabbling, etc. We should not introduce a law that victimizes cell phone users under all conditions, while ignoring many other causes of accidents.

Research shows very little difference between using a handheld and a hands-free cell phone, in terms of impaired concentration and slower reaction times in braking tests. For some reason the brain treats a telephone conversation differently from talking to a passenger, perhaps because the passenger is also aware of possible road hazards in a way the telephone caller cannot be and, accordingly, stops talking when the driver needs to concentrate. In any case, voice-activated technology is often unreliable, thus frustrating drivers, who lose concentration as a result. Banning one kind of cell phone while allowing the use of another kind would be inconsistent. In addition, hands-free cell phones cause just as many accidents.

Hands-free cell phone sets, with earpieces and voice-automated dialing, are the answer. These allow drivers to communicate freely without taking their hands off the controls or their eyes off the road. Effectively there is no difference between talking to someone on a hands-free cell phone and holding a conversation with a passenger next to you; in fact, the latter is more dangerous as you may be tempted to turn your head to directly address the passenger.

Existing laws are inadequate; driving without due care and attention is a limited charge that can be very difficult to prove. In any case, every time a driver of a moving vehicle uses a cell phone, a potentially dangerous situation is created. This justifies a specific offense being introduced.

Society has no need for a specific law relating to cell phone use; almost every country has laws against driving without due care and attention. Thus if someone is driving dangerously because of inappropriate use of a cell phone, the laws to prosecute are already on the books. The police should enforce the existing rules more consistently. Such enforcement could be coupled with energetic advertising campaigns to warn people of a range of potentially dangerous driving habits.

New laws would be enforceable because billing records show when a phone has been in use. Technological improvements in photography may also allow the automatic detection of drivers breaking laws against cell phone use at the wheel. In any case, just because a law is not completely enforceable does not mean that it should be scrapped.

Banning cell phone use by drivers will be unenforceable—often it will just be a policeman's word against a driver's. This is especially true of hands-free phones, where accused motorists could simply claim to be singing along to the radio or talking to themselves. In any case, the widespread introduction of speed cameras in many countries and an increased public fear of violent crime have led to the redeployment of the traffic police who would be needed to enforce such laws.

Using a cell phone in the car is unnecessary—everyone coped without them 10 years ago, and little else about life has changed radically enough to make them indispensable, so no real loss of personal liberty occurs with the banning of cell phone use while driving. Drivers always have the choice of pulling over and calling from a parked vehicle. The ban will also protect drivers from pressure from bosses who call them while on the road, requiring their employees to risk their lives for the company.

Using cell phones on the road could improve safety, for example, by allowing delayed employees to call the office rather than drive recklessly in an effort to arrive on time. Drivers now often use cell phones to report accidents to the emergency services and alert the police to others driving dangerously, stray animals, unsafe loads, etc.

The state's authority to control the actions of drivers is already accepted, for example, through speed limits or rules against drunk driving. Dangerous driving meets

The state has no right to interfere so blatantly in our personal liberties. Cell phones don't kill people, bad driving does, and simply banning the use of phones

the classic liberal test by endangering not just the individual but others, including drivers, passengers, and pedestrians thus society has a right to intervene to protect the innocent. A new law signals social unacceptability and will send a message to drivers; the New York ban has already been highly effective.

while driving will penalize the many good drivers without removing the dangerous ones.

Sample Motions:
This House would ban drivers from using mobile phones.
This House would do more to promote road safety.
This House would tame technology.

Web Links:
• Cell Phones Bans May Not Make Roads Safer. <http://my.webmd.com/content/article/1728.82343>
Article on WebMDHealth, discussing how "hands-free" devices, suggested as alternatives to traditional cell phones, may cause even more problems.
• Driving with Cell Phones: What Have Highway Safety Researchers Learned? <http://www-nrd.nhtsa.dot.gov/PDF/nrd-13/BentsF_doc.pdf>
Summarizes findings of highway safety experts on the use of cell phones while driving.
• Insurance Institute for Highway Safety. <http://www.hwysafety.org/sr.htm>
Contains information on all aspects of highway safety, including the use of cell phones.

CRSO

CENSORSHIP OF THE ARTS

While all modern democracies value free expression, freedom of speech is never absolute. The restrictions a nation puts on speech are a product of its experience and culture. The United States views free speech as the cornerstone of American civil liberties and has few restrictions on expression. Nevertheless, conservatives have called for some type of censorship of art that they find morally offensive, such as Robert Mapplethorpe's sadomasochistic and homoerotic images of adult men and pictures of nude children. Many people are also disturbed by studies that show a correlation between watching violent films and television shows and violent behavior.

PROS

An individual's rights end when they impinge on the safety and rights of others. By enacting laws against incitement to racial hatred and similar hate speech, we acknowledge that freedom of expression should have limits. Art should be subject to the same restrictions as any other form of expression. By making an exception for art, we would be creating a legal loophole for content such as hate speech, which could seek protection on the grounds that it was a form of art.

Certain types of content (e.g., sexual content) are unsuitable for children despite their artistic merits. We should be able to develop a system of censorship, based on age, that protects our children.

CONS

Civil rights should not be curtailed in the absence of a clear and present danger to the safety of others. Furthermore, as long as no illegal acts were committed in the creative process, the public should have a choice in deciding whether to view the resulting content. Arguments about child pornography displayed as art are irrelevant because child pornography is illegal.

An age-rated system is a very blunt tool. It does not take into account differing levels of education or maturity. Censorship also deprives parents of the right to raise their children as they see fit. Adults have the right to vote, bear arms, and die for their country. Why should

PROS	CONS
	they be deprived of the ability to decide what they or their children see? Finally, we have to remember that people are not forced to view art; they don't have to look at something they think is offensive.
Censorship may actually help artists. The general public is far more likely to support erotic art if it knows that children won't see it!	Censorship is far more likely to hurt the arts. If the government labels art as unsuitable for children, the general public is not going to want to fund it.
Many forms of modern art push the boundaries of what is acceptable or aim for the lowest level of taste. This type of content is unacceptable, and governments should have the right to ban it.	Content that we consider acceptable today would have been regarded as taboo 50 years ago. If a novel or controversial piece of art is out of touch with society, society will reject it.
Excessive sex and violence in the media lead to similar behavior in viewers. This alone should justify censorship.	The correlation between watching violence and committing violent crimes is still not established. These studies are not exhaustive, and often are funded by special interest groups. We must also realize that correlation is different from causation. An alternative interpretation is that people with violent tendencies are more likely to be connoisseurs of violent art. Even if we believe that some people are likely to be corrupted, why should all of society be penalized? There are far better ways of reducing the crime rate, with far less cost in civil liberties, than censorship.
Even if some individuals manage to circumvent censorship laws, government has sent an important message about what society considers acceptable. The role of the state in setting social standards should not be underestimated, and censorship (be it through bans or minimum age requirements) is an important tool in this process.	Censorship is ultimately not feasible. Try censoring art on the Internet, for example! In addition, censoring art merely sends it underground and might glamorize the prohibited artwork. It is far better to display it so that people can judge for themselves.

Sample Motions:
    This House supports censorship of the arts.
    This House believes that nude art is lewd art.
    This House fears that artistic license is a license to kill.
    This House believes that you are what you see.

Web Links:
    • American Civil Liberties Union. <http://www.aclu.org>
    Offers information on laws, court cases, and challenges to free speech.
    • PBS: Culture Shock. <http://www.pbs.org/wgbh/cultureshock/>
    A companion site to a PBS series on art, cultural values, and freedom of expression.
    • University of Pennsylvania: Banned Books Online. <http://digital.library.upenn.edu/books/banned-books.html>
    On-line exhibit of books that have been the objects of censorship and censorship attempts.

Further Reading:
    Dubin, Stephen. *Arresting Images: Impolitic Art and Uncivil Actions*. Routledge, 1994.

CRಱಐ

CHEMICAL CASTRATION

Many people consider sexual abuse one of the worst crimes a person can commit. Some have suggested that sex offenders be punished by chemical castration in addition to a jail term. Chemical castration uses drugs to lower testosterone levels, blunting the sex drive. During the late 1990s several US states passed laws mandating or permitting judges to impose this treatment for certain kinds of paroled sex offenders.

PROS

Because sexual abuse is a horrific crime, damaging its victim both physically and psychologically, chemical castration is a suitable punishment. In many instances counseling cannot cure the psychological and physical urges behind these crimes. Chemical castration prevents repeat offenses (one of the main purposes of any punishment) and is a strong deterrent for prospective offenders.

Chemical castration will help offenders by freeing them from the urges that cause them to repeat their crimes. Many sexual criminals have said that they would like to be free of these urges but cannot control their actions, much like heroin addicts cannot control theirs. A chemical cure for these urges will free the offender.

Chemical castration will also stop the widespread stigmatization of and violence against sex offenders. In many cases, they are required to register with the police, who may post their names and addresses on Web sites or notify their neighbors. Some sex offenders who have served their sentences have been driven out of their homes. Sex offenders are also subject to violence from other prison inmates. If chemical castration were introduced, the public would no longer see such offenders as a threat, and they would be allowed to get on with their lives. Chemical castration removes both the public stigmatization and personal suffering of sex offenders.

CONS

Our justice system has rejected the barbaric practice of using physical pain or disfigurement as punishment in favor of a more enlightened system of reforming the offender. What would happen if the suspect were later found to be innocent? Imprisonment and counseling to prevent recidivism would be far more effective.

Even if chemical castration is combined with a jail term, it is still a far cruder and less effective treatment than prolonged psychotherapy. Also, the proposition's argument places the legal emphasis on helping the offender and may give the appearance of "coddling criminals."

There would be no such benefit. Witch hunts against sex offenders are not motivated by rational considerations. Chemical castration would not end public anxiety. Also, violence against sex offenders, both in and out of prison, is motivated by the desire to punish the original crime, not to prevent repeat offenses. Chemical castration is an unproven and unsubtle method that deserves no place in a modern penal system.

Sample Motions:
  This House would cure sex offenders by physical means.
  This House would use cure rather than prevention in dealing with sex offenders.
  This House would chemically castrate pedophiles.

Web Links:
  • American Civil Liberties Union (ACLU) Condemns Governor for Signing Mandatory Chemical Castration Law. <http://www.aclu.org/news/n091796b.html>
  ACLU press release presenting arguments opposing chemical castration.
  • Is Chemical Castration an Appropriate Punishment for Male Sex Offenders? <http://www.csun.edu/~psy453/crimes_y.htm>
  Information and links to articles in support of chemical castration.

Further Reading:
    Pallone, Nathaniel. *Rehabilitating Criminal Sexual Psychopaths.* Transaction, 1990.
    Prentky, Robert, and Anne Wolbert Burgess. *Forensic Management of Sexual Offenders.* Plenum, 1999.

ᚱᛊᚱ

CHILD OFFENDERS, STRICTER PUNISHMENT FOR

Most US states have separate justice codes and justice systems for juvenile offenders. Traditionally the main goal of these systems has been rehabilitation rather than punishment; courts have frequently sentenced delinquents to probation or counseling rather than jail. During the 1980s and early 1990s, the US experienced an unprecedented wave of juvenile crime, and although juvenile crime had dropped by the mid-1990s, a series of high-profile school shootings and murders by children as young as six kept the issue in the news. In response nearly every state passed laws making it easier for minors to be tried and incarcerated as adults.

PROS

The primary purpose of a justice system is the prevention of crime and the protection of the innocent. It is to achieve these purposes that children should not be entitled to lenient punishment. The purposes of punishment are proportional retribution, deterrence, and prevention of crime. Rehabilitation should at best be a secondary aim.

The "just desserts" theory of punishment argues that the retribution society takes against an offender should be proportional to the harm he has caused the victim. For example, a person who kills is more culpable than a person who robs or hurts. Because the harm children cause is the same as that caused by adults committing a similar offense, children should not receive special treatment. The assumption that children are not as morally culpable as adults is false.

Treating children more leniently than adults undermines the deterrent value of punishment. A 1996 survey in Virginia, for example, showed that 41% of youths have at various times either been in a gang or associated with gang activities. Of these, 69% said they joined because friends were involved and 60% joined for "excitement." This clearly shows that young adults do not take crime seriously because they think the justice system will treat them leniently.

The best way to prevent crime in the short run is to lock up the offenders. This stops them from immediately harming society. In the long term, these children will be reluctant to return to crime because of their

CONS

Child crime is different from adult crime. In most legal systems the offenders are not deemed to be fully functioning as moral agents. Thus, the best way to handle them is through rehabilitation rather than punishment.

Subjective culpability should play as important a part in punishment as the harm principle. That is why murder is punished more severely than negligent manslaughter, even though both cause the same harm. Children are not capable of making the same moral judgments as adults. It is the inability of children to form moral judgments that makes them less culpable and therefore worthy of lighter punishment.

The deterrence theory assumes that all crime is committed as a result of rational evaluation. If, indeed, 8- or 10-year-old children are capable of making rational calculations, then the prospect of spending several years in reform school should be no less a deterrent then spending the time in jail. It is still a curtailment of their liberty, and if they were rational, they would not want their liberty curtailed. The real problem is that most crimes are committed by people who do not make rational decisions.

This is an argument that would justify imprisoning people for life because that is the surest way to prevent them from harming anyone. Because this is plainly ridiculous, it must be accepted that locking a person up

memory of harsh punishment.

Rehabilitation (counseling and psychiatric treatment) is too lenient. It will make children believe that they are spending short periods of time at camp. In the US, more than half the boys who were ordered to undergo counseling rather than sentenced to detention committed crimes while in therapy. Rehabilitation programs should take place in a detention facility. Young offenders should be separated from hardened adult criminals, but they should not be given lighter sentences than adults who committed the same crimes.

is at best a short-term remedy. The long-term answer lies in rehabilitation.

The only long-term solution to juvenile crime is reform of the child. Children's characters are less formed and thus they are more amenable to reform. The rate of recidivism for child offenders in counseling in the US is significantly lower than that of adult offenders. Some children who have had counseling do return to crime, but a significant proportion does not. Putting children in prison with hardened adult offenders is likely to increase recidivism because they will be influenced by and learn from the adults.

Sample Motions:
This House would lower the age of criminal responsibility.
This House would punish children as if they were adults.
This House believes that sparing the rod spoils the child.

Web Links:
• Cornell Law Information Service: An Overview of Juvenile Justice. <http://www.law.cornell.edu/topics/juvenile.html>
Quick summary of the theory and current status of juvenile justice with links to specific statutes and court decisions.
• Juvenile Crime/Punishment Statistics. <http://crime.about.com/newsissues/crime/library/blfiles/bljuvstats.htm>
Offers links to statistics on juvenile crimes and arrests, juveniles in the court system, juveniles in adult jails, and juveniles and the death penalty.
• National Criminal Justice Reference Service—Juvenile Justice. <http://virlib.ncjrs.org/JuvenileJustice.asp>
Provides links to resources on a wide variety of juvenile justice topics, including alternatives to incarceration.

Further Reading:
Fagan, Jeffrey, and Franklin E. Zimring, eds. *The Changing Borders of Juvenile Justice: Transfer of Adolescents to the Criminal Court.* Chicago University Press, 1998.
Jensen, Gary, and Dean G. Rojek. *Delinquency and Youth Crime.* Waveland Press, 1998.
Lawrence, Richard, and Christopher Lawrence. *School Crime and Juvenile Justice.* Oxford University Press, 1997.
Morrison, Blake. *As If: A Crime, a Trial, a Question of Childhood.* Picador, 1997.
Vito, Gennaro, et al. *The Juvenile Justice System: Concepts and Issues.* Waveland Press. 1998.

CRSO

CHINA, FEAR OF

China's perceived threat to the West stems largely from its history under communist rule. Continuing human rights abuses and its violent suppression of democratic reform movements, as witnessed in Tiananmen Square in 1989, are not easily ignored. The nation's aggressive foreign policy during the Cold War years and its willingness to provide arms to rogue nations and leftist revolutionaries have created an image of China as a warmonger and powerbroker. In recent years China has worked to counter its image and to improve relations with the West. However, the fear of China continues. The 1999 Cox Report on Chinese espionage revealed that China had acquired American nuclear weapons technology, and China remains the only nation known to target its missiles at the United States.

PROS

China is an economic powerhouse that could dwarf Western nations. The biggest market on Earth, China already produces one-third of the world's toys and one-eighth of its textiles. Between 1951 and 1980, the economy of China grew at a 12.5% annual rate, which is greater even than the archetypal "Tiger" economy of Japan. America's huge trade deficit with China suggests that China could dominate the conventional trading relationships and suck in most Western economies.

Since the middle of the twentieth century, China has presented a formidable military threat. China has the world's largest standing army and poses a threat both in terms of technology and regional ambition. The Cox Report revealed that China had acquired modern nuclear warheads. In addition, China's arms sales, particularly to rogue states, threaten world peace. Its transfer of weapons to Pakistan has precipitated an arms race with India and conflict in Kashmir, resulted in two civil wars, and bolstered a military regime. We no longer have to fear terror from the East only, but terror from around the world that flows from China.

China acts as a destabilizing influence in East Asia. The threat posed to Taiwan is clear, not only in the aggressive statements made by Chinese leaders, but also in recent naval maneuvers designed to intimidate the Taiwanese. In 1997, China went so far as to launch missiles over Taipei.

China threatens the Western powers even in the United Nations. As a permanent member of the Security Council, China has repeatedly vetoed Western proposals, often for petty political objectives. For example, it vetoed peacekeeping operations for Guatemala and Macedonia on the ground that these nations trade with Taiwan. NATO had to intervene in Kosovo in part because China refused to authorize a UN operation there.

China is capable of forming a dangerous power bloc in East Asia that threatens Western interests. China remains both politically and economically close to many states that lack the support of Western powers: Vietnam, Cambodia, Burma, and North Korea.

CONS

China's economic growth is unremarkable. In 1997 it accounted for merely 3.5% of world GDP, as opposed to the leading economy, the United States, representing 25.6%. In terms of GDP per capita, China ranks eighty-first, just ahead of Georgia and behind Papua New Guinea. In terms of international trade, China is equivalent to South Korea and does not even match the Netherlands. In China's peak year for the receipt of "foreign direct investment," it received $45US billion. However, this was accompanied by record capital flight, in which $35US billion left the country.

People wrongly assume that a communist regime is a military threat. In terms of defense spending, China is insignificant, accounting for only 4.5% of the global total, as opposed to 33.9% spent by the United States. Similarly, China's arms dealing is also no cause for concern. At the end of the twentieth century, China's weapons transfers constituted 2.2% of the global total. The United States, by contrast, traded 45% of the world's weapons. China is a signatory to the Nuclear Non-Proliferation Treaty and the Comprehensive Test Ban Treaty. It has never detonated a nuclear weapon in conflict nor shown any inclination to do so.

China actually acts as a stabilizing force in a turbulent region. It has considerable influence over its neighbors, particularly North Korea. No one would deny that China has a right to practice military maneuvers. Moreover, it is by no means certain that China is exerting undue influence on Taiwan. Both the Taiwanese and the Chinese national constitutions state that Taiwan is a part of mainland China.

China actually has a much better Security Council record than either Russia or France. Disagreements that divide the globe should not be laid at China's door. China has made many efforts to promote international peace both within and outside the UN. In any case, whatever China does in the UN is of little consequence because the UN has very little real power.

China exerts an astonishingly small influence over other nations. As the largest recipient of international aid and a very reluctant donor, China is certainly not buying herself allies. For 2,000 years, China rejected the concept of international interdependence. Although economic globalization has modified this approach, there is no evidence that China has adopted an aggressive or expansionist philosophy.

Sample Motions:
   This House should regard China as a global power.
   This House thinks that China is merely a regional power.
   This House treats China as an equal power.

Web Links:
   • Cox Report. http://www.cnn.com/ALLPOLITICS/resources/1999/cox.report/>
   CNN summary of Cox Report on Chinese espionage.
   • Sinomania.com. http://www.sinomania.com
   News resource devoted to fighting fear of China.
   • The "State-to-State" Flap: Tentative Conclusions About Risk and Restraint in Diplomacy Across the Taiwan Straits.
   <http://www.fas.harvard.edu/~asiactr/haq/200001/0001a008.htm>
   Scholarly article from the *Harvard Asia Quarterly* on recent China-Taiwan relations.
   • US Has Much to Fear from China. <http://www.capo.org/opeds/china.html>
   1997 article from the Center for the Advancement of Paleo Orthodoxy discussing China from a conservative Christian perspective.

Further Reading:
   Lampton, David M., ed. *The Making of Chinese Foreign and Security Policy in the Era of Reform, 1978–2000.* Stanford University Press, 2001.
   Mann, James. *About Face: A History of America's Curious Relationship with China.* Vintage Books, 2000.
   Swaine, Michael D., and Ashley J. Tellis. *Interpreting China's Grand Strategy: Past, Present and Future.* Rand Corporation, 2000.

CIVIL DISOBEDIENCE

Civil disobedience is the deliberate disobeying of a law to advance a moral principle or change government policy. Those who practice civil disobedience are willing to accept the consequences of their lawbreaking as a means of furthering their cause. Henry David Thoreau first articulated the tenets of civil disobedience in an 1849 essay, "On the Duty of Civil Disobedience." He argued that when conscience and law do not coincide, individuals have the obligation to promote justice by disobeying the law. Civil disobedience was a major tactic in the women's suffrage movement, the campaign for independence of India, the civil rights movement, and the abolition of apartheid in South Africa.

PROS

Elections do not give the people sufficient opportunity to express their will. In certain circumstances civil disobedience is a powerful method of making the will of the public heard. If a law is oppressive it cannot be opposed in principle by obeying it in practice. It must be broken.

Civil disobedience has a history of overcoming oppression and unpopular policies where all other methods have failed. For example, Mohandas Gandhi's civil disobedience was instrumental in winning liberty for India, and Martin Luther King's tactics won basic rights for African Americans in the United States. In these cases no other avenue was open to express grievances.

CONS

The "voice of the people" is heard in many ways. Elections take place regularly, and members of the public can write their local, state, or national representatives expressing their opinion. Legislators are there to represent and serve the people. Because citizens have many ways to express their views, civil disobedience is unnecessary. Protests can be made perfectly well without breaking the law.

Peaceful protest is quite possible in any society—to go further into actual lawbreaking is pointless. Civil disobedience can devolve into lawlessness. Indeed, it can be counter-productive by associating a cause with terror and violence.

In actual fact, the conflict with the authority gives any protest its power and urgency and brings an issue to a wider audience. The women's suffrage movement in Britain and the civil rights movement in the United States are both examples of an eventually successful campaign that won by its confrontation with authority, where more sedate methods would simply not have succeeded.

Too often this "productive violence" is directed against innocent members of the public or against the police, often causing serious injuries. No cause is worth the sacrifice of innocent lives; protest must be peaceful or not at all.

Sample Motions:
    This House supports civil disobedience.
    This House believes the ends justify the means.
    This House would break the law in a good cause.

Web Links:
    • Civil Disobedience Index. <http://www.actupny.org/documents/CDdocuments/CDindex.html>
    Offers information on the history, theory, and practice of civil disobedience.

Further Reading:
    Arendt, Hannah. *Crises of the Republic.* Harvest Books, 1972.
    Thoreau, Henry David. *Civil Disobedience and Other Essays.* Dover, 1993.

CR80

CONSCRIPTION AND NATIONAL SERVICE

Many countries throughout Europe and the rest of the world have conscription or some type of required national service. This is normally for 18-year-olds and lasts between one and three years. Usually young people have the option of serving in the military or performing community service. Since the end of the Vietnam War, the United States has relied on a volunteer army. At age 18, young men are required to register with Selective Service, but there is no draft. Nevertheless, some believe that some type of obligatory national service would be good both for young people and the nation.

PROS

We accept the need for national service in wartime; service in peacetime is just an extension of the same idea. It would mean that the country was prepared for emergencies when they happen, rather than having to prepare after the fact.

National service develops valuable character traits. Young people learn respect for authority, self-discipline, teamwork, and leadership skills.

The military teaches important skills that help young people get jobs. In the long run this will reduce unemployment and help the economy.

National service helps to promote patriotism and a sense of nationhood.

CONS

No justification exists for compulsory military service. The armed forces as they stand are capable of carrying out their role without conscripts. In fact, the military prefers a volunteer army.

Forcing young people to go into the armed forces against their will fosters only resentment against authority and undermines any real chance at learning new skills.

The government would be better off establishing civilian training programs. The military is not an educational institution.

Patriotism should not be centered on the military. We have seen the detrimental effect a focus on the military has had in other nations, such as Germany. National pride should be fostered in other ways.

PROS	CONS
The individual has a duty to give something back to society, and national service allows this. Whether through protecting the country or helping with social or environmental projects, national service encourages the idea of working as a community.	A citizen has a duty to pay taxes and follow the rules of society. Any service to the community should be voluntary.

Sample Motions:
This House would reintroduce the draft.

Web Links:
- Corporation for National Service. http://www.cns.gov
US government site presenting information on public service programs.
- Draft Registration: The Politics of Institutional Immorality. <http://www.cato.org/pubs/pas/pa-214.html>
Essay in support of dismantling the Selective Service System.

Further Reading:
Danzig, Richard, and Peter Szanton. *National Service: What Would It Mean?* Lexington Books, 1986.
Evers, William M. *National Service: Pro and Con.* Hoover Institute Press, 1990.

CR80

CORPORAL PUNISHMENT: ADULTS

Nigeria, Malaysia, Brunei, Saudi Arabia, and Singapore have retained flogging as a punishment long after other countries have declared it a violation of human rights. In some fundamentalist Islamic countries the cutting off of a hand is also an acceptable sentence.

PROS

Criminals must be punished. All forms of punishment recognize that with the commission of criminal acts individuals surrender some of their human rights. Why, logically, is corporal punishment any more of an infringement of these rights than prison? Corporal punishment is an easy, strong, visible, and therefore effective deterrent. It is also a proportionate punishment for certain crimes.

Like all forms of punishment, flogging and whipping can and should be subject to regulation. In Singapore, for example, caning is confined generally to males between 16 and 50, with a maximum number of 24 strokes, which must be administered all at once.

CONS

Punishing with pain is barbaric, a throwback to societies built on military might, slavery, and the treatment of criminals as entities without any rights. The mark of civilized society is that it behaves better than its criminals. Prison is necessary as a method of punishment, prevention, and rehabilitation, but it does not (or at least should not) stoop to cruelty. This is why the UN Declaration of Human Rights forbids "torture or ... cruel, inhuman or degrading treatment or punishment."

Any regulation tends to be arbitrary and allow abuse. Singapore's list of crimes for which caning may be imposed includes the transport of fireworks or a third traffic offense. In 1995, a 48-year-old Frenchman was caned five times for overstaying his visa.

PROS

Corporal punishment is a useful deterrent against prisoners breaking prison rules. Since their freedom is already gone and their date of release may seem distant (or nonexistent), little else remains to help maintain order.

Corporal punishment is appropriate for some cultures, but not for others. Citizens of Western democracies find a great deal of state control and authority frightening, and hold very diverse views on acceptable behavior and appropriate punishment. In many Middle and Far Eastern countries, however, consensus is much greater on what is acceptable—and a harsher collective response exists toward those who breach society's norms. Singapore has very little crime in comparison with the US. Let the results of its justice system speak for themselves.

CONS

There are always alternative punishments that can be used in prison: solitary confinement, removal of privileges, extension of sentence, and so on. Prisoners are particularly vulnerable to abuse from prison supervisors who seek to maintain order through a climate of fear.

Societies with a collective mentality need less strict punishment laws than societies without. The US doesn't have more crime than Singapore because of the lack of corporal punishment but precisely because of the lack of a behavioral norm. The US and Britain allowed corporal punishment in the past; nevertheless, crime flourished.

Sample Motions:

This House would flog criminals live on national television.
This House would bring back the birch.

Web Links:

- World Corporal Punishment Research. <http://www.corpun.com>

Links to hundreds of sites providing historical and contemporary data on the subject.

Further Reading:

Newman, Graeme. *Just and Painful: A Case for the Corporal Punishment of Criminals.* Harrow & Heston, 1995.

CORPORAL PUNISHMENT: CHILDREN

The issue of "paddling" or spanking children is less about punishment in itself and more about punishment as a means of education. How can young children learn the difference between right and wrong? How can teachers establish order in the classroom and with it a better environment for learning? With the exception of the United States, Canada, and one state in Australia, all industrialized countries now ban corporal punishment in schools although they may permit parental spanking.

PROS

Corporal punishment, specifically spanking or similar actions, can be an effective punishment and deterrent for childish misbehavior. If children do not respond seriously to verbal warnings or light punishment from teachers or parents, then a short, sharp stimulus, which inflicts pain but no lasting damage, is the last resort to cause the child to associate misbehavior with punishment—a crucial association in a child's development.

CONS

Hitting a child is never right. The power of physical punishment to teach a child the difference between right and wrong is unproven. A young child may learn that the adult is displeased, but not why. Spanking will cause a state of extreme distress and confusion that makes children less likely to analyze their behavior with clarity. In older children disciplined at school, a physical punishment is likely to provoke resentment and further misbehavior.

Much of the argument against corporal punishment has a hysterical edge. Corporal punishment must be used as part of a wider strategy and at the correct time: when other immediate discipline has failed and after an initial warning and opportunity for the child to repent. The person delivering the punishment must not be angry at the time.

Serious physical injuries occur only where disciplined, strategic corporal punishment becomes child abuse. There is a strict line between the two and to ignore it is deliberately misleading.

Corporal punishment administered in the presence of at least two adults is much less likely to become violent or lead to sexual abuse. At school, another teacher should be present; at home, both parents.

"He who spareth his rod hateth his son, but he who loveth him is chasteneth him betimes." Proverbs 13:24.

No matter how orderly you make the beating of a child, adverse effects are numerous. Children lose trust in the adults who administer the beating; they learn that force is acceptable in human interaction; they feel humiliated and lose self-respect; and they build up resentment that may lead to severe misbehavior in the future.

The actual physical damage inflicted via corporal punishment on children can be horrifying. Examples can be found of students needing treatment for broken arms, nerve and muscle damage, and cerebral hemorrhage. Spanking of the buttocks can cause damage to the sciatic nerve.

The buttocks are a sexual zone. Adults can derive pleasure from administering punishment to that zone, and such a punishment can affect the psychosexual development of children being disciplined. Even the presence of another adult does not prevent the easy degeneration from punishment into child abuse. A notorious case from Arizona in 1995 involved school principal Michael Wetton, who had previous convictions for violence against children. He was convicted of abuse after forcing a 9-year-old boy and a 15-year-old girl to strip naked and be paddled. In the girl's case, her mother was present, but "too frightened to resist."

"The Devil can cite Scripture for his purpose." *Shakespeare.*
The Bible frequently condones practices that are outrageous to the modern sensibility.

Sample Motions:
This House would spank its children when necessary.
This House believes that it is never right to hit a child.

Web Links:
• Corporal Punishment of Children. <http://people.biola.edu/faculty/paulp/index.html>
Provides links and references to research on corporal punishment for children in the home and critiques of anti-spanking research.
• The Sexual Dangers of Spanking Children. <http://silcon.com/~ptave/sexdngr.htm>
Detailed 1996 article on the dangers of spanking.
• Ultimate Deterrent: Punishment and Control in English and American Schools. <http://www.hku.hk/cerc/2b.html>
1966 article examining disciplinary policy in British and American schools.
• World Corporal Punishment Research. <http://www.corpun.com>
Links to hundreds of sites providing historical and contemporary data on the subject.

Further Reading:
Hyman, Irwin. *The Case Against Spanking: How to Discipline Your Child Without Hitting.* Jossey-Bass, 1997.
Rosemond, John. *To Spank or Not to Spank: A Parent's Handbook.* Andrews McMeel, 1994.
Straus, Murray, and Denise A. Donnelly. *Beating the Devil Out of Them: Corporal Punishment in American Families and Its Effect on Children.* Transaction, 2001.

CR80

CORRUPTION, BENEFITS OF

Public corruption is generally viewed as an obstacle to the development of a country. Many governments, international organizations, and aid agencies as well as donor-states have special agendas to fight the problem. Yet, in the countries with high levels of corruption, arguments have been made that because corruption is pervasive it has to have some benefit. While definitely not something to be proud of, public corruption is seen as an unavoidable side effect of development.

PROS

Corruption reduces bureaucracy and speeds the implementation of administrative practices governing economic forces of the market. Corrupt public officials acquire incentives to create a development-friendly system for the economy. As a result, corruption starts a chain of benefits for all the economic actors, making overregulated, obstructive bureaucracies much more efficient.

Corruption is a Western concept and is not applicable to traditional societies, where corruption does not have such a negative meaning. Many traditional societies with a "gift culture" have a different understanding of civil responsibilities and etiquette. The social structure and political traditions of many countries are based on the beneficial effect of corruption and cannot survive in its absence.

Corruption is a condition of developing states, and should be seen as a childhood disease. Western countries themselves were once the most corrupted societies of the world. Not only is corruption endemic in underdeveloped nations, it is also an evolutionary level that precedes development and industrialization. Corruption is a side effect of emerging capitalism and a free market. Underdeveloped countries cannot combat corruption without having achieved the level of economic development necessary to fight it.

CONS

Countries with lower levels of corruption still have efficient bureaucracies and enjoy better economic well-being. Corruption in the public sector is the biggest obstacle to investment, causing misallocation of valuable resources and subversion of public policies. It is also an invisible tax on the poor people. GDP levels for deeply corrupted states could be much higher without corruption.

The very idea of corruption is unethical, regardless of one's traditions. Cultural relativism is just an attempt to legitimize corruption by the corrupted. Not enough evidence has been presented to support the suggestion that corruption is required by certain socio-cultural practices. Moreover, regarding corruption as an innate quality of human culture undermines the hope for any improvement and is inherently fatalistic, serving as an excuse for creating cultures of corruption and fear.

Corruption is universal, and the fact that a nation is economically developed does not mean that it has less corruption. Some First World countries have high rates of public corruption. Having a low level of corruption, however, gives a unique advantage to any developing nation. Appropriate policies can substitute for any positive effect of corruption.

Sample Motions:
This House declares that anticorruption efforts do more harm than good.
This House confirms that corruption is unethical.
This House should fight public corruption.

Web Links:
• Anti-Corruption Gateway. <http://www.nobribes.org>
Provides information about combating corruption in Europe and Eurasia.
• Global corruption report. <http://www.globalcorruptionreport.org>
Project of Transparency International provides an extensive report on corruption around the world.
• Transparency International. <http://www.transparency.org>
Global coalition against corruption.

Further Reading:
Anechiarico, Frank, et al. *The Pursuit of Absolute Integrity: How Corruption Control Makes Government Ineffective.* University of Chicago Press, 1998.
Della Porta, Donatella, and Alberto Vannucci. *Corrupt Exchanges: Actors, Resources, and Mechanisms of Political Corruption.* Aldine de Gruyter, 1999.
Rose-Ackerman, Susan. *Corruption and Government: Causes, Consequences, and Reform.* Cambridge University Press, 1999.

CRINGO

COVENANT MARRIAGE

Divorce is an unfortunate reality of American life. Recent statistics compiled by the US Census Bureau show that between 40% and 50% of marriages end in divorce. Divorce can have a negative effect on society; accordingly, advocates of divorce reform have suggested giving couples the choice of covenant marriage. Thus, couples could either marry under the current "no fault" system in which either party can, at any time, dissolve the marriage or they could choose the covenant marriage option if they want a marriage that is more difficult to dissolve. Before entering into a covenant marriage, premarital counseling would be required; counseling would also be required prior to granting a divorce By 2002, Louisiana, Arkansas, and Arizona had implemented covenant marriage laws; many other state legislatures are considering instituting covenant marriage as an option.

PROS

Covenant marriages might reduce the number of domestic violence cases. A 1991 Justice Department study concluded that current husbands/fathers account for only 9% of the cases of domestic abuse. The rest of the abuse was perpetrated by former husbands, boyfriends, or transient partners. Without divorce, women may be less likely to be involved with abusive men.

In a covenant marriage, the offended spouse is the only one who can ask for the divorce. This gives the offended spouse many benefits in negotiating the end of the marriage. A woman clearly has more to lose in assuming a marriage will last forever, especially if she puts her career on hold to care for children. A covenant marriage is a way for women to have more security in a marriage. Religious belief is only one reason to want marriages to succeed; society as a whole has an interest in stable families. Advocate for covenant marriage, Amitai Etzioni, founder and director of the Washington-based Communitarian Network, says, "One can be deeply concerned with strengthening the commitment of marriage without favoring traditional or hierarchical forms of marriages or denying women full equal standing."

The premarital counseling by a trained counselor that is a requirement of covenant marriage enables the future husband and wife to get to know each other well. Issues such as how to raise children, how to split housework,

CONS

In a covenant marriage, a partner must prove that abuse actually occurred to be permitted to end the marriage. This especially worries advocates for battered women who say that proving domestic abuse can be difficult and the waiting period makes women stay in abusive relationships longer. In addition, mental abuse is not seen as a legitimate reason to end a marriage.

Some feminists feel initiatives for covenant marriage simply conceal the hidden agenda of the antifeminist Moral Majority. Liberal commentator Katha Pollitt, a columnist for *The Nation*, says covenant marriages "enforce a narrow and moralistic vision of marriage by rendering divorce more painful and more punitive." Many advocates of covenant marriage laws are self-described conservative Christians; religious groups are major supporters of the covenant marriage laws. Louisiana NOW president Terry O'Neill points out that " 'Covenant' and 'covenant marriage' are terms with a very specific meaning in the Christian community." Conflating religious values with secular laws on marriage is wrong.

If partners enter a covenant marriage, they would not be able to divorce until they are separated for at least two years. People could get stuck in marriages and be unable to continue with their lives even when the mar-

and financial matters are discussed and explored with the counselor. Covenant marriages are more restrictive but allow for divorce in specific circumstances: adultery; physical or sexual abuse of a spouse or child; abandonment of at least one year; incarceration of a spouse for a felony conviction; spouses living separate and apart for two years; and a legal separation of one year, or 18 months if a minor child is involved.

Divorce is terrible for children. They lose stability and security. Children whose parents have divorced have higher rates of suicide. They are more likely to commit crimes and abuse drugs. Their education suffers, and they are less likely to graduate from college and more likely to drop out of high school. The detrimental financial effects of divorce also affect these children. Children of divorce must adapt to many changes in their family environment and are at greater risk of being abused. The American Academy of Matrimonial Lawyers summer 1997 newsletter says, "Only acts of war and the events of natural disasters are more harmful to a child's psyche than the divorce process."

Passage of no-fault divorce laws resulted in an onslaught of divorce and a breakdown of the American family. In 1968, the year before California adopted the nation's first no-fault divorce law, the US had 584,000 divorces (2.9 divorces per 1,000 Americans). After 30 years of no-fault divorce, the number of divorces had reached 1,135,000 annually, or 4.2 per 1,000. Covenant marriages are the answer. Research has shown that 33% to 45% of couples on the brink of divorce may reconcile if they are legally prevented from divorcing for six months as specified in a covenant marriage.

riage has produced no children and the spouses have no significant assets to divide. Also, covenant marriage lays the burden of proof on the spouse who files for divorce. A judge must be convinced that grounds for divorce actually exist. In addition, although a covenant marriage can be dissolved because of a felony conviction, a partner's string of misdemeanors is not grounds for divorce.

Covenant marriages force families in conflict to stay together, which has the potential to harm children more than divorce. Research shows that when parents stay in a high-conflict marriage, children fare worse than when their parents actually divorce. Children must be considered when parents divorce, but with appropriate nurturing and support, children can cope with divorce and eventually have strong marriages of their own. In fact, studies show that a child of divorced parents is no more likely than a child of married parents to divorce as an adult.

Covenant marriage laws are weak, and the resources do not exist to provide the counseling they mandate. The US Supreme Court ruled more than 50 years ago that the state of residence at the time of the divorce determines the laws governing that divorce. So if the covenant marriage partners move to a state without covenant marriage laws, they are free to use the no-fault system anyway. The mandated counseling both before marriage and before divorce could be costly. States that have passed covenant marriage laws have done little to provide low-cost or free counselors for those who cannot afford them. In addition, those who choose covenant marriages are the least likely to divorce anyway. Studies show that those in covenant marriages have higher incomes and education, are more involved with their churches, and take marriage more seriously than those who do not select covenant marriages. These traits are all predictors of a successful marriage, regardless of the requirements of covenant marriage.

Sample Motions:
    This House believes that couples should choose a covenant marriage instead of a traditional marriage.
    This House opposes covenant marriage laws.
    This House supports covenant marriage laws as the answer to America's divorce problem.

Web Links:
    • American Academy of Matrimonial Lawyers. <http://www.aaml.org>
    Web site with many articles related to marriage and divorce laws.

• Americans for Divorce Reform. <http://www.divorcereform.org>
Pro-divorce reform page offers many articles on divorce reform as well as a section on covenant marriages and sample legislation states could adopt to create covenant marriage laws.
• Covenant Marriage Movement. <http://www.covenantmarriage.com>
This Christian-based site gives information for couples considering covenant marriage and urges church congregations to support covenant marriage.

Further Reading:
Bennett, William J. *The Broken Hearth: Reversing the Moral Collapse of the American Family.* Doubleday, 2001.
Fineman, Martha Albertson. *The Illusion of Equality: The Rhetoric and Reality of Divorce Reform.* University of Chicago Press, 1991.
Hetherington, E. Mavis, and John Kelly. *For Better or for Worse: Divorce Reconsidered.* W. W. Norton, 2002.
Lowery, Fred. *Covenant Marriage: Staying Together for Life.* Howard Publishing, 2002.
Wilson, James Q. *The Marriage Problem: How Our Culture Has Weakened Families.* HarperCollins, 2002.

CREATIONISM IN PUBLIC SCHOOLS

In the mid-nineteenth century, Charles Darwin articulated his theory of evolution, which argues that human beings evolved, over the course of millennia, from more primitive animals. This theory conflicts with the account of man's creation in Genesis, wherein Adam is created by God as the first fully formed human, having no predecessors. Adam's creation is the act of an "intelligent designer," rather than the result of some natural evolutionary process. Although many believers think that evolution is compatible with the Bible, many others feel that the account in Genesis must be taken literally and that teaching evolution is an affront to their religious beliefs. Many states and school districts have tried to ban the teaching of evolution (most famously, the state of Tennessee, which prosecuted John Scopes in 1925 for violating its ban), but the Supreme Court ruled in 1968 that the purpose of such bans is religious and cannot be permitted in public schools. Nonetheless, believers in "intelligent design"—or "creationism"—have continued to insist that creationism should be taught alongside evolution in the classroom.

PROS

The Constitution forbids the establishment of any one religion, but it also guarantees freedom of religion, which means that the government cannot suppress religion. By teaching that evolution is true, schools are violating the religious beliefs of students.

Evolution has not been proved; it is a theory used to explain observable facts. But those facts can be explained just as well, and in some cases, even better, by intelligent design theory. Moreover, evolutionists do not acknowledge that the evidence essential for proving their ideas—e.g., fossil remains of transitional, evolving beings—simply does not exist. Creationism is a theory that is at least as worthy as evolution and should be taught along with it.

By teaching intelligent design theory, a school is not doing anything to establish any particular religion.

CONS

In practice, there is no question that the supporters of creationism depend upon one religious tradition—the Judeo-Christian—and upon the account of creation in its sacred texts. Teaching creationism establishes, in effect, only that specific religious tradition, to the detriment of other religions and of nonbelievers. Teaching creationism in a publicly funded school is clearly a violation of the Constitution.

Evolution is a theory that is based on verifiable scientific facts, but creationism is based on the revelations contained in scripture. Creationism cannot be taught as science because it is not consistent with standard scientific procedure.

All religions offer a creation story, varying from religion to religion and from culture to culture. A public school

Intelligent design is accepted by Christians, Jews, Muslims, Native Americans, Hindus, and many others. Therefore, it should not be forbidden by the establishment clause of the First Amendment.

might examine all of these beliefs in the context of a history of ideas course, rather than in a science course. In practice, however, creationists are not interested in exploring different beliefs; they are, rather, committed to putting one religious belief on equal footing with prevailing scientific thinking in the science classroom.

Creationism is not, as the Supreme Court has ruled, a religious belief. It is a scientific theory, and has been articulated by many philosophers and scientists, for example, Aristotle, in a completely secular context.

Creationism is not a scientific theory and is not accepted by the scientific community. Schools have a mandate to teach what is currently accepted by the country's scientists—that is, they must teach evolution, not material from outside the discipline of biology.

History has shown that scientific theories are often disproved over time; evolution, thus, should not be considered to be an unchangeable, unassailable truth. In the spirit of scientific inquiry and intellectual skepticism, students should be exposed to competing theories.

Science is morally and religiously neutral. It does not aim to uphold religious beliefs; it does not aim to debunk religious beliefs. Evolution is not taught as an attack on religion; it is taught as the best scientific explanation of available facts. Students are free to pursue their own private religious beliefs.

Sample Motions:
This House favors a curriculum free of creationism teachings in public schools.
This House believes that evolution ought to be taught instead of creationism.
This House thinks that teaching creationism in public schools is justified.

Web Links:
• Evolution vs. Creationism. <http://physics.syr.edu/courses/modules/ORIGINS/origins.html>
Site contains information on both sides of the debate, including links to articles, newsgroups, books, and frequently asked questions.
• Science and Creationism. <http://www.nap.edu/html/creationism/preface.html>
Detailed essay from the National Academy of Sciences summarizes the key aspects of evolution, describes the positions taken by advocates of creation science, and analyzes their claims.
• Scientific Creationism. <http://www.scientificcreationism.org>
Site outlines arguments in support of creationism.

Further Reading:
Binder, Amy J. *Contentious Curricula: Afrocentrism and Creationism in American Public Schools.* Princeton University Press, 2002.
Gilkey, Langdon. *Creationism on Trial: Evolution and God at Little Rock.* University Press of Virginia, 1998.

ॐ

CUBA, DROPPING OF US SANCTIONS ON

Fidel Castro and his communist government came to power in Cuba in 1959, much to the horror of the Eisenhower administration in the US. Cuba was supported throughout the Cold War by the Soviet Union and became a flashpoint for Cold War tensions, notably during the Cuban Missile Crisis of 1962, when Nikita Khrushchev sparked the most dangerous Cold War confrontation by attempting to place nuclear weapons on the island. America has maintained near total sanctions on Cuba since 1959, but before 1990 they were largely offset by the support, trade, and subsidy offered by the USSR. Since the collapse of the Soviet Union, the withdrawal of these subsidies has caused a 35% drop in Cuba's GDP. The decreased threat of communism has led to a reevaluation of the sanctions by the US, but so far the wounds of the twentieth century, and the electoral significance of Florida where most Cuban émigrés live, has steeled the resolve of the White House. Sanctions were, in fact, strengthened significantly in the Helms-Burton Act of 1996, although recent moves have made food and medicine a little easier to move from the US to Cuba.

PROS

The sanctions cause real and unacceptable harm to the Cuban people. In the 1990s Cuba lost $70US billion in trade and $1.2US billion in international loans because of US sanctions. Cuba is too poor a country not to suffer from these losses. The dominance of America in the pharmaceuticals industry, moreover, means that Cubans are unable to gain access to many drugs. America would be the natural market for most Cuban products, and its refusal to accept goods with even the most minor Cuban components from third nations damages Cuba's ability to trade with other countries. Other South American countries have recently relied on the types of loans that Cuba is denied to keep their economies on track.

Sanctions are pointless and counterproductive. They've made no political difference in the last 43 years, why would they now? They result the US being blamed for all the failures of the Cuban economy, and sanctions are also used to justify repressive measures for security. President George W. Bush claims to want to empower civil society in Cuba, but in 1998, while governor of Texas, he argued that the best way to achieve this in China was to trade and spread "American values."

No legitimate reason has been offered for singling out Cuba for sanctions. Cuba has no biological, chemical, or nuclear weapons and does not sponsor terror. Cuba holds fewer prisoners of conscience than China, Vietnam, Iran, or even Egypt. To maintain sanctions to encourage change in the form of government, as the US claims it is doing, is totally illegitimate under international law. Cuba has offered to compensate US citizens whose property was nationalized in 1959.

CONS

Sanctions didn't cause economic failure in Cuba. The communist political and economic system has been shown to lead inevitably to economic collapse with or without sanctions. Even if sanctions were lifted, lack of private ownership, foreign exchange, and tradable commodities would hold Cuba back. The International Trade Commission found a "minimal effect on the Cuban economy" from sanctions. In fact, the US can best contribute to an economic recovery in Cuba by using sanctions to pressure that nation into economic and political reforms.

Sanctions are a proven policy tool and can be used to pressure an extremely repressive regime into reforms. Aggressive US engagement and pressure contributed to the collapse of the Soviet Union. Sanctions are also, according to Secretary of State Colin Powell, a "moral statement" of America's disapproval for the Castro regime. Blaming America for all economic woes didn't fool ordinary Russians, and it won't fool Cubans. Now is exactly the time that the US should be tightening the screws so that Castro's successor is forced to make real changes.

Cuba is a repressive regime with one-party rule that holds political prisoners and stifles opposition and economic freedom through constant harassment. The Castro regime has refused to aid with the search for Al Qaeda suspects and is on the US list of sponsors of terror because it provides a safe haven to many American fugitives. Cuba is known to have a developmental biological weapons "effort" and is recorded as breaking international sanctions to export dual-use technologies to Iran. Finally, Cuba has failed to stop illegal drug shipments through its waters, and its government profits directly from resources stolen from US citizens in 1959.

Sanctions on Cuba are illegal and damage America's international standing. They violate the UN Charter, laws on the freedom of navigation, and repeated UN resolutions since 1992 (passed with only the US and Israel in opposition). Furthermore, some parts of the Helms-Burton Act are extraterritorial in their effects on the business of other nations and thus cause significant protest around the world. This makes a mockery of the US claim to be a guardian of international law, not only in its dealings with Cuba but also in the negotiations over the future of Iraq. America could achieve its goals internationally more easily if it were not for its own lack of respect for international law.

America is attempting to protect the rights enshrined in the Universal Declaration of Human rights for both its own citizens and citizens of Cuba. If the US breaks international law, it is only to more fully realize the true aims of international law. The UN resolutions condemning the sanctions have never passed the Security Council and therefore lack any authority. America's status as a guardian of human rights and an enemy of terror is enhanced by its moral refusal to compromise with a repressive government just off its own shores.

The US will also benefit from the opening of trade with Cuba economically. Midwest Republicans have voted to drop the embargo because of the potential for profits in their farming states. Further, if sanctions end, Americans will be able to stop pretending that they prefer Bolivian cigars!

Cuba will never account for more than a tiny percentage of America's trade, and it is able to source and sell all its products elsewhere. Even if Cuba were a vital market for American goods, it would be worth giving up some economic growth to maintain a commitment to the freedom of the Cuban people. As it is, the total Cuban GDP is a drop in the ocean.

Sanctions are not the will of the American people but of a small minority of embittered Cuban Americans in Florida who are being pandered to. National opinion generally expresses no preference about or opposes the ban. Congress recently voted 262–167 to repeal the travel ban to Cuba but will be thwarted by the insistence of President George W. Bush that the ban remain. This is electioneering government at its worst.

The people who care most about the Cuban question thoroughly oppose dropping sanctions. The Midwest Republicans who voted to drop the travel ban are no less blinkered than the Cuban Americans who vote to keep it. Opinion on sanctions wavers; the separation of powers is in place specifically to allow the White House to maintain a stable policy on issues of national security.

Sample Motions:
   This House would drop the sanctions on Cuba.
   This House would sanction sanctions.
   This House believes in Cuba Libre.
   This House condemns US foreign policy.

Web Links:
   • CIA Country Profile. < http://www.cia.gov/cia/publications/factbook/index.html>
   Quick overview of the government and economy of Cuba.
   • CubaNet. < http://www.cubanet.org>
   Provides latest news on Cuban domestic issues and international relations.
   • GlobalPolicy.org. <http://www.globalpolicy.org>
   Site offers extensive links to documents and articles on US sanctions against Cuba.
   • State Department Reports on Cuba. <http://www.state.gov/www/regions/wha/cuba/>
   Archive of State Department information on Cuba before 2001.

Further Reading:
Castro, Fidel. *Capitalism in Crisis: Globalization and World Politics Today.* Ocean Press, 2000.
Fontaine, Roger, and William E. Ratliff. *A Strategic Flip-Flop in the Caribbean: Lift the Embargo in Cuba.* Hoover Institute Press, 2000.
Schwab, Peter. *Cuba: Confronting the US Embargo.* Palgrave Macmillan, 1999.

CRO

CULTURAL TREASURES, RETURN OF

Debate has raged for almost two centuries about the ownership and display of cultural treasures that were frequently acquired from the (then) developing world by imperial powers in the eighteenth and nineteenth centuries and displayed in Western museums. This debate most often uses the Elgin, or Parthenon, Marbles, masterpieces of classical Greek sculpture that Lord Elgin removed from the Parthenon in 1801 and sold to the British Museum in 1816. Greece has consistently demanded their return since independence in 1830. The issue of who owns cultural treasures reemerged following World War II, when the victorious Allies, principally the Soviet Union, seized art from the defeated Axis powers. During the last decades of the twentieth century, Native Americans successfully waged a number of campaigns for the return of their sacred relics.

PROS

Cultural treasures should be displayed in the context in which they originated; only then can they be truly understood. In the case of the Elgin Marbles, this is an architectural context that only proximity to the Parthenon itself can provide.

Display of cultural treasures in Western museums is an unfortunate legacy of imperialism. It reflects the unacceptable belief that developing nations are unable to look after their artistic heritage. The display of imperial trophies in institutions such as the British Museum or the Louvre has become offensive.

Artifacts were often acquired illegally, through looting in war, under the duress of imperial force, or by bribing officials who were supposed to be safeguarding their country's artistic treasures.

CONS

Art treasures should be accessible to the greatest number of people and to scholars. In practice this means displaying them in the great museums of the world. Returning treasures to their original context is impossible. Too much has changed physically and culturally over the centuries for them to speak more clearly in their country of origin than they do in museums where they can be compared to large assemblies of objects from a wide variety of cultures. In any case, copies could be placed in original locations.

For whatever reason the treasures were first collected, we should not rewrite history; sending such artifacts back to their country of origin would set a bad precedent that could denude museums around the world. Placing great artifacts in a geographical and cultural ghetto—African sculptures could be viewed only in Africa, Egyptian mummies only in Egypt—would leave the world much poorer and reduce popular understanding of the achievements of such civilizations.

Although some art treasures may have been acquired illegally, the evidence for this is often ambiguous. For example, Lord Elgin's bribes were the common way of facilitating any business in the Ottoman Empire and do not undermine Britain's solid legal claim to the Parthenon marbles based upon a written contract made by the internationally recognized authorities in Athens at the time. Much art was freely sold to the imperial powers, indeed some art was specifically produced for the European market.

Some treasures, such as Native American buffalo robes, have religious and cultural associations with the area from which they were taken, but none for those who view them in sterile glass cases. Descendants of their creators are offended by seeing aspects of their spirituality displayed for entertainment.

This may be true, but religious artifacts may have been originally purchased or given in good faith, perhaps with the intention of educating a wider public about the beliefs of their creators. Descendants should not be allowed to second-guess their ancestors' intentions. Also, many cultural treasures relate to extinct religions and cultures; no claim for their return can be validly made.

In the past, countries may not have been capable of looking after their heritage, but that has changed. A state-of-the-art museum is planned in Athens to house the surviving marbles, while pollution-control measures have reduced sulfur dioxide in the city to a fifth of its previous level. At the same time the curatorship of institutions such as the British Museum is being called into question, as it becomes apparent that controversial cleaning and restoration practices may have harmed the sculptures they claim to protect.

In the case of the Parthenon marbles, Lord Elgin's action in removing them was an act of rescue because the Ottoman authorities were pillaging them for building stone. They cared nothing for the classical Greek heritage. Furthermore, had they been returned upon Greek independence in 1830, the heavily polluted air of Athens would by now have destroyed them. Similar problems face the return of artifacts to African or Native American museums. Delicate artifacts would be destroyed without proper handling and preservation techniques. These institutions frequently lack the qualified personnel or necessary facilities to preserve these treasures.

Sample Motions:
This House would return cultural treasures to their country of origin.
This House would return the Elgin Marbles.
This House believes a jewel is best in its original setting.
This House would lose its marbles.

Web Links:
• Elgin Marbles (*The Guardian*). <http://www.guardianunlimited.co.uk/elgin/0,2759,184528,00.html>
Provides interactive guide to the history of the Elgin Marbles as well as current articles about the controversy.
• The Melina Mercouri Foundation. <http://www.lofstrom.com/mercouri>
Site campaigning for the return of the Elgin Marbles.
• The Parthenon (Elgin) Marbles. <http://www.museum-security.org/elginmarbles.html>
Offers links to many sites dealing with the issue.
• Stolen Property or Finders Keepers. <http://home.att.net/~tisone/problem.htm>
General site offering information on the issues concerning many stolen historical artifacts.

Further Reading:
Hitchens, Christopher. *The Elgin Marbles: Should They Be Returned to Greece?* Verso Books, 1998.
St. Clair, William. *Lord Elgin and the Marbles.* Oxford University Press, 1998.
Vrettos, Theodore. *The Elgin Affair: The Abduction of Antiquity's Greatest Treasures and the Passions It Aroused.* Little Brown, 1998.

CURFEW LAWS

Over 300 US towns have passed local curfew laws making it illegal for youths to be out-of-doors between certain publicized times. In most cases cities imposed nighttime curfews, but a 1997 survey indicated that approximately one-quarter had daytime curfews as well. All curfews are aimed at proactively reducing juvenile crime and gang activity. Officials also see curfews as a way of involving parents and keeping young people from being victimized. Opponents say the curfews violate the rights of good kids to prevent the actions of a few bad ones.

PROS

Youth crime is a major and growing problem, often involving both drugs and violence. Particularly worrying is the rise of youth gangs, which can terrorize urban areas and create a social climate in which criminality becomes the norm. Imposing curfews on minors can help solve these problems. They keep young people off the street and out of trouble. Curfews are easy to enforce compared to other forms of crime prevention and are therefore effective.

The use of curfews can help protect vulnerable children. Although responsible parents do not let young children out in the streets after dark, not all parents are responsible. Inevitably their children suffer, both from crime and in accidents, and are likely to fall into bad habits. Society should ensure that such neglected children are returned home safely and that their parents are made to face up to their responsibilities.

Children have no good reason to be out unaccompanied late at night, so a curfew is not really a restriction on their liberty. They would be better off at home doing schoolwork and participating in family activities.

Child curfews are a form of zero-tolerance policing. The idea of zero tolerance comes from the theory that if the police ignore low-level crimes they create a permis-

CONS

Curfews are not an effective solution to the problem of youth crime. Research finds no link between reduction in juvenile crime and curfews. Although some towns with curfews did see a drop in youth crime, this often had more to do with other law-enforcement strategies, such as zero-tolerance policing, or with demographic and economic changes in the youth population. In any case, most juvenile crime takes place between 3 p.m. and 8 p.m., after the end of school and before working parents return home, rather than in the hours covered by curfews.

Youth curfews infringe upon individual rights and liberties. Children have a right to freedom of movement and assembly, which curfews directly undermine by criminalizing their simple presence in a public space. This reverses the presumption of innocence by assuming all young people are potential lawbreakers. They are also subject to blanket discrimination on the grounds of age, although only a few young people commit crimes. Furthermore, curfews infringe upon the rights of parents to bring up their children as they choose. Just because we dislike the way some parents treat their children does not mean that we should intervene. Should we intervene in families whose religious beliefs mean girls are treated as inferior to boys, or in homes where parents practice corporal punishment?

Children in their mid-teens have legitimate reasons to be out at night without adults. Many have part-time jobs. Others participate in church groups or youth clubs. Requiring adults to take them to and from activities is unreasonable. It will ensure many children do not participate in after-school activities either because adults are unwilling or are unable to accompany them. On a more sinister note, some children are subject to abuse at home and actually feel safer out on the streets.

Youth curfews have great potential for abuse, raising civil rights issues. Evidence suggests that police arrest far more black children than white for curfew viola-

sive atmosphere in which serious crime can flourish and law and order breaks down entirely. Child curfews can help the police establish a climate of zero tolerance and create a safer community for everyone.

tions. Curfews tend to be imposed in inner cities with few places for children to amuse themselves safely and legally. Curfews compound the social exclusion that many poor children feel with physical exclusion from public spaces. This problem is made worse by the inevitable deterioration in relations between the police and the young people subject to the curfew.

Child curfews can help change a negative youth culture in which challenging the law is seen as desirable and gang membership an aspiration. Impressionable youngsters would be kept away from gang activity on the streets at night, and a cycle of admiration and recruitment would be broken. By spending more time with their families and in more positive activities such as sports, which curfews make a more attractive option for bored youngsters, children will develop greater self-esteem and discipline.

Imposing curfews on children would actually be counter-productive because it would turn millions of law-abiding young people into criminals. More American children are charged with curfew offenses than with any other crime. Once children acquire a criminal record, they cross a psychological boundary, making it much more likely that they will perceive themselves as criminal and have much less respect for the law. This can lead to more serious offenses. At the same time, a criminal record decreases the chances for employment and so contributes to the social deprivation and desperation that breed crime.

We should try other ways of reducing youth crime, but they will work best in conjunction with curfews. If a troubled area develops a culture of lawlessness, identifying specific youngsters for rehabilitation becomes more difficult. A curfew takes the basically law-abiding majority off the streets, allowing the police to engage with the most difficult element. Curfews are a tool in the struggle to improve lives in rundown areas. They are likely to be used for relatively short periods to bring a situation under control so that other measures can be put in place and given a chance to work.

A number of alternative strategies exist that are likely to do more to reduce youth crime. Rather than a blanket curfew, individual curfews could be imposed upon particular troublemakers. Another successful strategy is working individually with young troublemakers. For example, authorities can require them to meet with victims of crime so that they understand the consequences of their actions. Youths can also be paired with trained mentors. Overall, the government needs to ensure good educational opportunities and employment prospects so that youngsters feel some hope for their futures.

Sample Motions:
This House would introduce child curfews.
This House would lock up its daughters.
This House believes children should be neither seen nor heard.

Web Links:
• American Civil Liberties Union. <http://www.aclu.org/cgi-bin/aclu/AT-aclu_sitesearch.cgi>
Links to articles on the legal status of curfews.
• Status Report on Youth Curfews in American Cities. <http://www.usmayors.org/uscm/news/publications/curfew.htm>
Summary of 1997 survey of 374 cities providing status of curfews and information on their effectiveness.

Further Reading:
Jensen, Gary, and Dean G. Rojek. *Delinquency and Youth Crime.* Waveland Press, 1998.

CR&O

DEVELOPING-WORLD DEBT, CANCELLATION OF

For many years, poor nations in Asia, Latin America, and particularly Africa, have borrowed heavily to reduce poverty and foster development. Over the years external debt payments increased dramatically, often forcing countries to choose between paying their debt and funding social, health, and education programs. By the beginning of the new millennium the situation had reached a crisis in some countries. Sub-Saharan Africa owed lenders approximately $200US billion, 83% of its GNP. Groups such as the International Monetary Fund (IMF) and the World Bank, with their Heavily Indebted Poor Countries initiative, are working toward a partial reduction or rescheduling of this debt, but demand adherence to strict economic reforms. Others, such as Jubilee 2000, are pressing for more immediate and more substantial action.

PROS

The burden of debt costs lives. Some of the most heavily indebted poor countries are struggling to pay even the interest on their loans, let alone paying down the principal. This massively distorts their economies and their spending priorities. African nations currently spend four times as much on debt repayments as they do on health. The reforms demanded by the IMF in return for rescheduled debt make this problem even worse. In Zimbabwe, spending on health care has dropped by a third, in Tanzania, school fees have been introduced to raise more money. Progress made in health and education over the past 50 years is actually being reversed in some countries. It is obscene that governments are cutting spending in these vital areas to repay debts. The debts must be cancelled now.

To raise the cash for debt repayments, poor countries have to produce goods that they can sell internationally. Often this means growing cash crops instead of the food needed to support their population. People in fertile countries can find themselves starving because they cannot afford to buy imported food.

Debt repayments often punish those who were not responsible for creating the debt in the first place. In a number of poorer countries, huge debts were amassed by the irresponsible spending of dictators in the past. They have now been overthrown, yet the new government and the people of that country still are required to pay the price for the dictator's actions. This is clearly unfair.

All poor countries need is the chance to help them-

CONS

There are many reasons for the current problems in the world's poorest nations. They may often have heavy debt burdens, but the debt is not necessarily the cause of the problems. Many countries spend huge amounts of money on weapons to fight local wars instead of investing in their people. Many are led by dictators or other corrupt governments, whose incompetence or greed is killing their own population. The money to pay for social programs and, at the same time, repay debt may well exist, but it is being wasted in other areas.

Again, there are many potential causes for starvation— famines are caused by war or by freak weather conditions, not by debt. While growing cash crops can seem to be counter-intuitive, the money they bring in helps boost the country's economy. The idea that a nation could and should be agriculturally and industrially self-sufficient is outdated.

This thinking has dangerous implications on an international level. Governments are always changing in democracies, but nations are expected to honor their debts. A crucial element in lending money is the promise that the debt will be repaid. If every new government could decide that it was not responsible for its predecessor's debts, then no one would ever lend money to a country. Developing countries in particular still need loans to invest in infrastructure projects. Canceling debt now would make lenders far less likely to provide loans on good terms in the future and would retard economic growth in the long term.

Reform must come first. Corrupt and incompetent

selves. While their economies are dominated by the need to repay debt, it is impossible for them to truly invest in infrastructure and education. By canceling debt, we would give them a fresh start and the opportunity to build successful economies that would supply the needs of generations to come.

The developed world has a moral duty to the developing world because of the historical background of developing world debt. In the rush to invest in the 1970s, many banks made hasty loans, pouring money into pointless projects without properly examining whether they would ever make a profit. Because of these bad investments, some of the world's poorest countries are so burdened with debts that they can now no longer realistically expect to pay them off and are instead simply servicing the interest. An important parallel may be made with bankruptcy: If an individual is unable to repay his or her debts, he or she is declared bankrupt and then allowed to make a fresh start. The same system should be used with countries. If they are unable to repay their debts, they should be given the opportunity to start again. A country making contributions to the world economy is far better than a country in debt slavery. At the same time, banks would be discouraged from making bad loans as they did in the 1970s.

governments and economic systems cripple many poor countries. Canceling debt would therefore make no difference, it would be the equivalent of giving a one-time payment to dictators and crooks, who would siphon off the extra money and become rich while the people still suffer. Even worse, dictators might spend more money on weapons and palaces, thus reincurring possibly even greater debt. A country's government must be accountable and its economy stable before debt reduction or cancellation is even considered.

The parallel with bankruptcy cannot work on a national scale. First, when an individual is declared bankrupt, most assets and possessions are seized to pay as much debt as possible. This is why banks find bankruptcy an acceptable option. In national terms, this would mean the total loss of sovereignty. Foreign governments and banks would be able to seize control of the infrastructure or the resources of the "bankrupt" country at will. No government could, or should, ever accept this. Second, the difference in scale is vitally important. Whereas the bankruptcy of a single individual within a country is unlikely to cause major problems for that country's economy, the bankruptcy of a nation would significantly affect the world economy. The economic plans of banks and nations currently include the interest payments on developing world debt; if this substantial revenue stream were suddenly cut off, economic repercussions could be catastrophic. Even if this debt relief would be helpful to the "bankrupt" countries in the short term, a world economy in recession would be in nobody's best interest.

Sample Motions:
This House would end developing world debt.
This House would kill the debt, not the debtors.
This House would break the chains of debt.

Web Links:
• International Monetary Fund: Debt Initiative for the Heavily Indebted Poor Countries (HIPCs). <http://www.imf.org/external/np/hipc/hipc.htm>
Offers information on IMF programs and progress for HIPCs.
• Jubilee 2000 Coalition. <http://www.jubilee2000uk.org/>
Research, analysis, news, and data on international debt and finance presented by an advocacy group dedicated to ending developing world debt.
• World Bank: HIPC. <http://www.worldbank.org/hipc>
Detailed information, including progress reports and country cases, on world debt and World Bank debt relief initiatives. Includes links to scholarly articles on the issue.

Further Reading:
Dent, Martin, and Bill Peters. *The Crisis of Poverty and Debt in the Third World.* Ashgate, 1999.
O'Cleireacain, Seamus. *Third World Debt and International Public Policy.* Praeger, 1990.

DNA DATABASE FOR CRIMINALS

DNA evidence is playing an increasing role in criminal cases both to convict the guilty and to clear the innocent. The federal government and the states are building interlinked computerized databases of DNA samples. Initially these samples were taken from people convicted of sex crimes and a few other violent offenses, but recently, there have been moves to include all convicted criminals. Some officials, such as former attorney general Janet Reno, have recommended expanding the database to include all individuals arrested. Some police officials, including former NYC police commissioner Howard Safir, want the database to include DNA from everyone. Many people view extending the database beyond convicted criminals as an invasion of privacy and a violation of civil liberties.

PROS

DNA detection has considerable advantages over conventional fingerprinting. Fingerprints attach only to hard surfaces, can be smeared, or can be avoided by using gloves. Comparison of even a clear print from a crime scene with a print in the national database requires significant scientific expertise. Scientists can build an accurate DNA profile from very small amounts of genetic data, and they can construct it even if it has been contaminated by oil, water, or acid at the crime scene. The accused should appreciate a novel fingerprinting technique that is both objective and accurate.

The use of a DNA fingerprint is not an affront to civil liberties. The procedure for taking a sample of DNA is less invasive than that required for taking a blood sample. The police already possess a vast volume of information; the National Crime Information Center Computer in the United States contains files relating to thirtytwo million Americans. A forensic DNA database should be seen in the context of the personal information that other agencies hold. Insurance companies commonly require an extensive medical history of their clients. Mortgage lenders usually demand a full credit report on applicants. Many employers subject their employees to random drug testing. If we are prepared to place our personal information in the private sector, why can we not trust it to the police? Law enforcement officials will use the DNA sample only in the detection of a crime. In short, the innocent citizen should have nothing to fear.

The creation of a DNA database would not require a disproportionate investment of time or public resources.

CONS

Although DNA detection might have advantages over fingerprint dusting, the test is nevertheless fallible. Environmental factors at the crime scene such as heat, sunlight, or bacteria can corrupt any genetic data. DNA evidence must be stored in sterile and temperature controlled conditions. Criminals may contaminate samples by swapping saliva. There is room for human error or fraud in analyzing samples. The accuracy of any genetic profile is dependent upon the number of genes examined. The smaller the number, the greater the possibility of error. In 1995 an 18-month investigation was launched into allegations that the FBI Crime Lab was "drylabbing" or faking results of DNA comparisons. Even a complete DNA profile cannot indicate the length of time a suspect was present at a crime scene or the date in question. The creation of a database cannot be a panacea for crime detection.

DNA fingerprinting would have to be mandatory, otherwise those liable to commit crime would simply refuse to provide a sample. Individuals consent to pass personal information to mortgage or insurance agencies. When citizens release information to outside agencies they receive a service in return. In being compelled to give a sample of DNA, the innocent citizen would receive the scant benefit of being eliminated from a police investigation. Moreover, the storage by insurance companies of genetic information remains highly controversial because of the potential abuse of that information. Finally, creation of the database would change the attitude of government toward its citizens. Every citizen, some from the moment of their birth, would be treated as a potential criminal.

The initial and continuing expense of a DNA database would be a gross misapplication of finite public

The requisite computer and laboratory technology is already available. The United States has developed the Combined DNA Index System (CODIS). The expense of sampling the entire population of most countries would be substantial and is unlikely to be offset by any subsequent saving in police resources, but this is part of the price for justice. Popular support for "law and order" suggests that the public puts a very high premium on protection from crime.

Persons who create violent crimes are unlikely to leave conventional fingerprints. However, the National Commission on the Future of DNA Evidence estimates that 30% of crime scenes contain the blood, semen, or saliva of the perpetrator. DNA detection can identify the guilty even when the police have no obvious suspects.

A DNA database is not intended to replace conventional criminal investigations. The database would identify potential suspects, each of whom could then be investigated by more conventional means. Criminal trials frequently feature experts presenting scientific evidence. The jury system is actually a bastion against conviction on account of complicated scientific facts. If the genetic data and associated evidence is not conclusive or is not presented with sufficient clarity, the jury is obliged to find the defendant not guilty. O.J. Simpson was acquitted of the murders of Nicole Brown Simpson and Ron Goldman in spite of compelling DNA evidence linking him to the scene of the crime.

The increased use of DNA evidence will minimize the risk of future wrongful convictions. An FBI study indicates that since 1989 DNA evidence has excluded the initial suspect in 25% of sexual assault cases. Moreover, forensically valuable DNA can be found on evidence that has existed for decades and thus assist in reversing previous miscarriages of justice.

resources. Public confidence in the criminal justice system will neither be improved by requiring individuals to give time and tissue to the police nor by the creation of a bureaucracy dedicated to administering the database. The funds would be better spent on recruiting more police officers and deploying them on foot patrol.

The most serious violent crimes, notably rape and murder, are most commonly committed by individuals known to the victim. When the suspects are obvious, DNA detection is superfluous. Moreover, it is harmful to suggest that crimes can be solved, or criminals deterred, by computer wizardry. Unless the DNA is used to identify a genetic cause for aggression, violent crimes will continue.

There is a serious risk that officials will use genetic evidence to the exclusion of material that might prove the suspect innocent. Moreover, there is the possibility that not only the police, but also the jury, will be blinded by science. It seems unlikely that juries will be able to comprehend or, more importantly, to question the genetic information from the database. The irony is that forensic evidence has cleared many wrongly convicted individuals but might now serve to create miscarriages of its own.

We do not need a database to acquit or exclude non-offenders. When the police have identified a suspect they ought to create a DNA profile and compare it to the crime scene data. Likewise, a DNA sample should be taken if there is concern that an individual was wrongly convicted of a crime.

Sample Motions:
This House would have a criminal DNA database.
This House would give away its DNA.
This House would catch a crook by his genes.

Web Links:
- National Commission on the Future of DNA Evidence - http://www.ojp.usdoj.gov/nij/dna/
  Part of the larger National Institute of Justice website, this section furnishes information to law enforcement providers on how to maximize the value of forensic DNA evidence
- Shadow Article, Anti-DNA Database - http://shadow.autono.net/sin001/dna.htm
  Detailed essay outlining the reasons for opposing a broad forensic DNA database.

- "From Crime Scene to Courtroom" - http://www.ornl.gov/hgmis/publicat/judicature/article9.html
  A 1999 essay stressing the benefits of and problems involved in the Combined DNA Indexing System (CODIS) by the executive director of the National Commission on the Future of DNA Evidence.
- How Stuff Works - http://www.howstuffworks.com/dna-evidence.htm
  Detailed explanation of DNA fingerprinting for the layperson.
- Genelex, DNA Profilers - http://www.genelex.com/paternitytesting/paternitybook5.html
  Detailed discussion of the use of DNA evidence in the courtroom.

Further Reading:
Norah Rudin and Keith Inman. *Introduction to Forensic DNA Analysis.* 2nd ed. CRC Press, 2001.
Gerald Sheindlin. *Genetic Fingerprinting: The Law and Science of DNA.* Routledge, 1996.

CR✿SO

DRILLING IN THE ARCTIC NATIONAL WILDLIFE REFUGE

In 2002, the US Congress rejected a motion that would allow oil drilling in the Arctic National Wildlife Refuge (ANWR) on grounds that the area was ecologically sensitive. Oil developers and environmentalist have never had a more highly charged and symbolic debate to engage in. Supporters of drilling claim that growing foreign dependence on oil threatens American security and that drilling in ANWR would help reduce that dependence. Opponents of drilling maintain that US dependence on foreign oil is inevitable and that drilling in ANWR would not significantly reduce dependence.

PROS

An oil pipeline runs through ANWR and the same argument (ecology) was used to attempt to oppose that pipeline's construction; however, the pipeline actually increased caribou numbers. Perhaps "keystone" species are not as "key" as has been supposed.

Substantial amounts of time and energy are needed for drilling (in some cases years). If we do not put the exploration and drilling structure in place now, they won't be at hand in times of crisis.

Consumption is inevitable. Proponents of renewable energy have not made clear how opening ANWR would delay a transition to renewable energy. Opening ANWR could speed up the transition by making the US more dependent on foreign oil in the future (once the ANWR reserves were depleted) and thus give more of an incentive to convert.

Proposed development may need to be spread out, but drilling can be made seasonal to avoid disruptions to

CONS

Drilling would disrupt certain ecologically sensitive areas. Alaska has caribou herds that moved north to ANWR seasonally, and drilling carries the risk of diverting and potentially reducing the herd. Sources have also revealed that other key species live on Alaska's shoreline.

Drilling would undercut a vital reserve that we may need in the future. The US is without long-term recourse, it is dependent on foreign oil; in times of crisis, however, drilling in ANWR could regulate prices for a limited time. So we should not drill now, we need to hold those reserves for an emergency.

Oil development is unjustified because it further exacerbates the problems of consumption. The more we rely upon fossil fuels, the longer we delay the inevitable: the vital shift to renewable energy. Other action should be taken to limit fuel consumption, such as an increased use of hybrid cars.

Proposed "limited development" will still intrude hundreds of miles into pristine areas. Alaska doesn't have a

animal migration. Caribou herds move into ANWR during specific and predictable times, thus drilling can be scheduled, which would reduce the effect of oil drilling.

major reserve under ANWR; rather, ANWR contains several reserves. Thus, even with "minimal" development, the damage would cover thousands of acres.

Sample Motions:
This House supports measures to allow oil development in ANWR.
This House believes ecology should be valued over development.
This House maintains that limited development in the ANWR is justified.

Web Links:
• ANWR. <http://www.anwr.org/>
This introductory-level Web site provides justifications for oil development, giving up-to-date information on the status of prospects for drilling in the Arctic. Offers links to fact sheets and various other information in support of drilling.
• DOE Fossil Energy—Strategic Petroleum Reserve. <http://www.fe.doe.gov/spr/>
Government-sponsored neutral site provides a basic history and analysis of Strategic Petroleum Reserves (SPR) and what function they serve. Contains quick facts and an up-to-date status of SPRs.
• Save the Arctic National Wildlife Refuge. <http://www.savearcticrefuge.org/>
This site provides a detailed analysis of the issues involved.

Further Reading:
Hiscock, Bruce. *The Big Caribou Herd.* Boyds Mills Press, 2003.
House Committee on Resources, *Hearings on Arctic Coastal Plain Leasing*, 104th Cong., 1st sess., August 3, 1995.

CR80

DRUGS IN SPORTS

Over the past decades, the Olympic Games have focused the world's attention on the use of performance-enhancing drugs in sports. Delegations have quietly withdrawn on the eve of the Games, and Olympic champions such as sprinter Ben Johnson have been stripped of their medals as a result of testing positive for banned drugs. During 2002, major league baseball players Jose Canseco and Ken Caminiti alleged that a large percentage of players used steroids to enhance their performance. Their allegations led to demands for mandatory drug testing for professional baseball players; professional football and basketball players are routinely tested for drugs.

The use of steroids has not been confined to professional athletes. Young athletes have died as a result of steroid use, leading to bans on performance-enhancing drugs in high school and college programs. Nonetheless, doubts remain about the effectiveness of these tests and the fairness of some of the resulting bans. Some people argue that the whole approach is deeply flawed.

PROS

Using performance-enhancing drugs is an issue of freedom of choice. If athletes wish to take drugs in search of improved performances, let them do so. They harm nobody but themselves and should be treated as adults capable of making rational decisions on the basis of widely available information. We should not forbid them performance-enhancing drugs even if such drugs have long-term adverse effects. We haven't outlawed tobacco and boxing, which are proven health risks.

What is the distinction between natural and unnatural

CONS

Once some people choose to use these drugs, they infringe on the freedom of choice of other athletes. Athletes are very driven individuals who go to great lengths to achieve their goals. To some, the chance of a gold medal in two years time may outweigh the risks of serious long-term health problems. We should protect athletes from themselves and not allow anyone to take performance-enhancing drugs.

Where to draw the line between legitimate and illegiti-

enhancement? Athletes use all sorts of dietary supplements, exercises, equipment, clothing, training regimes, medical treatments, etc., to improve their performance. There is nothing "natural" about taking vitamin pills or wearing whole-body Lycra suits. Diet, medicine, technology, and even coaching already give an artificial advantage to those athletes who can afford the best of all these aids. As there is no clear way to distinguish between legitimate and illegitimate artificial aids to performance, they should all be allowed.

Legalizing performance-enhancing drugs levels the playing field. Currently, suspicion about drug use surrounds every sport and every successful athlete. Those competitors who don't take performance-enhancing drugs see themselves as (and often are) disadvantaged. There are no tests for some drugs, and, in any case, new medical and chemical advances mean that cheaters will always be ahead of the testers. Legalization would remove this uncertainty and allow everyone to compete openly and fairly.

Legalizing these drugs will provide better entertainment for spectators. Sport has become a branch of the entertainment business, and the public demands "higher, faster, stronger" from athletes. If drug-use allows athletes to continually break records or makes football players bigger and more exciting to watch, why deny the spectators what they want, especially if the athletes want to give it to them?

Current rules are very arbitrary and unfair. For example, the Olympics forbids athletes from using cold medicines, even in sports where the stimulants in these medicines would have minimal effects on performance. There is also the possibility that some positive tests are simply the result of using a combination of legal food supplements. Cyclists legally have heart operations to allow increased circulation and thus improve performance, but they would be banned if they were to use performance-enhancing drugs.

In many countries bans on performance-enhancing drugs fail to stand up in court. The legal basis for drug testing and the subsequent barring of transgressors from further participation is open to challenge, both as restraint of trade and invasion of privacy. Sports

mate performance enhancement? Difficult though that may be, we should nonetheless continue to draw a line: first, to protect athletes from harmful drugs; second, to preserve the spirit of fair play and unaided competition between human beings at their peak of natural fitness. Eating a balanced diet and using the best equipment are clearly in a different category from taking steroids and growth hormones. We should continue to make this distinction and aim for genuine drug-free athletic competitions.

Legalization is very bad for athletes. The use of performance-enhancing drugs leads to serious health problems, including "steroid rage," the development of male characteristics in female athletes, heart attacks, and greatly reduced life expectancy. Some drugs are also addictive.

Spectators enjoy the competition between athletes rather than individual performances; a close race is better than a no-contest in a world record time. Similarly, they enjoy displays of skill more than simple raw power. In any case, why should we sacrifice the health of athletes for the sake of public enjoyment?

What about the children? Even if performance-enhancing drugs were legalized only for adults, how would you control the problem among children? Teenage athletes train alongside adults and share the same coaches. Many would succumb to the temptation and pressure to use drugs if these were widely available and effectively endorsed by legalization. Young athletes are unable to make fully rational, informed choices about drug-taking, and the health impact on their growing bodies would be even worse than for adult users. Legalization of performance-enhancing drugs would also send a positive message about drug culture in general, making the use of "recreational drugs" with all their accompanying evils more widespread.

Legalization discriminates against poor nations. Far from creating a level playing field, legalization would tilt it in favor of those athletes from wealthy countries with advanced medical and pharmaceutical industries. Athletes from poorer nations would no longer be able

governing bodies often fight and lose such court cases, wasting vast sums of money.

If drugs were legal, they could be controlled and monitored by doctors, making them much safer. Athletes on drugs today often take far more than needed for performance enhancement because of ignorance and the need for secrecy. Legalization would facilitate the exchange of information on drugs, and open medical supervision will avoid many of the health problems currently associated with performance-enhancing drugs.

to compete on talent alone.

Reform is preferable to surrender. The current testing regime is not perfect, but better research, testing, and funding, plus sanctions against uncooperative countries and sports could greatly improve the fight against drugs in sports.

Sample Motions:
This House would legalize the use of performance-enhancing drugs for athletes.
This House would win at all costs.
This House believes your pharmacist is your best friend.

Web Links:
- Performance Enhancing Drugs. <http://esc.calumet.purdue.edu/athletic/ performance_enhancing_drugs.htm#Performance%20Enhancing%20Drugs>
Provides links to information on steroids, blood doping, and performance-enhancing drugs as well as articles relating to performance-enhancing drugs of all types.
- Sports Supplements Danger. <http://www.consumerreports.org/main/ derail.jsp?CONTENT<>cnt_id=59279&FOLDER<>folder_id=18151&bmUID=992904313175>
Overview of issues surrounding the use of sports supplements.

Further Reading:
Kuhn, Cynthia, Scott Schwartzwelder, and Wilkie Wilson. *Pumped: Straight Facts for Athletes about Drugs, Supplements, and Training.* Norton, 2000.
Yesalis, Charles, and Virginia S. Cowart, *The Steroids Game.* Human Kinetics, 1998.

CR∞

DRUG-TESTING IN SCHOOLS

The right of schools to randomly test students for drugs has been debated in the courts for years. In a landmark 1995 decision Vernonia School District v. Acton, *the US Supreme Court ruled that schools could test student athletes for drug use. Three years later the US Court of Appeals for the Seventh Circuit (covering Illinois, Indiana, and Wisconsin) extended the right to test all participants in extracurricular activities, but in 2000 the Indiana Supreme Court banned such testing where the student concerned was not suspected of taking drugs. In 2002 the US Supreme Court ruled that drug testing was permissible for students involved in "competitive" extracurricular activities. Does society's desire to combat a growing drug problem override the right to privacy?*

PROS

Drug use among teenagers is a clear and present problem. Current measures to tackle drugs at the source (i.e., imprisoning dealers and breaking the supply chain) are not succeeding. It is especially important to protect teenagers at an impressionable age and at the time when

CONS

Our justice system is based on the principle that a person is innocent until proven guilty. To enforce random drug testing (thereby invading the privacy of students who are not suspected of drug use) is to view them as guilty until proven innocent. Nothing justifies

PROS	CONS
their attitude to education greatly affects their entire lives. Some sacrifice of human rights is necessary to tackle the drug problem.	the sacrifice of the human rights of innocent people.
Students who do not take drugs have nothing to fear.	Innocent students do have something to fear—the violation of privacy and loss of dignity caused by a drug test.
The purpose of random drug testing is not so much to catch offenders but to prevent all students from offending in the first place.	Other methods of preventing drug abuse are less invasive. These include encouraging extracurricular activities, fostering better relations with parents, tackling the problems of poverty and safety, and so on.
Peer pressure is the primary cause of experimentation with drugs. Discouraging drug use among athletes, model students, etc., sends a powerful message to the entire student body.	Teenagers, especially drug-taking teenagers, are attracted by rebellion and the chance of beating the system. Draconian, Big Brother–style tactics of random drug testing will only provoke resentment and encourage students to break the law. Peer pressure increases as they unite against school authorities.
Urine, hair, and breath samples can be used to detect use of most common drugs, including marijuana, cocaine, heroin, and methamphetamines.	Drug users will only turn to drugs that are more difficult to test, such as "designer" drugs, or use masking agents before being tested.

Sample Motions:
This House supports random drug testing in schools.
This House believes in a student's right to privacy.

Web Links:
• Reported Drug Use by Potential Targets of Random School Drug Testing Policies. <http://www.drugs.indiana.edu/drug_stats/athlete.html>
Short essay presenting evidence that random drug testing in schools is unlikely to detect much drug use.
• Substance Abuse Resource Center. <http://www.jointogether.org/plugin.jtml?siteID=AMBIOMED&P=1>
General site offering links to current news on drug-related topics as well as resources on issues, laws, and government policy.

Further Reading:
Ligocki, Kenneth B. *Drug Testing: What We All Need to Know.* Scarborough, 1996.

CREO

ECONOMIC DEVELOPMENT VS. ENVIRONMENT

The issue of economic development versus environmental conservation can also be seen as the First World vs. the Third World. Industrialized nations, ironically those that are most responsible for current environmental problems, fear that unregulated economic development in the Third World will have disastrous long-term environmental effects on the planet. They point out that massive clearing of tropical forests for farmland is threatening biodiversity and may impact world climate, while a reliance on heavy industry to fuel economic growth adds more pollutants to the air, ground, and water. Developing countries counter that they must make industrialization and economic development a priority because they have to support their growing populations. Developing countries must address current problems; they cannot afford to worry about the distant future.

PROS

Taking care of the millions of people who are starving is more important than saving natural resources, most of which are renewable anyway.

The industrialized world's emphasis on protecting the environment shackles developing countries and contributes to and widens the great divide between the First and Third Worlds. By limiting the development of profitable but polluting industries like steel or oil refining, we are sentencing nations to remain economically backward.

Economic development is vital for meeting the basic needs of the growing populations of Third World countries. If we do not permit industrialization, these nations will have to implement measures to limit population growth just to preserve vital resources such as water.

Obviously the world would be better if all nations abided by strict environmental rules. The reality is that for many nations such adherence is not in their larger interests. For example, closing China's massive Capital Iron and Steelworks, which ecologists point to as a major polluter, would cost 40,000 jobs. The uniform application of strict environmental policies would create insurmountable barriers to economic progress.

Rapid industrialization does not have to put more pressure on the environment. Technological advances have made industries much safer for the environment. For example, nuclear generating plants can provide more energy than coal while contributing far less to global warming. We are also exploring alternative, renewable types of fuel.

The "Green Revolution" has doubled the size of grain harvests. Thus, cutting down more forests or endangering fragile ecosystems to provide more space for crops is no longer necessary. We now have the knowledge to feed the world's increasing population without harming the environment.

CONS

We have wasted and destroyed vast amounts of natural resources, and in so doing have put Earth in jeopardy. We must preserve Earth for future generations.

No one wants to stop economic progress that could give millions better lives. But we must insist on sustainable development that integrates environmental stewardship, social justice, and economic growth. Earth cannot support unrestricted growth.

Unchecked population growth has a deleterious effect on any nation and on the entire planet. Limiting population growth will result in a higher standard of living and will preserve the environment.

Nations are losing more from polluting than they are gaining from industrialization. China is a perfect example. Twenty years of uncontrolled economic development have created serious, chronic air pollution that has increased health problems and resulted in annual agricultural losses of billions of dollars. Thus, uncontrolled growth is not only destructive to the environment, it is also unsound economically.

Technological progress has made people too confident in their abilities to control their environment. In just half a century the world's nuclear industry has had at least three serious accidents: Windscale (UK, 1957), Three Mile Island (US, 1979), and Chernobyl (USSR, 1986). In addition, the nuclear power industry still cannot store its waste safely.

The Green Revolution is threatening the biodiversity of the Third World by replacing native seeds with hybrids. We do not know what the long-term environmental or economic consequences will be. We do know that in the short run, such hybrid crops can indirectly cause environmental problems. The farmer using hybrid seed, which is expensive, must buy new seed each year because the seed cannot be saved to plant the following year's crops. Farmers using hybrid seeds in what once was the richest part of India went bankrupt. As a result, fertile lands lay idle and untilled, resulting in droughts and desertification.

Sample Motions:

This House believes that environmental concerns should always take precedence over economic development in both the First and Third Worlds.

This House believes that economic growth, even at the expense of some environmental degradation, is justified by the need to feed the rising world population.

Web Links:
- Center for International Environmental Law. <http://www.ciel.org>
Offers a review of major international environmental agreements as well as information on the impact of globalization and free trade on sustainable development.
- International Institute for Sustainable Development. <http://www.iisd.org>
Describes institute activities and offers reports and research materials on different aspects of sustainable development.
- United Nations Environmental Programme: Division of Technology, Industry and Economics. <http://www.uneptie.org>
Presents information on UN programs associated with sustainable development.

Further Reading:
Bartelmus, Peter. *Environment, Growth and Development: The Concepts and Strategies of Sustainability.* Routledge, 1994.
Cole, Matthew A. *Trade Liberalisation, Economic Growth and the Environment.* Edward Elgar, 2000.
Kageson, Per. *Growth Versus the Environment: Is There a Trade-Off?* Kluwer, 1998.
Lomborg, Bjorn. *The Skeptical Environmentalist: Measuring the Real State of the World.* Cambridge University Press, 2001.

CRISD

ECONOMIC SANCTIONS VS. ENGAGEMENT

Economic sanctions are one of the most controversial ways whereby the international community seeks to influence a nation's internal policy and democratize countries. Sanctions helped end apartheid in South Africa, but the 40-year-old US embargo of Cuba has not brought down its communist government. China has a terrible human rights record, nevertheless sanctions have not been imposed on it. The question of whether to use trade to effect change is a subject of continuing debate. Meanwhile, international sanctions on Iraq seem to be hurting that country's civilian population more than Saddam Hussein.

PROS

Free trade brings about democratization in three ways: It permits a flow of information from Western countries; it raises a nation's standard of living; and it facilitates the growth of a middle class. These factors generate internal pressure and consequent political change—economic freedom leads to political freedom. Free trade helped bring about the downfall of communism in Eastern Europe and is beginning to increase freedoms in China. When the United States linked most favored nation (MFN) status to improvements in human rights, China made only token gestures to improve its rights record to maintain MFN status. Deep structural changes in human rights in any country come only with unlimited free trade.

Sanctions are ineffective. For example, France and Russia currently have openly breached international sanctions against Iraq because of their complete failure. Sanctions against Cuba, Haiti, and Burma have also proved useless because many nations do not recognize them. In addition, once sanctions are in place,

CONS

Most dictatorial oligarchies welcome free trade as it usually increases their wealth. The West no longer has any leverage over them once they have been accepted into the free trade arena. Although the international community chose not to impose sanctions on China because it is a valuable economic and strategic partner, trade, specifically MFN status, can still be used to force China to improve human rights. Believing that free trade can lead to democratization is naïve. Governments against which sanctions are imposed will not permit the growth of a middle class or let wealth filter down to the people. In reality free trade has worsened Chinese living standards by putting domestic industries out of business and forcing people to work for multinational corporations that pay little.

Sanctions are effective as a long-term tool. They worked in South Africa and they worked in the former Rhodesia. Granted, they can lead to mass suffering of the very people they are designed to help, as they did to the black population of South Africa. However, Nelson Mandela has said that the suffering was worthwhile

the government of the country being sanctioned keeps all available resources, ensuring that sanctions adversely affect only the people. In the case of Iraq, sanctions have led to terrible suffering.

because it helped end apartheid.

Sanctions block the flow of outside information into a country, thus permitting dictators to use propaganda to strengthen their own position. People cannot believe such propaganda is false when there are no competing external claims.

Sanctions send a strong message to the people of a country that the Western world will not tolerate an oppressive regime.

Sample Motions:
This House would put trade relations above human rights.
This House believes in free trade.
This House would make money not war.
This House would engage, not estrange, nondemocratic nations.

Web Links:
• Cato Institute Center for Trade Policy Studies. <http://www.freetrade.org/>
Site advocating free trade includes essays on China, the Cuban embargo, and the failure of unilateral US sanctions.
• Iraq: Sanctions: The Private Weapon. <http://www.iacenter.org/iraq.htm>
Site advocating the lifting of US and UN sanctions against Iraq.
• USA Engage. <http://usaengage.org/>
Information on current US sanctions and potential sanctions by coalition of American business and agriculture opposing unilateral US action.
• A User's Guide to Economic Sanctions. <http://www.heritage.org/library/categories/trade/bg1126.html>
Essay on the effectiveness of economic sanctions from a conservative perspective.

Further Reading:
Crawford, Neta, and Audie Klotz, eds. *How Sanctions Work: Lessons from South Africa.* Palgrave, 1999.
Simons, Geoff. *Imposing Economic Sanctions: Legal Remedy or Genocidal Tool?* Pluto Press, 1999.

CR&O

ELECTORAL COLLEGE, ABOLITION OF

The presidential election of 2000 gave new prominence to the Electoral College. Although Al Gore received more popular votes than George W. Bush, Bush won the election because his victory in Florida gave him a majority of electoral votes. To some observers, this outcome demonstrated clearly that the Electoral College should be abolished. They feel it is an anachronism that has outlived its usefulness. To others, however, the result demonstrated that the Electoral College is both good and necessary, and that the system had worked as it was designed to do.

PROS

The president should be the person chosen by the greatest number of Americans, via the popular vote. The Electoral College violates this mandate in principle and sometimes in practice.

The Electoral College was established at a time when the people were not trusted to choose wisely; senators, too, were initially not chosen by popular vote. The

CONS

The Electoral College ensures that the person elected president has broad support throughout the country. Without the college, candidates could win by appealing only to heavily populated urban areas.

The principle behind the Electoral College is similar to the principle that determines the composition of the Senate, wherein every state is deemed equal, no matter

PROS	CONS
system should be changed to trust the wisdom of the American people.	its size. The college is an integral part of the system of federalism, which gives the states distinct and important rights.
The Electoral College system gives greater weight to votes cast in lightly populated states. The result is that a vote cast for the president by a New Yorker counts less than a vote cast by a North Dakotan; this inequality is inherently unfair.	The Electoral College forces candidates to campaign broadly throughout the country to gain the electoral votes of as many states as possible. If it is eliminated, candidates will spend all their time campaigning in the states with the greatest number of voters and ignore smaller states.
The lightly populated states that are privileged by the Electoral College system are overwhelmingly white. In effect, the system discounts the worth of votes cast by minorities living in urban areas and exacerbates the racial imbalance of power in the country.	Minority voters could be safely ignored by candidates in a national election that depended only on receiving a popular majority. But because these voters can determine who wins a majority—and the electoral votes—in a given state, their influence is significant in the present system.
The current winner-take-all system effectively eliminates third-party candidates, as they cannot win enough Electoral College votes to gain office. The result? The electoral process is predisposed to the status quo, and change and progress are discouraged.	Because no candidate can win the presidency without an absolute majority of electoral votes, the Electoral College promotes the strength of the two-party system and that system promotes the political stability of the country.
Too much latitude is given to electors in the present system; in some states, electors are not required to cast their votes for the candidates who have won the popular vote in their states. Electors should not have the power to disregard the will of the people.	The Constitution designed the US government to include a series of checks and balances, and the Electoral College is part of that system. The Electoral College is meant to limit the "tyranny of the majority" that is possible in unrestrained democracy.

Sample Motions:

This House supports the abolition of the Electoral College.

This House values the will of the people over the rights of the states.

Web Links:

• Center for Voting and Democracy: The Case Against the Electoral College. <http://www.fairvote.org/op_eds/electoral_college.htm>

Web site argues for abolition, with news items and links to other sites.

• The Electoral College. <http://www.fec.gov/pages/ecmenu2.htm>

The Web site of the Federal Election Commission explains what the electoral college is and how it works, and offers essays in favor of retaining the Electoral College.

• In Defense of the Electoral College. <http://www.cato.org/dailys/11-10-00.html>

Think tank Web site offers essay in favor of retaining College.

Further Reading:

Abbott, David W., and James P. Levine. *Wrong Winner: The Coming Debacle in the Electoral College.* Praeger, 1991.

Hardaway, Robert M. *The Electoral College and the Constitution: The Case for Preserving Federalism.* Praeger, 1994.

Pierce, Neal R., and Lawrence D. Longley. *The People's President: The Electoral College in American History and the Direct-Vote Alternative.* Yale University Press, 1981.

ENVIRONMENTALLY LINKED AID

Many parts of the developing world have begun industrializing without regard to the environmental consequences. In light of growing environmental concerns, some individuals and groups have suggested tying aid to environmental goals including curbing emissions of carbon dioxide and chlorofluorocarbon. The international community would still give emergency aid in response to disasters, but it would tie development aid to environmental standards set by the United Nations Environmental Program (UNEP). Countries with especially low emissions would receive extra aid.

PROS

The scientific community is almost unanimous in believing that emissions are seriously damaging the world ecosystem. The most serious threat is climate change. The effects of global warming include increasing desertification and rising sea levels. In addition, the El Niño phenomenon occurs more often. Air pollution has also resulted in increased acid rain and a growing hole in the ozone layer.

The industrialization of the small number of developed countries caused virtually all the problems laid out above. If developing countries, which have about five times the population of the developed world, were to industrialize unchecked, the effect could be catastrophic. For example, rising sea levels would flood millions of homes in low-lying areas such as Bangladesh. Increased crop failure would kill many more by starvation. Developed countries might be able to protect themselves from these effects, but developing countries would not. The developing world has not acted to prevent environmental disaster and so the developed world must act to save literally billions of lives.

The UN could design initial standards so that all developing countries could meet the goals and receive aid. If they spend this development aid wisely, developing countries could industrialize in an environmentally clean way. In the long run, the combined approach of extra rewards for successful countries and serious sanctions for unsuccessful countries should ensure success.

Developed countries should be guardians of the planet expressly because they have a terrible history of polluting. They must prevent unhindered industrialization elsewhere.

Even if environmentalists have exaggerated their claims,

CONS

Environmental pressure groups seriously overstate the evidence for climate change. Even if climate change is occurring, pollution is not necessarily the cause. It may result from natural variations, which the fossil record indicates have occurred in the past.

This is just a new form of imperialism. Developing countries have the right to develop economically and industrially just as developed countries have. Industrialization will improve the living standards of billions of people throughout the globe. In addition, industrialization will lead to economic stability for the world's poorest countries. This, in turn, will increase democratization in these nations.

Developed countries are hypocritical in trying to restrict emissions from developing countries when they do so little themselves. The United States, which is still the world's biggest polluter, consistently refuses to ratify environmental treaties because its own economic self-interest does not appear to be served by doing so. What right does the developed world have to preach to the developing world about emissions?

Asking the UNEP to set emission standards is unfeasible because both developed and developing countries would try to influence the agency. Developed countries would lobby for very restrictive emission standards to decrease the threat from cheap imports. Developing countries would demand standards so lax that they would have no effect.

This proposal has serious consequences for world sta-

the threat from environmental pollution is still great enough to require action. The potential benefit of acting to save the planet's ecosystem far outweighs any downside. (We are not conceding that the claims are exaggerated, merely that it does not matter even if they are.)

bility. First, developed countries would certainly not enforce regulations against China (an important trading partner and the linchpin of regional stability), the world's fastest growing polluter. Second, the developing countries, particularly those that fail to meet the standards, would resent such outside intrusion. In addition, withholding aid could cause economic collapse and the subsequent rise of dictatorships. Rogue nations might form alliances that threatened world stability. In their rush to develop, these states would increase pollution because developed countries would have no influence over them.

Sample Motions:
This House would link aid to emissions reductions.
This House believes that the environment must come first.

Web Links:
• World Bank Development Education Program. <http://www.worldbank.org/html/schools/depweb.htm>
Information on sustainable development for teachers and students.
• World Bank: Environmentally and Socially Sustainable Development. <http://www-esd.worldbank.org/>
Information on World Bank initiatives promoting sustainable development.

Further Reading:
Bossel, Hartmut. *Earth at a Crossroads: Paths to a Sustainable Future*. Cambridge University Press, 1998.
Carty, Winthrop, and Elizabeth Lee. *In the Shadow of the First World: The Environment as Seen from Developing Nations*. Chicago Review Press, 1995.
Daly, Herman. *Beyond Growth: The Economics of Sustainable Development*. Beacon, 1997.
Gupta, Avijit. *Ecology and Development in the Third World*. Routledge, 1998.
Miller, Marian A. L. *The Third World in Global Environmental Politics*. Lynne Rienner, 1995.

CRSO

ETHICAL FOREIGN POLICY

For centuries, the foreign policy of most Western nations was based on realpolitik, doing whatever necessary to forward the self-interest of the nation. In the United States, which traditionally has seen itself as holding to a higher standard, tension has always existed between realpolitik and a desire to act out of humanitarian concern or to preserve liberty. During the 1990s, ethnic cleansing in the Balkans and genocide in Africa forced Western nations to confront the question of ethics in foreign policy. Should nations whose self-interests are not threatened intervene in other countries solely for humanitarian reasons?

PROS

Western governments must pursue an ethical foreign policy. This translates into the philosophy that impels us to act whenever there is a moral imperative to do so.

Lobbyists should not influence foreign policy. It should

CONS

If "ethical foreign policy" means active intervention whenever there is a "moral imperative," then it is a hopelessly naïve notion. Governments are constrained by practical concerns. For example, selling arms to certain nations might be unethical, but if the government stops such sales, citizens lose jobs—and the weapons are purchased elsewhere.

In a representative democracy discounting these groups

PROS	CONS
be above special interests and should focus on doing what is right.	is impossible. Moreover, the "right thing to do" for the nation may be what special interests demand.
The argument for ethical foreign policy is strongest when the West confronts heinous crimes in foreign lands, such as genocide in Rwanda or ethnic cleansing in the Balkans. In both places, the West had a clear moral imperative for active involvement—our action could save lives and free people from oppression.	We concede the principle but reject the practice. Intervening might make matters worse. We also have to be mindful of broader concerns, like the situation in the foreign country and what action might do to our image in other nations. Taking an active and moralistic stance toward African problems, for example, may make the West look like neo-imperialists.
In many cases, such as that of Kosovo in the 1990s, the humanitarian imperative demands intervention: We must act because if we don't people will suffer and die. Taking the pragmatic approach based on a careful assessment of national interests costs lives.	Intervention before a situation is fully assessed may cost more lives in the long run. Being starkly utilitarian is horrible, but foreign policy must solve problems for the long term; it cannot be based on a knee-jerk reaction to an immediate situation.
Ethical foreign policy means standing up to regimes that discriminate among their people. We must send a clear message about our values.	The West is inconsistent in applying ethical values to foreign policy. We intervened in Kosovo to prevent genocide, but we have not intervened to prevent the persecution of minorities in Russia or China. Our guiding force is what is possible, not what is principled. Why lie about it?

Sample Motions:
   This House would have an ethical foreign policy.
   This House believes politics is the art of the necessary not the possible.

Web Links:
   • Foreign Policy. <http://www.foreignpolicy.com>
   Journal specializing in analysis and comment on foreign policy issues.
   • Foreign Affairs. <http://www.foreignaffairs.org>
   Journal sponsored by the Council on Foreign Relations, exploring foreign policy issues.

Further Reading:
   Forsythe, David P. *Human Rights in International Relations.* Cambridge University Press, 2000.
   Hitchens, Christopher. *The Trial of Henry Kissinger.* Verso, 2001.

CRSO

EUROPEAN DEFENSE FORCE

In recent years, particularly in light of the wars in the Balkans during the late 1990s, members of the European Union (EU) have debated the creation of a European Defense Force (EDF). Such a standing armed force would be drawn from EU members and operate under EU control, in contrast to NATO, which is dominated by the United States. Debates on the EDF often revolve around the proposed role of NATO in the post–Cold War era. Note well: The significance of the EDF may spread beyond the borders of the European Union.

PROS

The EU must have a defense policy independent of NATO. With its origins in the Cold War and its domination by the United States, NATO carries a great deal of historical and geopolitical baggage. NATO cannot easily intervene in Eastern Europe without incurring Russia's displeasure. The EDF will allow the EU to deal with crises in Eastern and Central Europe more effectively than can NATO because the EU will not have to tiptoe around Russia.

The EU has achieved significant integration of and convergence in the political and economic spheres. Integration of defense policy and the establishment of a European Defense Force are the logical next step.

NATO has shown the EU that a standing multinational defense force is possible. The proposed EDF could follow its example and complement it.

With the growing industrial and economic maturity of the EU and its members, the EU could now afford to have a standing defense force. The proposed EDF would also create a great many jobs for European defense industries.

CONS

NATO has successfully defended the interests of Western Europe for decades. Why rock the boat? What problem could a European Defense Force solve that NATO could not? In any case, the EU will always have to consider Russia's sensibilities when engaged in Eastern Europe. Far better to have America's bargaining power and geopolitical clout backing the EU in negotiating with Russia. Creating a European Defense Force will marginalize NATO and the United States. This will lead to reduced US engagement in Europe, which may, in turn, diminish the EU's influence with Russia.

EU members frequently disagree on political and economic issues. Member interests are even more divergent on the thorny area of defense policy. This difference in priorities will ultimately lead to deadlock because no country wishes to see its soldiers dying on a battlefield that is not strategically important to it.

NATO and the proposed EDF are designed to address very different concerns. NATO exists to deal with significant situations in which Western European nations are likely to adopt a common defense policy. In contrast, the EDF is targeted at smaller geopolitical incidents that would be "beneath" NATO's notice. By their nature, these incidents would not have uniform effects on EU members. Therefore the EU is unlikely to achieve consensus on how to deal with them.

Even if we assume that the EU could bear the massive costs of a standing military force, there are significant political and economic barriers to establishing it. Among these barriers are: How will the EU develop a common defense policy? Will the force's mandate be only defense or will it include peacekeeping? What is the nature of its command structure? Who will choose its supplies and equipment? What language will its members use? These questions involve political and economic considerations that are likely to result in continuous contention that will ultimately yield a stillborn EDF.

Sample Motions:
This House believes in a European Defense Force.
This House believes that Europe should defend itself.

Web Links:
• Jane's: Defence. <http://www.janes.com/defence>
Offers news on European defense concerns.

Further Reading:
Nye, Joseph. *Understanding International Conflicts*. Longman, 2002.

EUROPEAN FEDERALIZATION

The members of the European Union (EU) are currently debating the next step in the evolution of a European government. One suggestion is the creation of a federal structure similar to that of the United States. Under such a system, a European government would be responsible for defense, foreign affairs, economic policy, agriculture, external trade, and immigration. The lowest appropriate authority—in some cases the individual nations of the EU—would exercise power over areas such as culture, law and order, and education, as American states do. Supporters of devolution want to take this one step further, devolving certain responsibilities to regional and local authorities, further weakening the nation-state.

PROS

A federal Europe would build on the success of the EU and its predecessors. It would tame the nationalism that caused so many horrors in the twentieth century and realize the vision of its founders for an "ever-closer union." While national governments exist they will regard policy making as a competitive business, damaging the potential prosperity of all of Europe's citizens. A federal European state can build on the shared history and culture of its members to further the common good while accommodating regional differences.

A federal system in which decision making occurs at the lowest appropriate level combines maximum effectiveness with maximum accountability. Citizens gain the advantages of living in an economically, militarily, and politically powerful state and increase individual opportunities for work, study, etc. At the same time, they preserve the advantages of living in a smaller state: connection to the political process; respect for local cultural traditions; and responsiveness to differing economic and physical situations. The checks and balances of a federal system prevent tyranny and increase willing obedience to laws.

A federal Europe is better equipped to promote the interests of its citizens internationally because it will have more influence than the sum of its individual states do now. Furthermore, Europe has a lot to contribute to the world in terms of its liberal traditions and political culture, providing both a partner and a necessary balance to the United States in global affairs.

The success of other federal states in providing peace and prosperity for their citizens while safeguarding democracy points to the advantages of this model. The United States, Australia, and Canada have standards of

CONS

National identity and differences remain far more important than supposedly shared European values. Existing national governments operate on different models. These recognize the historical, cultural, and economic distinctiveness of each nation and provide an important focus for the loyalty of their citizens. The further power is removed from the citizens, the more detached they are from the democratic process, the less accountable power becomes, and the more likely government is to make both bad decisions and decisions badly. A federal system can damage the interest of tens of millions of people.

Forcing people in a direction they do not wish to go is fraught with danger. An ill-advised dash to build a federal Europe could raise dormant nationalist feelings, promote the rise of populist politicians with xenophobic agendas, and endanger the stability of the EU. A "Europe of Nations," not a federalized government, preserves the current benefits of the EU without the risks of further unwanted political integration.

A federal Europe may damage the security of its citizens. Russia would almost certainly view a new super state composed of its traditional enemies as a threat. A European state would result in the collapse of NATO, making current NATO members outside the EU more insecure. Inevitably, it would result in rivalry rather than partnership with the United States, which currently pays a disproportionate amount of Europe's defense costs.

Europe is not Australia, which was settled by culturally homogeneous immigrants. Canada's relations with Québec show that cultural and linguistic differences can be politically destabilizing. Federal states such as

living that most Europeans would envy, while India is the best example of a long-term democratic success in the developing world.

Brazil and the Soviet Union have seen dictatorship, human rights problems, and retarded economic development. EU members often have no commonality of interests in what would be key federal issues, including defense and foreign policy, agricultural reform, and trade.

Federalism allows for regional identities—e.g., for Spain's Basques—in a way national states cannot. In a federal Europe minority groups would not feel under threat from a dominant culture. Long-running conflicts could be resolved because issues of sovereignty would be less relevant within the new political structure.

Existing states can decentralize successfully, as Britain and France have both showed in the 1990s and as Germany has done since 1945. Spain's problem with separatist terrorists in the Basque region shows that even a great deal of regional autonomy fails to satisfy extremists.

National sovereignty is increasingly irrelevant as a result of globalization. The global economy demands that multinational corporations, which can pit national governments against each other in search of economic advantage, be tamed. A federal Europe would be powerful enough to demand high standards of behavior from such companies and could make a greater difference on environmental issues like global warming.

Europe should be wider, not deeper, in its political development. Peace and prosperity can be most surely provided by the accession of all European states to the EU. Given the former communist and Soviet-dominated past of many of these nations, they are unlikely to again give their independence away. The EU's focus on the creation of a single currency in the 1990s has already delayed enlargement. It may be lost altogether if deeper integration becomes the new priority.

Sample Motions:
This House would create a United States of Europe.
This House believes in a federal Europe.
This House would pursue an ever-closer union.
This House would go deeper.

Web Links:
• The Bruges Group. <http://www.eurocritic.demon.co.uk/brughome.htm#Top>
British organization offering articles and speeches in opposition to a centralized EU government.
• The European Movement. <http://www.euromove.org.uk>
Information about the European Movement, an organization calling for a more democratic EU government accountable to citizens.
• The European Party. <http://www.europeanparty.org>
Information on the party, which supports reform of the current governing structure of the EU.
• The Federal Trust. <http://www.cix.co.uk/~fedtrust>
Provides summaries of major speeches on the EU issues including increased federalization.

Further Reading:
Brown-John, C. Lloyd, ed. *Federal-Type Solutions and European Integration.* University Press of America, 1995.
Siedentop, Larry. *Democracy in Europe.* Columbia University Press, 2001.

CRISD

EXTREMIST POLITICAL PARTIES, BANNING OF

Extremist political parties can be taken to mean either those on the extreme left or those on the extreme right. For a group to be considered extremist, usually the members must promote hate speech or condone the use of violence to promote political goals. In the past few years a number of groups that have been labeled as extremist have received increased support in elections in many European countries.

PROS

Free speech does not exist in a vacuum. It can be restrained specifically in this case on grounds of harm. Extremism as hate speech that causes harm to minorities is a justifiable reason for curbing free speech.

Private and public thought and speech are intrinsically different. The former is to be preserved, but the latter has an impact on other people that can be harmful; it is this speech we are seeking to restrain.

The recent rise in popularity of right-wing extremist parties across Europe, exemplified by the success of Jean-Marie Le Pen in the initial round of the French presidential elections, shows that appealing to voters on extremist grounds can be a successful strategy. We have a duty to act against a threat to our society in the form of extremism.

Merely by being allowed to advocate their views, extremist parties are given a veneer of respectability. The fact that the vast majority of people disagree is irrelevant. Extremists cannot be allowed on the same democratic ticket as respectable, pro-system groups, because their mere presence tarnishes the system.

Those who talk of parties going underground if they are banned are wrong. Banning such extreme political parties will mean that the vast majority of people in a nation never hear of them or their views. Such parties will never get anywhere without mass support and publicity.

We have the right to make a moral judgment on society and its actions. We can declare things abhorrent and not justified in decent society. Such a function is a role for government in making any laws. A removal of this moral dimension from lawmaking would lead to extreme moral relativism and anarchy.

CONS

We already have laws that regulate the conduct of free speech—slander, libel, etc. Yet the basic premise of free speech in a democracy must be protected at all costs, else we risk turning into the kind of society that these extremist groups support.

Delineating such a difference is misleading and dangerous. If one is invited into someone's home, does this make what would be public speech now private? In any case, although politicians in extremist parties may promote intolerance and discriminatory policies, very rarely do they directly call for violent action, so what impact are we seeking to avoid?

What rise in extremism? Le Pen achieved success when he moderated his extremist message; his success was a result of the fracturing of the Left in French politics, and his Front National Party won no seats in the Assembly. The draconian law proposed would be a disproportionate response to a limited threat.

No one is disputing the fact that extremist views are repellent, often shallow, and not logically thought through. Meeting their views and combating them in open and honest debate are the most effective ways of highlighting the flaws in their thinking and solutions.

Such parties benefit from going underground. They can present themselves as martyrs and as being persecuted by the establishment, which is denying their chance to have a say. Such antistate rebellious sentiment will be very attractive to a cross section of the dispossessed and dispirited in society.

Moral judgments are fine, but the very strength—and weakness of a democracy—lies in allowing anyone to challenge it and mold it. If a democratic system regulates itself by declaring who can challenge it, then that democracy betrays its very basis. Categorizing a party as "extremist" or "far right" is very subjective. In addition to repellent views on race, these parties may advocate policies worthy of serious political debate.

Sample Motions:
This House would ban extremist political parties.
This House believes an open society must have the right to protect itself from its enemies.

Web Links:
• Enduring Freedoms. <http://www.enduring-freedoms.org/breve.php3?id_breve=380>
Site reports on threats to freedoms, including challenges to extremist political parties.
• European Monitoring Centre on Racism and Xenophobia. <http://www.eumc.at/>
Site maintained by an organization established by the European Union to combat racism, xenophobia, and anti-Semitism in Europe.
• Searchlight. < http://www.searchlightmagazine.com/>
Site maintained by an organization formed to combat racism, neo-Nazism, fascism, and other forms of prejudice.

Further Reading:
Fraser, Nicholas. *The Voice of Modern Hatred: Tracing the Rise of Neo-Fascism in Europe.* Overlook Press, 2001.
George, John, and Laird M. Wilcox. *American Extremists: Militias, Supremacists, Klansmen, Communists & Others.* Prometheus, 1994

CR£O

FLAT TAX

The slogan, "No taxation without representation" is a part of US history. From our earliest days as a colony, taxation was controversial. The first income tax law was passed in 1862 to support the Civil War. This was a graduated or progressive tax, meaning that the percent of income paid in taxes depended on level of income. Over the next half-century the income tax was repealed and levied again multiple times. In 1913, the 16th Amendment to the Constitution made the federal income tax a permanent fixture of American tax law. Since its inception, the federal income tax has been graduated. Now, calls for a flat tax are being heard in the United States. A flat tax uses the same percentage rate for everyone, whatever their income.

PROS

US citizens waste too much time and money filling out tax forms. Just filling out a standard 1040 form takes over 13 hours. Overall, taxpayers spend 6.2-billion hours filling out IRS forms and paperwork. If the government paid citizens minimum wage to do their taxes, that would amount to $32 billion a year. When you add in the cost of tax professionals, the cost of compliance could be as high as $194 billion according to the Tax Foundation. Clearly, these costs are too high and drain too many resources from the economy.

The only homeowners who will be negatively affected by the flat tax will be the rich. A paper, "The Flat Tax and Housing Values," written by J. D. Foster,

CONS

Asking citizens to complete tax forms is a small price to pay for having a government that does so much for its citizens. Tax dollars pay for many things: roads, the military, social programs, and foreign aid, among them. For most citizens, filing their taxes is not pleasant, but recently the IRS has enacted many policies designed to help taxpayers. It has a toll-free number for questions and a comprehensive Web site. The high costs of tax professionals are usually the result of companies and individuals trying to find ways to pay less in taxes. A flat tax would limit or do away with deductions and could increase taxes for those with lower incomes.

The current tax system allows homeowners to deduct the interest they pay on their mortgages from their income taxes. This creates an incentive for people to

Tax Foundation executive director and chief economist, says that owners of homes currently priced at around $100,000 or below should actually see a significant increase in the value of their home. Foster says that owners of homes in the $200,000 range similarly have little to fear even with a pure flat tax, as the net effect of the various proposed tax changes seems to leave them with little hope of a windfall, but little fear of a significant loss. Only owners of homes that cost more than about $300,000 may see a modest decline in the value of their home.

A flat tax would increase privacy. In the current system, IRS employees have access to many details about a person's savings, investments and assets, property holdings, and retirement savings. Corporations also must disclose details of their businesses. With a flat tax, all profits from assets would be lumped together, and individual assets would not need to be listed. Getting rid of the estate tax would mean that when people die, the IRS won't need to go through their assets.

The flat tax would treat everyone equally. The current tax system forces low-income individuals and families to pay a larger percentage of their income in taxes than do the rich. The flat tax is different. It allows people to deduct an allowance based on their family size from their income, and then the rest of their earnings are taxed at a standard rate, no matter what their income. Individuals owe taxes only on the income above the standard allowance. People who are in the low- or middle-income ranges will receive the largest reduction in average taxes because their personal allowance will make up a greater percentage of their income. Some low-income individuals and families will pay no taxes at all.

This system will reduce the costs to the government and make people pay their fair share. It will result in people keeping more of their hard-earned money and being able to spend more on items they want and need. Studies of the flat tax project a large increase in per capita income if it is implemented. Consumer spending will stimulate the economy and this will improve the US economy.

become homeowners, thus strengthening the economy and neighborhoods. If this incentive is removed, fewer people will want to purchase homes, and people selling homes will lose money.

Citizens are protected by many federal laws that regulate the privacy of the information provided to the IRS. When applying for loans or other financial transactions, similar types of information must be provided. The IRS has an excellent track record on privacy, especially considering the number of tax returns that are submitted each year.

If this provision is added to the flat tax package, then poor people will live outside the income tax system. In many people's minds, they will become second-class citizens who contribute nothing to our country. Graduated taxation lets poor people do their small part to finance the government. Without graduation, you could be paying no tax one year, and start paying 17% on your raise the next year.

The idea that cutting taxes for the rich will lead to economic growth is fallacious. History has shown that supply-side policies, like the flat tax, do not actually boost the economy. The flat tax will reduce the amount of taxes paid by businesses. Even President Ronald Reagan, a huge proponent of supply-side policies, closed loopholes that businesses were using to avoid taxes. Economic theory offers no proof that supply-side policies work, and many historical facts indicate that the economy would be better off with the current tax system.

Sample Motions:
This House would adopt a flat tax system.
This House believes a flat tax system would be better for the US.

Web Links:
• Citizens for Tax Justice. <http://www.ctj.org/index.html>
Site maintained by an organization advocating a greater voice for citizens in the development of tax laws; includes many articles opposing a switch to a flat tax, which it maintains would hurt middle-income families.
• Citizens for a Sound Economy. <http://www.cse.org>
Site maintained by an organization advocating less government; it offers many pro-flat tax articles.
• National Center for Policy Analysis (NCPA). <http://www.ncpa.org>
NCPA, which promotes private alternatives to government regulation and control, offers information on the flat tax from a pro-flat tax perspective.
• Tax Foundation. <http://www.taxfoundation.org>
The site offers a lot of information regarding tax policies from an organization that supports a flat tax.

Further Reading:
Armey, Richard K. *The Flat Tax: A Citizen's Guide to the Facts on What It Will Do for You, Your Country, and Your Pocketbook.* Fawcett Columbine, 1996.
Hall, Robert E., and Alvin Rabushka. *Flat Tax.* Hoover Institution Press, 1995.
Hall, Robert Ernest, ed. *Fairness and Efficiency in the Flat Tax.* AEI Press, 1996.
Hicko, Scott E. *The Flat Tax: Why It Won't Work for America.* Addicus Books, 1996.
McCaffery, Edward J. *Fair Not Flat: How to Make the Tax System Better and Simpler.* University of Chicago Press, 2002.

CR80

FREE SPEECH, RESTRICTIONS ON

Freedom of speech is one of the basic tenets of democracy. A fundamental right enshrined in the US Bill of Rights, the United Nations Declaration of Human Rights, and the European Convention on Human Rights, freedom of speech is, nevertheless, not an absolute. Most nations have laws against sedition, libel, or speech that threatens public safety. Where a nation draws the line between protected and unprotected speech is a continuing subject for debate.

PROS

Free speech is an inherently ambiguous concept that requires definition and interpretation; it is the job of governments to clarify these ambiguities.

As Justice Oliver Wendell Holmes wrote, "the most stringent protection of free speech would not protect a man in falsely shouting fire in a theatre and causing a panic." We accept limitations on free speech when it may threaten public safety. Therefore, freedom of speech is never absolute.

Speech leads to physical acts. Pornography, hate speech, and political polemic are linked to rape, hate crimes, and insurrection.

CONS

The limits to free speech are too important to be determined by government. If speech is to be regulated, it should be done by an independent body.

The tyranny of the majority is a good reason to resist government censorship. A healthy democracy recognizes that smaller groups must be heard; to guarantee that they have a public voice, no restrictions should be put on speech.

Society is self-regulating. The link between speech and action is a false one. Yes, people who commit hate crimes are likely to have read hate literature, and people who commit sex crimes are likely to have watched pornography. But viewing pornography or reading hate speech does not necessarily lead to crime. In addition, exposing hate speech and extreme political polemic to societal scrutiny increases the likelihood that it will be discredited and defeated, rather than strengthened through persecution.

Government must protect its citizens from foreign and internal enemies. Thus, governments should be permitted to curb speech that might undermine the national interest during war.

Regardless of the situation, the public has the right to a free exchange of ideas and to know what the government is doing.

Some views are antithetical to religious beliefs. To protect the devout, we should ban this type of offensive speech.

We must defend the right of the nonreligious to express their views.

We need to protect children from exposure to obscene, offensive, or potentially damaging materials.

We all agree that government must protect children, but that does not mean that government should have the right to censor all material.

Sample Motions:
This House would restrict freedom of speech.
This House would muzzle the press.
This House would censor the Internet.
This House would ban books.

Web Links:
• American Civil Liberties Union. <http://www.aclu.org>
Offers information and resources on a wide variety of rights issues.
• Banned Books Online. <http://digital.library.upenn.edu/books/banned-books.html>
On-line exhibit of books that have been the object of censorship or attempted censorship.
• First Amendment Cyber Tribune. <http://w3.trib.com/FACT/>
Resource with links to hundreds of sites dealing with First Amendment issues.

Further Reading:
Curtis, Michael Kent. *Free Speech, "The People's Darling Privilege": Struggles for Freedom of Expression in American History.* Duke University Press, 2000
Eastland, Terry. *Freedom of Expression in the Supreme Court.* Rowman and Littlefield, 2000.
Hensley, Thomas R., ed. *Boundaries of Freedom of Expression and Order in American History.* Kent State University, 2001.
Irons, Peter, and Howard Zinn. *A People's History of the Supreme Court.* Viking, 1999.
Kennedy, Sheila, ed. *Free Expression in America: A Documentary History.* Greenwood, 1999.

CRSO

FREE TRADE

Economists and politicians have praised the virtues of free trade for over 200 years. By allowing everyone equal access to all markets, the theory goes, you guarantee the most efficient allocation of resources and the cheapest prices for consumers. Can such a theory work in practice? Specifically, could it help the least-developed countries achieve a better quality of life? Western rhetoric says it can and points to international institutions like as the World Trade Organization (WTO) and the World Bank that foster free trade and help these nations. However, as long as the West continues to protect its own agriculture and industries from the international market, its position is arguably hypocritical.

PROS

Interlocking trade relationships decrease the likelihood of war. If a nation is engaged in mutually beneficial relationships with other countries, it has no incentive to jeopardize these relationships through aggression. This promotes peace, which is a universal good.

A tariff-free international economy is the only way to maintain maximum global efficiency and the cheapest prices. Efficient allocation of the world's resources means less waste and, therefore, more affordable goods for consumers.

Free trade might lead to domestic layoffs, but the universal good of efficiency outweighs this. We should not subsidize uncompetitive industries; we should retrain workers for jobs in other fields. Subsidizing inefficiency is not sound economic practice. Moreover, the jobs we subsidize in the West are more needed in the developing world, to which they would inevitably flow if free trade were observed.

The growth of the developing world is a universal good because improving the quality of life of millions of people is clearly a moral imperative. Free trade helps countries by maximizing their comparative advantage in free trade circumstances.

Free trade permits developing countries to gain ready access to capital in liberalized international financial markets. This gives them the opportunity to finance projects for growth and development.

CONS

Free trade does not promote peace. Trading countries have gone to war against each other. This argument might apply to a good-natured trading relationship, but not necessarily to one that is just tariff free.

International economics isn't as simple as increasing the efficiency of global resource allocation above all else. Tariff revenue is a perfectly legitimate and useful source of government income. Without tariffs governments cannot protect the jobs of their citizens.

Job security is a legitimate concern of governments. The destruction of jobs is clear testimony against free trade serving a "universal good." Free trade supporters fail to factor in the political ramifications of job losses. A starkly utilitarian understanding of "universal good" may dictate that jobs flock to the developing world, but political considerations may dictate a more localized definition of the "good."

Defending pure, unadulterated free trade is a pointless exercise. Textbook ideas are always mediated by practical constraints. In reality, the conditions developing countries must meet just to join the "not quite free trade" WTO are stringent and may cost the equivalent of the nation's entire annual humanitarian budget. Poor nations have social and development programs that must take priority over trade issues.

If capital flow were rational, it would be beneficial. In practice, liberalized capital flow can destabilize developing economies, which are prone to speculation based on investor whim rather than economic fundamentals.

Sample Motions:
    This House believes free trade serves a universal good.
    This House believes free trade is good for the developing world.

Web Links:
    • International Monetary Fund (IMF). <www.imf.org>
    General site providing statistics and background on the IMF; offers information on trade and monetary issues and legal issues involving trade; and presents evaluations of IMF programs.
    • The World Bank Group. <www.worldbank.org>
    Broad site linking to development statistics, documents and reports, programs, research, and World Bank publications.
    • World Trade Organization (WTO). <http://www.wto.org>
    Offers general information on the WTO, international trade and trade agreements, and WTO programs.

Further Reading:
    Bhagwati, Jagdish N. *Free Trade Today.* Princeton University Press, 2002.
    Das, Bhagirathlal. *World Trade Organisation: A Guide to the Framework for International Trade.* Zed Books, 1999.

Irwin, Douglas. *Free Trade Under Fire.* Princeton University Press, 2002.

Rorden Wilkinson, *Multilateralism and the World Trade Organisation: The Architecture and Extension of International Trade Regulation.* Routledge, 2001.

Schott, Jeffrey. *Prospects for Free Trade in the Americas.* Institute for International Economics, 2001.

CRSO

GAY ADOPTION

At present, US states are divided on the issue of gay adoption. California, Connecticut, Illinois, Massachusetts, and New York have approved the practice, while Arkansas, Florida, and Utah, among others, have outlawed it. In 2000, Mississippi passed a law not only banning gay and lesbian couples from adopting children but also forbidding Mississippi to recognize gay adoptions from other states. Civil rights groups are currently challenging bans on gay adoption in federal courts.

PROS

Society is changing, and the traditional idea of the nuclear family with married mother and father is no longer the only acceptable alternative. Many states are beginning to award legal rights to gay couples because the stability of such relationships is now recognized. Such couples can provide a stable and loving upbringing for children.

Nature has shown in many species that, when one or both parents die, an uncle or aunt frequently takes on the child-rearing role.

Some babies (both human and of other species) are born with a predisposition to homosexuality, and their upbringing will not affect their sexuality. Attempting to suppress this genetic predisposition has resulted in great misery for many. We should embrace all gay people fully—which must include celebrating gay role models, especially as responsible parents.

In many cases where one of the partners is the biological parent, gay couples are currently responsibly rearing children. Allowing adoption by the other partner merely confers legal rights on an already successful, if informal, family model.

Homophobia is wrong and must be fought wherever encountered. Only through the full inclusion of gays in society and all its institutions can we hope to overcome prejudice.

CONS

The traditional nuclear family is still the ideal. Where its breakdown is inevitable, a close substitute, with maternal and paternal influences, is the only alternative. Evolution and nature have shown that the natural development of the young is aided by both these influences. Research published in the *University of Illinois Law Review* in 1997 found that children raised in homosexual households are significantly more likely to be gay themselves.

While exceptions occur, the norm in nature is that both mother and father nurture offspring. To legally allow adoption by gay couples is to encourage what is an unnatural upbringing.

A child's primary role models are his or her parents. Bringing a heterosexual child up in a gay household gives the child a distorted view of a minority sexuality, just as a girl brought up by two men would fail to benefit from a female influence.

While the law should not penalize gay relationships, it also exists to encourage the nuclear family as the ideal for child raising. Legal prohibition of gay adoption is a natural step toward this ideal.

Homophobic language and behavior is still common in society. Placing a child too young to have an opinion of his own in the care of a gay couple exposes him to this prejudice and subjects him to ridicule or violence. Whatever ideal we might have, the psychological and physical welfare of the child must come first.

Sample Motions:
   This House would allow gay couples to adopt children.
   This House would explode the nuclear family.

Web Links:
   • American Civil Liberties Union: Gay and Lesbian Rights. <http://www.aclu.org/issues/gay/hmgl.html>
   Provides information on gay rights and the status of legal issues facing the gay community.
   • Children of Lesbians and Gays Everywhere. <http://www.colage.org/research/index.html>
   Site offering sociological information on gay families for children of gay parents.

Further Reading:
   Savage, Dan. *The Kid: What Happened When My Boyfriend and I Decided to Go Get Pregnant: An Adoption* Story. Plume, 2000.
   Sullivan, Ann. *Issues in Gay and Lesbian Adoption.* Child Welfare League of America, 1995.
   Tasker, Fiona, and Susan Golombok. *Growing Up in a Lesbian Family: Effects on Child Development.* Guilford Press, 1998.

CRSO

GAY CLERGY

Debates over the ordination of gays have dominated—and divided—major American Protestant groups for years. Most denominations formally oppose the ordination of gays. In practice, however, many church leaders follow a "don't ask, don't tell" policy. Some church leaders who have openly ordained gays have been dismissed from their posts. American Roman Catholics debated the issue during 2002 as a result of the sex abuse scandal that engulfed the church.

PROS

Leviticus also permits polygamy, bans tattoos, and prohibits the wearing of clothes made of blended textiles. Most Christians accept that parts of the Bible reflect the societal attitudes of the time and are not relevant today. The only New Testament comments about homosexuality come from Paul; Jesus does not address the issue.

Scientists are now confident they have isolated the "gay gene" that makes individuals homosexual. Since science is part of nature, homosexuality must be part of God's plan.

Condemning homosexuality as sex outside marriage and therefore adultery is unfair because most denominations do not recognize same-sex unions. Were they to do so, gays could enjoy sex within loving relationships, sanctified by the church, just as heterosexuals do. Jesus' main teaching was clear: "Love your God and love your neighbor." You cannot equate homosexual behavior with adultery; the former causes pain and

CONS

The Bible considers homosexuality "a grievous sin" (Genesis 18:20); a capital crime (Leviticus 20:13); and punishable by exclusion from the Kingdom of Heaven (1 Corinthians 6:9–10). Christians—especially the clergy—must accept the Bible as the ultimate authority. Christian ministry is therefore incompatible with homosexuality. Jesus was a radical teacher who overturned Jewish tradition where he thought it necessary. His silence on homosexuality indicates that he saw no need in this case.

While homosexuality certainly has a genetic component, the existence of a "gay gene" has not been proven. Also, genes create only predisposition; if one identical twin is gay, the probability that the other twin will be gay is only 52%. Genetic pre-dispositions to alcoholism and pedophilia have also been found, but society does not accept these conditions as normal.

The Bible and Jesus strongly condemn sex outside of marriage. Although Jesus spent time in the company of adulterers, he loved "the sinner, not the sin" and ordered them to cease their behavior. His response to homosexuals would have been just as unequivocal.

has a victim (the betrayed partner), the latter can be a purely loving relationship.

Priests have a responsibility to represent the members of their congregations. A large number of Christians are gay, and they can receive better spiritual direction from gay ministers than from heterosexuals who do not understand their lifestyles or relationships.

Over the centuries, the church has revised its stand on social issues as it seeks to reinterpret and re-explain God's message of love in terms of modern society. The acceptance of homosexuality and ordination of openly gay priests is a necessary next step.

Priests act as representatives of God for members of their congregation. Some people oppose women priests because, while women are children of God and part of the church, they cannot represent Jesus because he was male. The same applies to gays; they cannot represent Jesus because he was heterosexual.

The church is not a political institution, changing and catering to the views of the electorate. It acts as the curator of God's word and maintains its principles no matter how unfashionable. Christianity will survive in an increasingly secular age by maintaining a clear, consistent message.

Sample Motions:
This House believes in the ordination of gay clergy.
This House calls for a representative clergy.

Web Links:
• BeliefNet. <http://www.beliefnet.com>
Multi-faith site offering information on various religions and on religious issues.
• ReligiousTolerance.Org: The Bible and Homosexuality. <http://www.religioustolerance.org/hom_bibl.htm>
Summarizes the conservative and liberal interpretations of biblical passages that might relate to homosexuality.
• What Does the Bible Say About Sexuality and Homosexuality? <http://www.christianity.com/CC/article/
0,,PTID4211|CHID102753|CIID234127,00.html> Article on the topic from a conservative perspective.

Further Reading:
Didl, Herman. *The Antigay Agenda: Orthodox Vision and the Christian Right.* University of Chicago Press, 1997.
Kader, Samuel. *Openly Gay, Openly Christian: How the Bible Really Is Gay Friendly.* Leyland, 1999.
Keith, Hartman. *Congregations in Conflict: The Battle over Homosexuality.* Rutgers University Press, 1996.
Siker, Jeffrey. *Homosexuality in the Church: Both Sides of the Debate.* Westminster John Knox, 1994.

CRSO

GAY MARRIAGE

American society increasingly supports equal rights for gays and lesbians in areas such as housing, employment, and public accommodations. Yet national polls consistently show that public opinion does not support granting homosexuals the right to marry or to formally register their unions with the state. In 2000 Vermont became the first state to grant gay and lesbian couples marriage-like status, but 30 states have passed laws specifically blocking recognition of same-sex unions. In contrast, the Netherlands passed a law permitting gay marriages in 2000.

PROS

The refusal of governments to permit gays to marry is one of the last areas of discrimination against gays. The state should permit gay couples to marry as a means of professing their love to and for each other. Societal views ought to change with the times.

CONS

While contemporary society should reject discrimination in general, some forms of discrimination can be objectively justified. Society has always viewed marriage as a heterosexual institution, the religious and/or civil union between a man and a woman.

PROS	CONS
Permitting gay couples to marry would enable them to take advantage of the various financial benefits accorded to heterosexual married couples.	Many of the financial benefits that married couples enjoy are not designed to encourage marriage per se but to promote the conventional family.
We must modify religious attitudes to reflect changes in society. Many religious views are no longer justifiable (e.g., the notion that women are inferior to men). Conversely, if religious institutions oppose gay marriage as against their beliefs, they should accept civil marriages.	Historically marriage has been a religious institution. Because most major world religions frown on homosexuality, they would find gay marriage unacceptable.
Marriage is not merely an institution for raising children. Many married couples do not have children. In addition, the number of single-parent families is increasing. In any case, many countries permit gay singles and couples to adopt. Advances in medical science also enable gay couples to have children through artificial insemination and the use of surrogate mothers.	Historically society has viewed child rearing as the major purpose of marriage. Because gay couples are unlikely to have children, they have no need for marriage.
A "registered union" is an alternative to gay marriage. However, this arrangement is unacceptable because gay couples still would not enjoy the same rights as married heterosexual couples. Moreover, registering would imply that gay couples had an inferior status to married heterosexual couples, thereby giving rise to discrimination.	Finland, Sweden, Denmark, Belgium, and Spain permit the registered union of gay couples. Registered couples are entitled to joint insurance coverage and enjoy inheritance and tenants' rights. Registration makes no incursions into the sanctity of the institution of marriage. Consequently it should prove acceptable to the religious sections of society.

Sample Motions:

This House would allow gay couples to marry.

This House would give homosexuals equal rights.

This House believes that discrimination can never be justified.

Web Links:

• Gay Marriage. <http://www.pe.net/~bidstrup/marriage.htm>

Essay in support of gay marriage that also presents the arguments used to oppose it.

• GayMarriedMen.Org. <http://www.gaymarriedmen.org>

Web site for gays in heterosexual marriages.

• Legal Gay Marriages in the Netherlands. <http://news.bbc.co.uk/hi/english/world/europe/newsid_922000/922024.stm>

BBC story on the Dutch parliament's passage of a bill giving gay marriage the same legal status as heterosexual marriage.

• RainbowGuide.Com. <http://www.rainbowguide.com>

Offers news on a variety of issues of interest to gays and lesbians.

• Right to Marry Resource Page. <http://www.grasshopperdesign.com/gay_marriage/>

Information on current issues surrounding gay marriage with state-by-state summaries of the status of legislation and lawsuits promoting gay marriage.

Further Reading:

Lehr, Valerie. *Queer Family Values: Debunking the Myth of the Nuclear Family.* Temple University Press, 1999.

Lewis, Ellen. *Recognizing Ourselves: Ceremonies of Lesbian and Gay Commitment.* Columbia University Press, 1998.

McNeill, John J. *Freedom, Glorious Freedom: The Spiritual Journey to the Fullness of Life for Gays, Lesbians, and Everybody Else.* Beacon, 1996.

Warner, Michael. *The Trouble with Normal: Sex, Politics and the Ethics of Queer Life.* Harvard University Press, 2000.

CR£O

GAYS IN THE MILITARY

In 1993 President Bill Clinton attempted to remove the long-standing ban on gays in the US military but was forced to compromise in the face of powerful military and congressional opposition. The Clinton administration reached a compromise known as "Don't Ask, Don't Tell." While the ban remained, the compromise permitted gays to serve if they did not disclose their sexual orientation or engage in homosexual behavior. The military was also prohibited from trying to discover the sexual orientation of its personnel. The United States is the only NATO country to maintain such a ban. The United Kingdom had a ban until January 2000, when it changed its policy after the European Court of Human Rights declared it illegal.

PROS

No one now can realistically doubt that gay men or women are as hard working, intelligent, or patriotic as heterosexuals. Only sheer bigotry would deny the opportunity to join the military (and suffer its pervasive homophobia) to those who want to do so.

Much of the argument against the admission of gays is based on homophobia, which is maintained and encouraged by continued segregation. Permitting straight soldiers to see how effective gays can be will reduce prejudice.

Many other professions require a bond of trust and intense living conditions among employees. Gays are not barred from any of them.

If the armed forces accepted gays, they would not have to remain in the closet, thus reducing the risk of blackmail. In any case this risk is diminishing as society increasingly accepts homosexuality.

Gays and lesbians frequently come to terms with their sexuality in their late teens or early twenties, which might be long after they had enlisted. A ban would require the firing of personnel who had joined in good faith. This is discrimination at its worst.

CONS

This debate is about soldiers defending their country while sharing close quarters. Their effectiveness depends on mutual trust and uncomplicated camaraderie. Sexual relations or tension between soldiers, no matter the gender, undermine this bond.

Not all gay applicants will have a vocational calling to the military. A disproportionate number of gays, lesbians, and bisexuals may apply because the high concentration of individuals of one gender in military units makes them a fruitful source of sexual partners. Using the military for this purpose will provoke even more homophobia.

The military is a special case. Its members work in life-or-death situations where any mental distraction could be fatal. Men and women aren't sent into combat together; why should gays and heterosexuals be?

Closeted homosexuals run the risk of blackmail, which could have implications for national security.

The problem is not so much the concept of a ban but the halfhearted enforcement of it. If a ban is well publicized and if people understand that encouraging sexual interest among military personal is inappropriate, then gays are not being misled.

Sample Motions:
This House would not admit gays into the armed forces.
This House believes that the military and sexuality do not mix.

Web Links:
• The Ban on Gays in the Military: Links. <http://www.california.com/~rathbone/links001.htm>
Links to history of "Don't Ask, Don't Tell" policy, articles on gays in the military, and resources for gays.
• Issues and Controversies: Gays in the Military. <http://www.facts.com/icof/i00062.htm>
Offers comprehensive overview of issue from 1992 to 1998.

Further Reading:
 Eidsmoe, John. *Gays and Guns: The Case against Homosexuals in the Military.* Vital Issues Press, 1993.
 Halley, Janet. *Don't: A Reader's Guide to the Military's Anti-Gay Policy.* Duke University Press, 1999.
 Herek, Gregory. *Out in Force: Sexual Orientation and the Military.* University of Chicago Press, 1996.
 Wells-Petry, Melissa. *Exclusion: Homosexuals and the Right to Serve.* Regnery Publishing, 1993.

CRThERD

GENE PATENTING

The pioneering research of the Human Genome Project has given us the ability to isolate our genes. This has engendered hope that scientists may be able to use genetic research to treat or cure disease. By the end of the twentieth century, the US Patent Office had granted more than 1,500 patents on fragments of human DNA. The patents are not on DNA in its natural state, but on the process of discovering and isolating certain strings of DNA, and on DNA developed in the laboratory. But legal—and ethical—questions arise when commercial companies attempt to patent genetic research. Many people fear that these companies are coming close to patenting the building blocks of life itself.

PROS

Companies engaged in genomic research are legally entitled to patent genes, so why should they be prevented from doing so?

If companies are not allowed to patent the products of their research, other companies will exploit their findings. Without the safeguards that a patent provides, companies will end their research because they see no future profit.

An inventor must be able to protect his or her invention. Private companies will continue genomic research because it promises to be extremely lucrative. Competitors will be willing to pay royalties to the patent holder for use of the material because they, too, can foresee future profit.

Patents are granted for a limited time in the United States, 17 years. Companies need this time to recoup their investments. If another company wishes to pursue a project in a patented area, it can always consult the patent owner.

CONS

Genes are the very basis of human life, and to claim that anyone has the right to be regarded as the "owner" of a particular gene shows a basic disregard for humanity. Patenting treatments based on genetic research is morally acceptable, but patenting genes is not.

Most genetic research is not conducted by private companies. The publicly funded Human Genome Project has contributed, by far, the greater amount of knowledge in this area. Patenting stifles research. We need to ban patenting in order to protect the public investment in genome research.

Facts do not support this contention; the Myriad Company, which holds patents on isolating BRCA 1 & 2, genes connected with breast cancer, prevented the University of Pennsylvania from using a test for these genes that was substantially cheaper than the company's own screening procedure. Companies are putting private profit before public good. Instead of protecting their research investment, companies have a moral duty to facilitate the development of inexpensive treatments and screening procedures.

Patenting discourages research because scientists fear costly lawsuits by patent holders. Medical and biotech patent holders frequently exploit their monopolies, charging what they like for their drugs and treatments. It was only after immense public protest, for example, that companies cut the prices of their AIDS medicines for African countries.

PROs	CONS
Profit has proved to be the most practical means of promoting medical advances. It is unrealistic and ill conceived to criticize an incentive that has brought us such benefits.	The Human Genome Project makes its research readily available to ensure the free flow of information and stimulate further research. The only barriers to genetic research should be those of conscience.

Sample Motions:
This House would allow the patenting of genes.
This House believes that genes are inventions.

Web Links:
- Celera. <http://www.celera.com/>
Biotech company site includes statement of its mission in genomic research.
- GeneLetter.Com. <http://www.geneletter.com/archives/dna1.html>
Offers clear summary of genetic patenting in the United States.
- The National Human Genome Research Institute (US): Division of Extramural Research. <http://www.nhgri.nih.gov/HGP/>
Excellent source of research on all aspects of the Human Genome Project.

Further Reading:
Matare, Herbert. *Bioethic: The Ethics of Evolution and Genetic Interference.* Bergin & Garvey, 1999.

CREsO

GENETIC SCREENING

Francis Galton coined the term "eugenics" in 1883 during his work on the genetic basis of intelligence. Literally meaning "good breeding," the term referred to the restructuring of the characteristics of the human race through selective mating (and subsequent reproduction) of the higher echelons of society. Some people, including Theodore Roosevelt, embraced the idea at the turn of the nineteenth century, but it lost favor as a result of its association with Nazi Germany, which took the idea to its extreme. Today, as a result of advances in biotechnology, we can screen fetuses to determine their predisposition to certain congenital disorders. In 2000, a baby boy, Adam Nash, was born after having been genetically screened as an embryo, from several embryos created by in vitro fertilization by his parents. They chose that embryo because tests showed that it was genetically healthy and the baby would be able to act as a bone marrow donor for his sister, who had a genetic disease. The case sparked heated moral debate.

PROS

Testing embryonic cells can help to identify potentially debilitating illnesses or inherited disorders. It can also determine the sex of a baby, allowing parents who carry a sex-linked genetic disorder to have children without passing on the disorder to their children. It is eminently sensible to use this technology to ensure that children are as healthy as possible.

We have a duty to give a child the best possible start in life, and if the technology is available to determine whether a baby will have a genetic disease such as Huntington's we should use it. This is not a case of engineering a child.

CONS

Embryonic testing could become a slippery slope for future exploitation of the process. It must not develop into the widespread abuse of screening to create "designer babies" chosen for aesthetic or other qualities considered desirable. This is morally wrong.

Are we not presuming that those born with physical or mental defects or genetic predispositions to certain diseases do not enjoy a quality of life as high and a life as fruitful as those born without? To suggest that they be bred out of society is presumptuous and abhorrent. More to the point, many "defective" genes confer advantages of a different nature, e.g., the sickle cell anemia allele protects somewhat against malaria.

PROS	CONS
When a number of embryos are created through in vitro fertilization, the embryos not chosen after screening may be offered up for "adoption." Human life will not be thrown away, and childless couples can benefit.	The proposition holds sinister overtones of treating embryos like commodities. Even more morally dubious is the idea of disposing of those embryos that do not conform to the requirements of health.

Sample Motions:
    This House would choose its babies.
    This House would genetically engineer its children.
    This House calls for more genetic screening.

Web Links:
    • The Bioethics.
    <http://library.thinkquest.org/29322/mainpage1.htm>
    Broad site on bioethics, offering information on medical developments and ethical problems.
    • Bioethics.Net. < http://www.med.upenn.edu/~bioethic>
    Maintained by the University of Pennsylvania, the site provides links to resources in bioethics.
    • Designer Babies. < http://www.bbc.co.uk/horizon/designer_babies.shtml>
    The site, connected with a BBC television series *Horizon*, offers a transcript of a program on human engineering.

Further Reading:
    Andrews, Lori B. *Future Perfect.* Columbia University Press, 2001.
    Chadwick, Ruth, Darren Shickle, and Henk Ten Have. *The Ethics of Genetic Screening.* Kluwer, 1999.
    Rothman, Barbara Katz. *The Book of Life: A Personal Guide to Race, Normality and the Implications of the Human Genome* Project. Beacon, 2001.

ᘓᘔᘓ

GLOBALIZATION AND THE POOR

Globalization is the process that spreads economic, political, social, and cultural activity across national boundaries and increases the integration of internationally dispersed activities. Foreign media often focus on the spread of American culture (characterized as fast food restaurants, Hollywood movies, etc.), but academic debates center around more fundamental economic issues. While globalization may have benefited industrialized nations and transnational corporations (TNCs), has the trend eroded global and national solidarity and increased the poverty and isolation of developing nations?

PROS

Globalization marginalizes the poor. It is a means of exclusion, deepening inequality and reinforcing the division of the world into core and periphery. It is a new form of Western imperialism that dominates and exploits through TNC capital and global governance by institutions such as the World Bank and the International Monetary Fund (IMF).

Globalization has intensified global and national inequality. The economic and social gaps within countries and between countries are widening, with the rich becoming richer and the poor becoming poorer. Globalization is an uneven process causing world fragmentation. Trade has also seen increasing inequality. Because of increasing globalization the value of world

CONS

Globalization is eroding the differences between developed and developing nations, sometimes called the North-South divide. It is a progressive force for creating global prosperity. Through free trade and capital mobility, globalization is creating a global market in which prosperity, wealth, power, and liberal democracy are being diffused around the globe.

Globalization has increased world prosperity, and organizational efforts to stabilize the world economy have shown significant progress. By historical standards global poverty has fallen more in the last 50 years than in the previous 500, and the welfare of people in almost all regions has improved considerably during the past few decades. Globalization will bring about the end of

trade is 17 times greater than 50 years ago, but Latin America's share has fallen from 11% to 5% and Africa's from 8% to 2%. The terms of trade have increasingly moved against developing nations.

Globalization exploits developing nations and their poor through TNCs. Globalization is a euphemism for transnationalization, the spread of powerful companies to areas that best suit corporate interests.

Increased global integration means that poorer countries become more vulnerable to world financial markets. The East Asian economic crisis of the 1990s, a direct result of globalization, increased and intensified poverty. The crisis shows that even the strongest developing states are at the mercy of global economic forces that serve the interests of the dominant capitalist powers. Globalization also resulted in the speedy transition of the crisis to the other East Asian countries— the "contagion effect"—with devastating human consequences. The benefits of the global market accrue to a relatively small proportion of the world's population. The stronger become stronger and the weak become weaker.

Globalization is a form of disempowerment. Outside interference from the World Bank and the IMF has weakened the economies of poor nations and constrained development. International negotiations to reduce and eliminate foreign debt have led to increasing exports of capital and deeper indebtedness in developing nations.

the Third World. The fall in the developing nations' share of world trade is due to internal economic, social, and political conditions in individual countries.

Globalization promotes development by spreading technology and knowledge to poor nations. The poorest nations are those countries bypassed by globalization.

Globalization has brought about huge benefits. The emergence of a single global market, free trade, capital mobility, and global competition has permitted the diffusion of prosperity, wealth, and power. Globalization has opened up new opportunities and is the harbinger of modernization and development. It was the force that led to the successful development of East Asia and its "economic miracle." Far from making developing nations more vulnerable, increased global integration means that better organizational structures are in place to address world political, economic, and social problems.

The policies of institutions such as the IMF and the World Bank have reinforced the global market. Outside intervention allows the dissemination of effective economic management strategies to less developed areas.

Sample Motions:
This House believes that globalization marginalizes the poor.
This House believes that globalization will bring about the end of the Third World.
This House believes that globalization is a euphemism for transnationalization.

Web Links:
• Government Report: Making Globalisation Work for the Poor. <http://www.globalisation.gov.uk/homecontents.htm>
British government report on globalization and developing nations.
• Poverty and Globalisation. <http://news.bbc.co.uk/hi/english/static/events/reith_2000/lecture5.stm>
Part of the BBC lecture series, Respect for the Earth. Lecture emphasizes the impact of globalization on food producers, particularly women.

Further Reading:
Allen, Tim, and Alan Thomas. *Poverty and Development into the 21st Century.* Oxford University Press, 2000.
Dicken, Peter. *Global Shift: Transforming the World Economy.* Guilford Press, 1998.
World Bank. *Entering the 21st Century: World Development Report 1999/2000.* World Bank, 2000.

CR&O

GLOBAL WARMING

Since the 1980s, a growing body of evidence has suggested that industrialization is affecting Earth's climate. As a result, in 1997 the industrialized nations of the world agreed to reduce their carbon dioxide emissions under the Kyoto Protocol. The protocol has come under attack from both sides—many environmentalists feel that it does not really address the threat of global warming, while many in industry feel it is an unnecessary burden. Although the United States signed the agreement, in 2001 President George W. Bush announced that the United States would abandon its commitment to the protocol as it was not in the nation's best economic interests. Global warming is a particularly difficult issue because it demands a worldwide response. Many developing nations are understandably angered that a problem that seems to have been created by the rich, developed nations will have the most impact on the Third World. A global consensus remains far off.

PROS

Over the past 100 years, humankind has been burning increasing quantities of fossil fuels to provide energy. This has released large volumes of gases into the atmosphere, particularly CO_2. At the same time, the world's remaining large forests, which help absorb CO_2, are being rapidly felled. Overall, the levels of carbon dioxide in the atmosphere have increased by 30% during the last century. When in the atmosphere, CO_2 and other gases are thought to cause a "greenhouse effect": They allow sunlight to pass through, but absorb heat emitted by the Earth, trapping it and leading to global warming. Weather records seem to support this theory. Average temperatures have increased by 0.6°C since the nineteenth century; the four hottest years since accurate records have been kept have all been in the 1990s. Unusual weather patterns such as floods and droughts have also been on the increase, with the uncharacteristically strong El Niño events of recent years causing widespread disruption. The Intergovernmental Panel on Climate Change (IPCC), an international body set up to study possible global warming, has concluded that ". . . the balance of evidence suggests that there is a discernible human influence on global climate."

Computer models predict that continued global warming could have catastrophic effects. Changes in temperature could devastate wildlife when local vegetation dies off. Patterns of disease could change. Already isolated cases of malaria have been reported far north of traditional danger zones as warmer weather allows the mosquitoes that carry the disease to spread. Most important, a portion of the polar ice caps might melt and lead to a rise in sea level, which has already increased by between 10 and 25 cm in the last 100 years. Giant cracks have been found in the Larsen ice shelf in Antarctica, which suggest that it is breaking apart; a section 48 miles wide and 22 miles long drifted free and melted as early as 1994. If, as experts believe, temperatures rise

CONS

Scientists have not yet proved conclusively that humankind is causing global warming. Although average temperatures rose during the twentieth century, temperatures actually dropped slightly between the 1930s and the 1970s. This was not associated with a reduction in fossil fuel consumption; emissions actually increased over this period. If the "greenhouse gases" are responsible for global warming, how do you account for this? Accurate records simply do not cover a long enough period to be useful. The Earth's average temperature varies naturally through time, and we have few good explanations of the Ice Ages. Indeed, there was a "mini–Ice Age" around 400 years ago, during which the River Thames in England repeatedly froze over in winter. This was followed by an intense but natural period of "global warming." We do not have enough information to say that current trends are not simply a natural variation.

Again, our computer models for predicting climate change are far from reliable. Weather is a hugely complex system that we are only beginning to understand. It is affected by many factors, including solar activity, volcanic eruptions, ocean currents, and other cycles that we are gradually discovering. Very slight changes in the computer model result in immense differences in predictions. Some scientists, for example, have suggested that global warming could actually cause a drop in sea level as rainfall patterns and ocean currents shift. Indeed, refinements in the models used by the IPCC have caused it to modify its predictions. In 1990, the IPCC estimated that by 2100 the average temperature would rise by 3°C and the sea would rise by about

a further 3°C over the next century, low-lying areas and even entire countries, such as Bangladesh, could disappear under the waves.

Technology has now reached the point where we can continue to increase standards of living without burning fossil fuels. Renewable sources of energy, such as wind or solar power, are ripe for development, but have yet to see the levels of investment needed to make them truly effective. More efficient use of energy is also vital. Encouraging the development of electric cars or promoting better insulation of houses could make a substantial difference in CO_2 levels in the long run.

Global warming is a worldwide catastrophe waiting to happen. The emission of greenhouse gases affects everyone. It is, therefore, vital that the entire world respond now. The targets set by the Kyoto Protocol will barely scratch the surface of the problem. The developed world agreed to only minimal reductions in carbon dioxide emissions, and no agreement was reached involving the developing world, which is producing a greater percentage of greenhouse gas emissions every year. Gases like CO_2 remain in the atmosphere for centuries. If we wait until we can see the results of global warming, it may be too late. The damage will have been done. We must act now, and we must act globally. Developed countries must do all they can to reduce their use of fossil fuels. They must assist developing nations to do the same, by sharing technology or perhaps through "emissions trading," allowing poorer countries to sell their quota of pollution in return for hard cash. International pressure must be exerted against those countries that do not cooperate, even if this slows economic growth. The poorest regions of the world would suffer most from more droughts and floods and rising sea levels. However difficult it may be in the short term, such actions now may save millions of lives in the future.

65cm; in 1995, it revised its estimates to 2°C and 50 cm. The more research that takes place, the less catastrophic global warming seems to be. The media always report the predictions of doom most widely.

Of course greater energy efficiency is important. However, most alternative fuels are simply not effective. They can also cause their own problems. Nuclear power creates unacceptable radioactive waste; hydroelectric power projects, such as the Three Gorges dam in China, lead to the flooding of vast areas and the destruction of the local environment; solar and wind power often require the covering of large areas of natural beauty with solar panels or turbines. Environmentalists often paint an idealistic view of renewable energy that is far from the less romantic reality.

The evidence for global warming is not strong enough to merit this kind of response. The changes over the past century may certainly have been purely natural. Environmentalists in the developed world can afford the luxury of demanding government action because reducing pollution will have a minimal impact on their technology-based economies. Those in the developing world are not so lucky. Industrialization is a key part of building successful economies and bringing prosperity to the world's poorest people; heavy industry is often the only area in which developing nations can compete. Global action on greenhouse gas emissions would sustain the inequalities of the status quo. The developing world would have to depend on multinational corporations to provide the technology needed to keep pollution levels low, or else they would have to stop expanding their economies. Having apparently caused the problem through the industrialization that made them powerful, developed countries would be pulling the ladder up behind them, depriving other countries of the chance to grow. This is simply unacceptable. In the modern world, one of our first priorities must be to help the poorest people achieve the prosperity they need to support themselves. The current evidence for global warming does not begin to merit endangering this goal.

Sample Motions:
　This House believes that Kyoto didn't go far enough.
　This House calls for urgent action on global warming.
　This House fears a global greenhouse.
　This House believes that global warming demands global action.

Web Links:
- Global Warming Central. <http://www.law.pace.edu/env/energy/globalwarming.html>
Site maintained by Pace University School of Law offers current news, documents, and resources on global warming.
- Intergovernmental Panel on Climate Change. <http://www.ipcc.ch>
Offers reports assessing scientific, technical, and socioeconomic information related to human-induced climate change.
- Kyoto Protocol. <http://www.cnn.com/SPECIALS/1997/global.warming/stories/treaty/>
Full text of the Kyoto Protocol.
- World Meteorological Organization. <http://www.wmo.ch>
UN organization provides information on meteorological issues as well as a statement on the status of the global climate.

Further Reading:
Drake, Frances. *Global Warming: The Science of Climate Change*. Edward Arnold, 2000.
Gelbspan, Ross. *The Heat Is On: The Climate Crisis, the Cover Up, the Prescription*. Perseus, 1998.
Houghton, John. *Global Warming: The Complete Briefing*. Cambridge University Press, 1997.

 C380

GOD, EXISTENCE OF

This is the "Big" question, the ultimate metaphysical debate. It has occupied the world's best minds for centuries. Followers of many religions have offered proofs of the existence of God. Below are arguments from within the Judeo-Christian and Islamic traditions.

PROS

The world is so magnificent and wonderful, so full of variety and beauty that it is inconceivable that it could have come about purely by chance. It is so intricate that a conscious hand must have been involved in its creation. Therefore, God exists as the creator of the world.

If you saw a watch lying on the sand, you would think that someone must have made the watch—a watch-maker. Similarly, we human beings are so complicated and amazing that we must conclude that we had a conscious maker.

Only human beings are capable of rational thought. That we are here at all is amazing. One infinitesimal change in the world and life would not have evolved. Getting something so amazing, on such long odds, smacks of intention.

God must be perfect if he exists. But a thing that exists is more perfect than a thing that doesn't exist. But nothing can be more perfect than God. So God must exist.

CONS

You cannot infer from the variety and beauty of the world that God was the creator. The conception of God contains many extra attributes that are not necessary for a world creator. Just because the world is beautiful and varied does not mean it was consciously designed. Why can't beauty happen by accident?

The difference between a watch and humans is that the watch serves a purpose—to tell time. Therefore, seeing something so perfectly serving a purpose suggests design. What purpose do we serve? We don't, we just exist. And even if we were designed for a purpose, the earlier argument applies: A purposeful designer isn't necessarily God.

The argument from probability does not work. It relies on there being something special about us. What is so special about us? We are rational—so what?

This ontological argument can be rebutted by rejecting the idea that existence is a perfection. Something either exists or it doesn't. The argument is a disguised conditional. You say "if God exists then he must be perfect, and if he must be perfect he must therefore exist." But all this rests on the initial "if God exists." If God doesn't exist, we don't have the problem and the argument doesn't work.

Everything in the universe has a cause. It is inconceivable that time is one long chain of cause and effect without beginning, but it must be because we cannot conceive of something happening uncaused. Therefore, God exists as the uncaused first cause.

The cosmological argument doesn't work. For a start, an uncaused first cause still doesn't necessarily have all the attributes it would need to be called God, e.g., omnipotence, benevolence, and omniscience. More important, an uncaused first cause is just as incomprehensible to us as an endless chain of cause and effect. You are just shifting the incomprehension one stage back.

Sample Motions:
This House believes that God exists.
This House believes that reports of God's death have been greatly exaggerated.

Web Links:
• Counterbalance. <http://www.counterbalance.com>
Contains summary of debate about the existence of God from the cosmological standpoint.
• The Existence of God and the Beginning of the Universe. <http://www.leaderu.com/truth/3truth11.html>
An academic paper employing the cosmological argument for the existence of God.
• First Things: The Journal of Religion and Public Life.
 <http://switch2.netrics.com/cgi-bin/likeit.cgi>
Links to articles from the journal dealing with various arguments on the existence of God.
• New Advent. <http://www.newadvent.org/cathen/06608b.htm>
Detailed essay on a Roman Catholic Web site, outlining the various proofs for the existence of God.

Further Reading:
Hume, David. *Dialogues Concerning Natural Religion.* New ed. Routledge, 1991.
Yandell, Keith. *Philosophy of Religion: A Contemporary Introduction.* Routledge, 1999.

CR80

GREENHOUSE GASES: TRADING QUOTAS

A number of methods have been proposed to reduce the emissions of the so-called greenhouse gases that lead to global warming. The European Union has always favored taxing heavy polluters, while the United States has supported Tradable Pollution Quotas (TPQs). The 1997 Kyoto Protocol laid the foundation for TPQs. Under this agreement developing countries are exempt from the emission standards and cannot take part directly in pollution trading. Each country in the TPQ plan is initially permitted to produce a certain maximum amount of each polluting gas. Countries that want to exceed their quotas can buy the right to do so from other countries that have produced less than their quota. Furthermore, countries can also "sink" carbon (by planting forests to remove carbon dioxide from the atmosphere) to offset some of their pollution quotas. Interestingly, two usually opposing groups are against TPQs. Industries claim that they go too far and that such stringent regulation is unnecessary. Environmentalists maintain that they are too lax.

PROS

The scientific community agrees that something must be done to curb emissions of greenhouse gases that may be the cause of global warming. The possible consequences of global warming include crop failure, mass flooding, and the destruction of entire ecosystems with the possible loss of billions of lives. Other consequences of pollution include acid rain and the enlargement of

CONS

The environmental lobby has hugely overestimated the claims for pollution damaging the environment. The fossil record indicates that climate change has occurred frequently in the past, and there is little evidence linking climate change with emissions.

the hole in the ozone layer.

The TPQ plan is the only practical way to reduce emissions of greenhouse gases globally. It will guarantee that global levels of these gases are kept below strict targets and is more realistic than expecting heavy polluters to cut their emissions overnight.

The TPQ plan ensures more pollution in the long run than if limits were strictly enforced for each country and punitive taxes imposed on those exceeding their quotas. Without TPQs, the environment would benefit further if a country kept well below its emissions quota. Adopting the TPQ plan means that this benefit is lost because the right to this extra pollution is bought by another country.

Emissions are a global problem. The emission of the main greenhouse gas, carbon dioxide, for example, affects the entire planet regardless of where the gas is produced. This validates the use of TPQs, which act to limit the total amount of each polluting gas globally. TPQs are much more effective than the alternative of taxing emissions, because rich companies or countries will be able to pay the tax and still pollute.

Stating that it does not matter where pollution is produced is simplistic and completely untrue for many gases, which do affect the region in which they are created. Furthermore, to permit developing countries to industrialize, they have been exempted from the protocol. This seriously undermines its efficiency. Furthermore, if taxes on pollution were set high enough, big companies would stop polluting because it would be prohibitively expensive. In addition, the introduction of TPQs will make later reductions in global emissions much harder. Once trading in TPQs has started, countries that have bought extra emission rights would certainly not voluntarily give them up to help reduce global emissions further.

TPQs are tried and tested. The United States has used them successfully since they were introduced in 1990. Therefore, we have good reason to expect them to succeed on a global scale.

TPQs have had some success in the United States, but they failed in Europe for two reasons. First, the European plans were poorly conceived, as was the Kyoto Protocol. Second, whereas the American solution to pollution was always trading emissions, the main European solution was, and still is, to produce new technology to clean the emissions. Extending the TPQ plan to the entire globe will slow the technological developments needed to reduce greenhouse gases.

Progress in the field of emission control is remarkably difficult because of the opposition from the industrial lobby, most notably in the United States, which sees such restrictions as harmful to its economy. TPQs are the one method of control acceptable to these lobby groups and, more significant, to the US government. As the world's biggest polluter, the United States must be included in any meaningful treaty. Therefore, TPQs are the only practical way forward.

The Kyoto Protocol lacks a comprehensive enforcement mechanism and is thus ineffective. In addition, assessing the effect that an individual country's carbon "sink" is having on the atmosphere is impossible. This merely creates a loophole that allows a country to abuse the protocol and produce more than its quota of gases.

TPQs cause less damage to an economy than any other emission control regime. Individual companies and countries can trade TPQs on the free market until they have struck the right balance between the cost of paying to pollute and the cost of cleaning up their industry.

TPQs will hit employment hard. Even developed countries are not so rich that they can simply buy enough quotas to avoid pollution; neither can they afford to install the expensive cleaning technology. Growth will consequently decline and with that decline will come a drop in living standards in developed countries.

Sample Motions:
This House would buy the right to pollute.
This House supports tradable pollution quotas.
This House believes that Kyoto got it right.

Web Links:
• The Kyoto Protocol: An Economic and Game Theoretic Interpretation. <http://www.feem.it/web/resun/wp/72-99.html>
Technical article discussing the economic issues involved in the Kyoto Protocol.
• Pollution For Sale. <http://www.npk.gov.pl/cordis/www.cordis.lu/euroabstracts/en/august99/energy1.htm>
Provides clear explanation of emissions trading.

Further Reading:
Grubb, Michael et al. *Kyoto Protocol: A Guide and Assessment.* Royal Institute of International Affairs, 1999.
Victor, David G. *The Collapse of the Kyoto Protocol and the Struggle to Slow Global Warming.* Princeton University Press, 2001.

GUN CONTROL

The issue of gun control has divided American society for years. Supporters insist that tighter measures are needed to curb crime and to prevent tragedies like the recent wave of school massacres where students used guns to kill other students and teachers. Opponents insist that they have the constitutional right to carry guns, and that people, not guns, cause crime. Long considered a uniquely American problem, gun control has become an issue in many European nations as a result of incidents including the school massacre in Erfurt, Germany, in 2002.

PROS

The only function of a gun is to kill. The more instruments of death and injury we remove from our society, the safer we will be.

The legal ownership of guns by law-abiding citizens inevitably leads to many unnecessary and tragic deaths. Legally held guns end up in the hands of criminals, who would have greater difficulty in obtaining weapons if they were less prevalent. Guns also end up in the hands of children, leading to tragic accidents and terrible disasters like the Columbine massacre.

Shooting as a sport desensitizes people to the lethal nature of all firearms, creating a gun culture that glamorizes and legitimizes unnecessary gun ownership. The minority who enjoy blood sports should not be allowed to block the interests of society as a whole in gun control.

CONS

Prohibition is not the answer. Banning guns would not make them disappear or make them any less dangerous. Citizens have the right to own weapons to protect themselves, their families, and their property. Many people also need guns for other reasons; farmers, for example, need them to protect their stock and crops.

Guns don't kill people; people kill people. Restricting gun ownership will do nothing to make society safer. Most crimes involve illegal weapons.

Shooting is a major sport enjoyed by many law-abiding people. Sportsmen have the right to continue their chosen leisure activity. Spending on guns and ancillary equipment puts large sums into the economy. Hunters also put food on the table.

Burglary should not be punished by vigilante killings. No amount of property is worth a human life. Keeping firearms in the home for protection leads to accidental deaths. And, perversely, criminals may be more likely to carry weapons if they think they are in danger from homeowners.

There is a correlation between the leniency of a country's gun laws and its suicide rate—not because gun owners are depressive, but because the means of quick and effective suicide is at hand. The state should discourage and restrict the ownership of something that wastes so many lives.

Law-abiding citizens deserve the right to protect their families in their own homes. Would-be rapists and armed burglars will think twice before attempting to break into a house where owners may keep firearms.

A country is more able to defend itself if many of its citizens are proficient with firearms. Some countries require adult citizens to maintain weapons and periodically train in their use. Of course, such widespread ownership of weapons is also a safeguard against domestic tyranny.

Sample Motions:
This House calls for stricter controls on gun ownership.
This House believes there is no right to bear arms.

Web Links:
• American Civil Liberties Union (ACLU): Gun Control. <http://www.aclu.org/library/aaguns.html>
Article explaining the ACLU's stand on gun control.
• Guide to Gun Laws, Gun Control and Gun Rights. <http://www.jurist.law.pitt.edu/gunlaw.htm>
The site, maintained by the Legal Education Network, offers resources on all sides of the gun control debate.
• Hodgdon. <http://www.hodgdon.com/liberty/gcn.htm>
Site outlines a campaign for stricter gun control in the United Kingdom.
• National Rifle Association of America. <http://www.nra.org/>
America's most powerful pro-gun lobby offers information on campaigns to limit gun control.

Further Reading:
Bruce, John M., and Clyde Wilcox, eds. *The Changing Politics of Gun Control.* Rowman and Littlefield, 1998.

CRℰSͻ

HATE SPEECH ON CAMPUS

Over the past few decades, a number of American colleges have reported incidents of verbal abuse and hate speech directed against minorities and homosexuals on their campuses. In response, many schools have adopted codes prohibiting speech that is racist, sexist, homophobic, or offensive to religious groups.

PROS
The rights we enjoy come with responsibilities. Minorities have a right to be free from verbal abuse and fear. If such rights are not informally respected, the college administration has the right and obligation to adopt codes prohibiting offensive speech.

CONS
Free speech is one of our basic rights and should be upheld at all costs. College administrations may abuse these speech codes, using them to silence those whom they consider disruptive. Upholding the right to hate speech will protect the free speech of everyone. Colleges should outlaw hate crimes, not hate speech. While we may abhor such views, it would be wrong to censor them.

PROS	CONS
The constant repetition of hate speech promotes offensive racial stereotypes. If children and youths grow up without hearing such views, they will mature without the bigoted attitudes engendered by constantly hearing hate speech.	Stereotyping is a result of the underrepresentation of minorities among students, faculty, and administrators on most campuses. University authorities should recruit more members of these minorities.
Adopting a speech code sends a strong message. It shows minorities that the authorities support them and, thus, will help in minority recruitment. It also shows bigots that their views will not be tolerated and helps marginalize and punish them.	Codes can often lead to resentment that can cause a backlash against minorities.
Minority students cannot learn in an environment full of fear and hatred. If all students are to achieve their full potential, they must be allowed to work without harassment.	Ensuring freedom of speech is especially critical in universities. The needs of education are served best in an environment in which free thought and free expression are actively encouraged.

Sample Motions:
This House would censor hate speech on campus.
This House may not agree with what you say, but will defend to the death your right to say it.

Web Links:
• American Civil Liberties Union (ACLU): Hate Speech on Campus. <http://www.aclu.org/library/pbp16.html>
Section of the broad ACLU Web site explaining its stand on hate speech on campus.

Further Reading:
Fiss, Owen. *The Irony of Free Speech*. Harvard University Press, 1996.
Heumann, Milton, Thomas W. Church, and David P. Redlawsk. *Hate Speech On Campus: Cases, Case Studies, and Commentary.* Northeastern University Press, 1997.
Shiell, Timothy. *Campus Hate Speech On Trial.* University Press of Kansas, 1998.

CRSO

HEALTH CARE, UNIVERSAL

The provision of health care to the citizens of the United States has been a contentious issue for decades. Currently, some people are covered under government health plans through programs like Medicaid, Medicare, and CHIP (Children's Health Insurance Program). But approximately 40 million people in the United States do not have health insurance. The health statistics for the uninsured are far worse than the statistics for those with insurance. Almost every industrialized country has a system of universal health care. These systems are single-payer programs: The government is the single payer for health care services. Citizens of those countries pay for their own health insurance, but they do not pay as much as we do in the United States. The cost of insurance is income-sensitive, so you pay more if your income is higher. Some believe that the United States should move to a system of universal health care so all our citizens can have access to quality medical care. Others say there are better ways to fix the system.

PROS

With universal health care, people are able to seek preventive treatment. For example, in a recent study 70% of women with health insurance knew their cholesterol level while only 50% of uninsured women did. Ultimately, people who do not get preventive health care will get care only when their diseases and illnesses are more advanced and their care will cost more.

Health insurance premiums are very high. Even employer-subsidized programs are expensive for many Americans. These plans often have high co-payments or deductibles. For those without insurance, a relatively minor illness can be financially ruinous. Incremental plans like the ones currently in existence, which cover only individuals who meet certain age or income criteria, will never provide true universal coverage. Even the Children's Health Insurance Program, which was intended to extend health insurance benefits to more children, has not been able to meet the needs of our nation's children. Since CHIP was enacted, the number of uninsured children has increased.

The current system of health maintenance organizations (HMOs) has destroyed the doctor-patient relationship and patient choice of health care providers. Patients find that their doctors are not on their new plan and are forced to leave doctors with whom they have established a trusting relationship. Also, patients must get approval to see specialists and then are permitted to see only selected doctors. Doctors usually can't spend enough time with patients in the HMO-controlled environment. Patients would have many more choices in a universal health care system. The HMOs that put profits before people would become obsolete.

The United States as a whole spends 14% of GDP on health care. This includes the amount spent by the federal government, state governments, insurance companies, and private citizens. Many studies have shown that a single-payer system would cut costs enough to enable everyone in the United States to have access to health care without the nation spending any more than currently. Medicare, a government-administered health care program, has administrative costs of less than 2% of its total budget.

In the current system the employee and the employee's family often depend on the employer for affordable health insurance. If the employee loses his or her job, the cost to get new health insurance can be high and is often unaffordable. Even with the current federal

CONS

Universal health care will cause people to use the health care system more. If they are covered, they will go to the doctor when they do not really need to and will become heavier users of the system. As seen in other countries, this heavier utilization results in delays and ultimately the rationing of care.

Many programs are already available where people can get care. Many employers offer health insurance plans. Health insurance plans can be purchased by individuals with no need to rely on an employer. Low-income individuals qualify for Medicaid and seniors qualify for Medicare. Eligible children benefit from the Children's Health Insurance Program. Health insurance is a necessity and, like other necessities, people must pay for their fair share and not expect the government to provide for them.

With government control of health care, ceilings on costs will be placed and many doctors will not be rewarded for their long hours and important roles in our lives. The road to becoming a doctor is long and hard; without the monetary rewards in place, good people will not enter the field of medicine. Current doctors may find that they do not want to continue their careers in a government-controlled market. The American Medical Association does not endorse a government-controlled, single-payer universal health care system.

The US government cannot afford to fund universal health care. Other universal social welfare policies like Social Security and Medicare have encountered major problems with funding. We should not add another huge government-funded social program. The nations that provide universal health care coverage spend a substantial amount of their GDP on the service.

The current system of offering group insurance through employers covers many Americans with good quality health insurance. The group plan concept enables insurance companies to insure people who are high risk and low risk by mixing them into the same pool. The

laws related to transportability of health insurance, the costs to the employee are too high. With a single payer, universal health care system, health insurance would no longer be tied to the employer and employees would not have to consider health insurance as a reason to stay with a given employer.

issues of transportability of coverage are covered by federal laws that mandate that employers must continue to offer health insurance to qualified employees for at least 18 months after the employee leaves the company. These laws give employees time to find new insurance or to find a new job if they leave or lose their job. These laws mandate that former employees will not have to pay substantially more for health insurance than employees who continue employment.

Moving to a system of universal health care would reduce the burden on human resources personnel in companies. Currently, they must comply with many federal laws related to provision of health insurance. With a single-payer system, these regulations would not apply and the costs of compliance would be eliminated.

Human resources professionals will still be needed to comply with the many other personnel regulations mandated by the federal government. Instead of employees being able to exercise control over their health care choices and work with people in their company, patients will be forced to deal with the nameless, faceless members of the government bureaucracy.

Sample Motions:
This House would adopt a universal health care system.
This House believes that universal health care is more important than financial concerns.
This House believes that it is immoral that US citizens do not have equal access to health care.

Web Links:
• American Medical Association. <http://www.ama-assn.org>
The American Medical Association (AMA) was founded more than 150 years ago to advocate for physicians. The AMA contributes to policy making through lobbying and by providing information to policy makers and the public. This site has a search feature that can be used to find information on the AMA's position on universal health care.
• Kaiser Family Foundation Commission on Medicaid and the Uninsured. <http://www.kff.org/content/2000/3013>
This site offers many articles with varied perspectives on the issue of health insurance and the uninsured. The foundation is an independent voice and source of facts and analysis for policy makers, the media, the health care community, and the general public.
• The 100% Campaign. <http://www.100percentcampaign.org/about.html>
This site is for the 100% Campaign in California. The goal of the campaign is to have 100% of the state's children enrolled in some type of health coverage. It offers information about why health insurance is so important for children.

Further Reading:
Anders, George. *Health Against Wealth: HMOs and the Breakdown of Medical Trust.* Houghton Mifflin, 1996.
Churchill, Larry R. *Self-Interest and Universal Health Care: Why Well-Insured Americans Should Support Coverage for Everyone.* Harvard University Press, 1994.
Woolhandler, Steffie, and David Himmelstein, M.D. *Bleeding the Patient: The Consequences of Corporate Healthcare.* Common Courage Press, 2001.

CRSO

HOLLYWOOD'S INFLUENCE

Many areas of the world have embraced Hollywood films. In 1998 the 39 most successful movies were American; in Europe, domestic film industries struggle to hold even 30% of their national market share. The issue of America's cultural influence is perhaps felt most profoundly in France, where President Jacques Chirac said in 1999 that France refused "to consider cultural products like ordinary goods, subject solely to the law of the market." This attitude is reflected in large subsidies (over $500US million) to French creative industries and by laws that limit the amount of foreign material in movie houses. Such cultural protectionism has become a major issue in World Trade Organization negotiations.

PROS

Hollywood films are poor, lowest-common-denominator pulp that rely on special effects and large quantities of sex and violence to mask preposterous plots, weak dialogue, and poor acting. The studios' addiction to market testing leads to unadventurous films, with compulsory happy endings and slushy morals.

Hollywood films glorify sex and violence. They attack the moral values of all societies and lead young people astray. Even American critics have attacked the ethical values they present.

Hollywood imposes American entertainment and its language on the world at the expense of indigenous cultures and languages and of domestic film industries. The globalization of entertainment threatens to result in a bland, American-flavored uniformity.

Hollywood promotes a biased and peculiarly American vision of the world. It offers a simplistic good vs. evil view of international conflicts, often presenting stereotyped and negative images of Muslims, Russians, South Americans, and others, as enemies of freedom and progress. Hollywood even distorts history, downplaying the contribution of other nations to the Allied victory in World War II films and including anachronisms in period dramas to show Americans in a favorable light.

Hollywood's major studios dominate the film industry through sheer size and financial power. They have the

CONS

Hollywood movies are internationally successful because people all over the world find them entertaining. Films made in Hollywood can be rubbish, but they can also be terrific. In any case, condemning films for lack of "artistic credibility" when they were made for lightweight escapism smacks of elitism. If the public wanted artistic credibility, it would be profitable and Hollywood would provide it.

Not all Hollywood movies are the same. Some are pornographic or gratuitously violent, but this is also true of films produced elsewhere. As a whole, Hollywood movies promote liberal values of universal significance: the rights of women; the importance of freedom; the independent worth of each human life; and the possibilities of individual success through hard work. The countries, e.g., China, that most wish to ban American films are those who least value these ideas.

Hollywood's success does not mean failure for other film industries. India's Bollywood is hugely successful, and the French-, Spanish-, Iranian-, and Chinese-language industries are thriving. Hollywood movies may help indigenous studios develop by creating the theaters, marketing methods, and audience that domestic filmmakers need to thrive.

Hollywood is far from typically or monolithically American. Instead its concentration of creative resources has made it an international center for the production of entertainment. Many of its most successful producers, directors, and stars have come to the United States either as refugees or because they sought the international audience Hollywood can provide. Recently acclaimed directors from a number of countries have brought new perspectives to Hollywood while creating internationally successful movies.

If money guaranteed success then small-budget films such as *The Full Monty* would never have become inter-

immense budgets needed for expensive special effects and for effective marketing. They can also pay huge salaries to foreign actors, who may be lost to their own film industry as a result. Hollywood has also lobbied the US government very effectively to ensure that cultural exports are classed as a form of trade in international agreements and to help it gain control over distribution networks abroad.

national hits and expensive box-office disasters like *Waterworld* would always succeed. The French government has been throwing money at its domestic film industry for years, yet the market share of American films in France has continued to rise. In any case, most of the major Hollywood studios are, or have recently been, owned by non-American companies.

Sample Motions:
This House would restrict the influence of Hollywood.
This House would practice cultural protectionism.
This House condemns cultural imperialism.

Web Links:
• Central Europe Review: Hungary v. Hollywood. <http://www.ce-review.org/kinoeye/kinoeye25old2.html>
Analysis of Hungarian films imitating Hollywood.

CRSO

HUMAN CLONING

The cloning of "Dolly" the sheep in 1997 generated worldwide reaction. The United States imposed a moratorium on human cloning and a ban on federal funding for cloning research, which will be reviewed every five years. One bill to make human cloning lawful and another demanding its prohibition were both rejected by Congress in 1999. The opposition of international organizations to human cloning is clear. The European Parliament, the Council of Europe, UNESCO, and the World Health Organization (WHO) have passed resolutions asserting that human cloning is both morally and legally wrong.

PROS

The technology is unsafe. The nuclear transfer technique that produced Dolly required 277 embryos, from which only one healthy and viable sheep was produced. The other fetuses were hideously deformed, and either died or were aborted. Moreover, we do not know the long-term consequences of cloning.

Cloning is playing God. It is not merely intervention in the body's natural processes, but the creation of a new and wholly unnatural process of asexual reproduction. Philosophers and clerics of many faiths oppose human cloning. They caution that the failure to produce scientific reasons against the technology does not mean we should deny our strong instinctive revulsion.

Reproductive cloning injures the family. Single people will be able to produce offspring without a partner. Once born, the child will be denied the love of one parent, most probably the father. Several theologians

CONS

Cloning is no different from any other new medical technology. Research is required on embryos to quantify and reduce the risk of the procedures.

This argument assumes that we know God's intentions. Moreover, every time a doctor performs lifesaving surgery or administers drugs he is changing the destiny of the patient and could be seen as usurping the role of God. Furthermore, we should be very wary of banning something without being able to say why it is wrong.

This argument is wholly unsuited to the modern age. Society freely allows single people to reproduce sexually. Existing practices such as sperm donation allow procreation without knowledge of the identity of the father.

have recognized that a child is a symbolic expression of the mutual love of its parents and their hope for the future. This sign of love is lost when a child's life begins in a laboratory.

Surely a mother would prefer to know the genetic heritage of her child rather than accept sperm from an unknown and random donor? It might be better for the child to be born into a happy relationship, but the high rates of single parenthood and divorce suggest that this is not always possible.

Many churches and secular organizations, including WHO, view reproductive cloning as contrary to human dignity.

When people resort to talking in empty abstract terms about "human dignity" you can be sure that they have no evidence or arguments to back up their position. Why is sexual intercourse to be considered any more dignified than a reasoned decision by an adult to use modern science to have a child?

Cloning will lead to eugenics. When people are able to clone themselves they will be able to choose the kind of person to be born. This seems uncomfortably close to the Nazi concept of breeding a race of Aryan superhumans, while eliminating those individuals whose characteristics they considered undesirable.

Eugenics is much more likely to arise with developments in gene therapy and genetic testing and screening than in human cloning. Clones (people with identical genes) would by no means be identical in every respect. You need only to look at identical twins (who share the same genes) to see how wrong that assumption is, and how different the personalities, preferences, and skills of people with identical genes can be.

Cloning will lead to a diminished sense of identity and individuality for the resultant child. Instead of being considered as a unique individual, the child will be an exact copy of his parent and will be expected to share the same traits and interests. His life will no longer be his own. This is an unacceptable infringement of the liberty and autonomy that we grant to every human person. The confusion of the offspring is likely to be compounded by the fact that the "parent," from whom he is cloned, will be genetically his twin brother. There is no way of knowing how children will react to having such a confused genetic heritage.

Children produced by reproductive cloning will not be copies of their parents. Different environmental factors will mean that children will not be emotionally or mentally identical to the people from whom they are cloned. You would have to apply the same objection to identical twins. A small proportion of identical twins do, indeed, suffer from psychological problems related to feelings of a lack of individuality. However, cloned children would be in a better position than traditional twins because they will be many years younger than their genetic twins, who are, of course, their parents. Therefore, they will not suffer from comparisons to a physically identical individual.

Cloning will lead to a lack of diversity in the human population. The natural process of evolution will be halted, and humankind will be denied development.

Any reduction in the diversity of the human gene pool will be so limited as to be virtually nonexistent. The expense and time necessary for successful human cloning mean that only a small minority will employ the technology. The pleasure of procreation through sexual intercourse suggests that whole populations will choose what's "natural" rather than reproduce asexually through cloning.

Human reproductive cloning is unnecessary. The development of in vitro fertilization and the practice of sperm donation allow heterosexual couples to reproduce where one partner is sterile. In addition, potential parents might better give their love to existing babies

The desire to have one's own child and to nurture it is wholly natural. The longing for a genetically related child existed long before modern reproductive technology and biotechnology, but only recently has medicine been able to sometimes satisfy that longing.

rather than attempt to bring their own offspring into an already crowded world.

Cloning treats children as commodities. Individuals will be able to have a child with desired characteristics as a symbol of status, rather than because they desire to conceive, love, and raise another human being.

The effort required to clone a human suggests that the child will be highly valued by its parent or parents. Furthermore, we should not pretend that every child conceived by sexual procreation is born to wholly well-intentioned parents.

Sample Motions:
This House would ban human cloning.
This House would not make a mini-me.
This House would not reproduce itself.

Web Links:
• American Life League. < http://www.all.org>
Pro-life organization offers information on a variety of reproductive topics.
• The Ethics of Reproductive and Therapeutic Cloning. <http://www.wits.ac.za/bioethics/genethics.htm>
Academic article arguing that there is no ethical reason to prevent research in reproductive cloning.
• Human Cloning Foundation. <http://www.humancloning.org>
Offers resources, books, and essays in support of human cloning.

Further Reading:
Burley, Justine, ed. *The Genetic Revolution and Human Rights.* Oxford University Press, 1999.
Harris, John. *Clones, Genes and Immortality: Ethics and the Genetic Revolution.* Oxford University Press, 1998.
Nussbaum, Martha, and Cass Sunstein. *Clones and Clones: Facts and Fantasies about Human Cloning.* Norton, 1998.

CRINO

HUMAN ORGANS, SALE OF

Advances in surgical and diagnostic techniques have substantially increased the success of organ transplant operations. In 2000, a total of 22,827 organs were transplanted in the United States. However, in the preceding decade, the gap between the number of available organs and the number of patients requiring a transplant increased significantly. The sale of human organs can be considered as a possible solution to the crippling shortage. The black market trade in human organs is already thriving. Entrepreneurs offer the opportunity for British patients to receive privately financed transplant operations in India and Malaysia, and Americans go to China, which has sold the organs of executed prisoners. In 1983, Dr. Barry Jacobs requested that the US government create a fund to compensate the families who donate the organs of deceased relatives. Dr. Jacobs also proposed setting up a business that would buy kidneys from living donors for transplantation, but the proposal ran into popular opposition. In 1984, Congress passed the National Organ Transplantation Act, which prohibits the sale of human organs from either dead or living donors.

PROS

The seriously ill are entitled to spend their money on saving their lives. It is preferable that some individuals receive organs, and survive, than that they die. The wealthy will not be the sole beneficiaries of a policy of organ purchase. For each successful kidney transplant operation, valuable hours on a dialysis machine will open up. The expense of palliative care for individuals

CONS

A single kidney has a black market price of $20,000. Consequently, the sale of organs will highlight and support the most egregious discrimination between rich and poor. Those who cannot afford to purchase an organ will have no opportunity to receive one. What family, if prepared to donate the organs of a relative, would decide to decline a payment of tens of thousands

requiring a transplant will be eliminated.	of dollars? Donated organs will disappear. The poor will die and only the rich will survive.
The donor of an organ, or his family, will benefit considerably from the sale. Both a kidney and a piece of liver can be removed without significant harm to the individual. Any assertion that an individual cannot make a reasoned decision to donate or sell these organs is patronizing. The family of a recently deceased individual also ought to be able to save the life of another and simultaneously receive remuneration.	The black market works in one direction—from the Third World to the First. The relative absence of regulation and the comparative value of the rewards mean that healthy individuals in Asia and Africa fall victim to scavenging organ merchants. The financial rewards make the decision to sell an organ one of compulsion rather than consent. Where colonialists raped the land, the neocolonialist surgeon steals from bodies.
Legalizing organ sales will eliminate the corruption that has led to reported executions and subsequent "thefts" of organs. A successful transplant operation is dependent upon medical knowledge of the donor. The black market cannot be regulated, but its purpose would be defeated once organ sales became lawful.	The sale of organs will lead to appalling human rights violations. Chinese judicial officials are reported to execute prisoners for their body parts. The lawful sale of organs would legitimize human sacrifice.
The transplant surgeon, the nursing staff, and even the pharmaceutical companies producing the anti-rejection drugs receive payment for each operation performed. Why should the donor of the organs, arguably the most important actor in any transplant, not also receive remuneration? What is remarkable is that a lifesaving treatment should apparently have no financial value.	Putting a price on the human body invites only exploitation by the unscrupulous.

Sample Motions:
This House would legalize the sale of organs.
This House would have a heart—with a price tag.
This House would buy body parts.

Web Links:
• Facts about Organ Donation and Transplantation.
http://www.inil.com/users/paulh/FACTS.HTM
A useful fact sheet, with statistics on organ donation and transplantation.
• Living Bank. <http://www.livingbank.org/main.html>
Site maintained by the largest donor education organization in the United States, it offers information designed to encourage organ donation.
• Organ Donor. <http://www.organdonor.gov/>
Provides information and resources on organ donation and transplant issues and promotes organ and tissue donation awareness.
• United Network for Organ Sharing. <http://www.unos.org/UNOS_redirect.asp>
The Web site of the organization that maintains the US organ transplant waiting list, it provides a wide variety of resources on transplantation and transplantation issues, including bioethical concerns.

Further Reading:
Chabot-Long, Lynn. *A Gift of Life: A Page From the Life of a Living Organ Donor.* Je Lynn Publications, 1996.
Green, Reg. *The Nicholas Effect: A Boy's Gift to the World.* O'Reilly and Associates, 1999.

HUMAN RIGHTS: EXISTENCE OF

The concept of human rights is central to modern Western culture. But what does "human rights" mean? Do we have such rights, and if we do, why are they needed? The United Nations adopted the Universal Declaration of Human Rights (UDHR) in 1948 in response to the savage inhumanities of World War II. This document sets out a declaration of fundamental entitlements including the political and civil rights common to Western democracies as well as economic, social, and cultural rights that Western nations have not historically considered fundamental. However, the document includes no enforcement mechanism, and states are obliged only to "move towards" a realization of these rights. Thus, while important steps have been made toward an international understanding of rights, there is a long way to go.

PROS

By their nature and birth, human beings possess certain inalienable rights. As Article I of the UDHR states, "All human beings are born free and equal in dignity and rights."

The simple sharing of a common humanity establishes human rights. We extrapolate from this humanity the norms that secure the basic dignity with which we all want to live.

Desires are not what grounds human rights. What human rights are based on is the universal need for basic security in our bodies, our possessions, and our relationships within society. This security isn't just desirable; it is vital. Human rights are those things that rationally assure these vital requirements. Thomas Hobbes recognized that all people benefit from this security because human beings are equal in their capacity to harm one another.

Our understanding of human rights has evolved over several hundred years. The rights contemporary Western societies consider basic are more extensive than those found in past societies because these Western societies have a higher standard of living. People often must experience the lack of something to appreciate how vital it is—this is true of human rights.

Human rights are not meant to be subject to artificial, academic analysis. They are practical guides to life, standards of how we should be able to live. They are an objective standard that people can use when calling on their governments for justice.

CONS

Do animals have the same inalienable rights by virtue of their nature and birth? Isn't this claim a bit arbitrary? Why should everyone have a "right" just because they are born?

This argument is arbitrary and nebulous. It bases fundamental human rights on extrapolating from "feelings." How accurate can this be? Furthermore, isn't this just a wish list of ways we want to be treated? A desire to be treated in a certain way doesn't give one the right to be so treated.

If human rights are requirements of reason, then why do we see so much ambiguity and confusion over what they are? There is huge debate over what rights we have, and many people cannot agree that we have basic economic or development rights. This seems odd if human rights are rational requirements that are vital to life.

This is a very subversive trail to start down. These "requirements of reason" are both subjective and dependent on specific circumstances. Does that mean that humans really don't have inalienable rights, but instead transform accepted standards of living into actual rights? In that case, two cultures could have radically different but valid interpretations of a specific human right. Can this be a satisfactory basis for concrete and actual rights?

This all suggests that human rights can be extremely useful. However, something can be useful, indeed necessary, without it being your right. None of these arguments establishes that human beings have inherent "rights."

Sample Motions:
This House believes in fundamental human rights.
This House believes rights are right.

Web Links:
• Amnesty International. <http://www.amnesty.org/>
Provides information on contemporary human rights issues.
• Human Rights Documents and Materials. <http://www1.umn.edu/humanrts/>
Site maintained by the Human Rights Library at the University of Minnesota providing links to over 7,000 documents on human rights.
• Human Rights Web. <http://www.hrweb.org/>
General site offering an introduction to human rights, biographies of individuals important in the human rights movement, documents relating to human rights, and links to other resources
• Universal Declaration of Human Rights. <http://www.un.org/Overview/rights.html>
Text of the document.

Further Reading:
Paine, Tom. *Common Sense, the Rights of Man and Other Essential Writings of Thomas Paine.* New American Library, 1988.
Savic, Obrad. *The Politics of Human Rights.* Verso, 2000.

CRSO

HUMAN RIGHTS: IMPOSITION BY FORCE?

During the 1990s the international community intervened to end massive human rights violations in the former Yugoslavia. But less dramatic infringements of human rights continue. China regularly cracks down on pro-democracy activists, Tibetans, and Christian groups, while civilians "disappear" in Colombia. How should those concerned about human rights address the issues? Intervention, whether by military force, through peacekeeping forces, or by diplomatic means, might curtail human rights abuses, but it poses practical and moral problems.

PROS

As good international Samaritans, we must intervene to halt human rights violations. The 1948 Genocide Convention calls on countries to "undertake to prevent and to punish" genocide.

Because all people have the same rights, countries with the best human rights records have the authority to impose their standards on other nations. Certainly, when one country perceives a breach of human rights as it understands them, it must use force to uphold these rights.

Careful planning can minimize the military violation of human rights. It is possible to hit military bases, runways, bridges, and so on without killing a single civilian or destroying anyone's personal property.

CONS

Using force to uphold human rights is hypocritical. Force inevitably involves infringing one right (to life or property) for the sake of another. For example, Indonesian intervention in East Timor involved the imposition of martial law: Amnesty International described this as "complaint and cure" being the same.

We cannot assume that Western ideas of human rights extend throughout the world. Buddhism, for example, places more emphasis on "human nature" and on the effects of individuals' actions than upon "rights." In any case, which country has the best human rights record? The United States often takes the initiative in launching intervention, but many nations see its use of the death penalty as a human rights violation.

This is totally impossible. Despite tremendous increases in the accuracy of weapons over the past decade, the US still hit civilians when bombing Afghanistan. The only safe answer is not to bomb.

PROS	CONS
Force need not mean "violence." Throughout its history the United Nations has deployed peacekeeping missions to stop violence and protect human rights. Individual nations, too, have carried out successful campaigns. If Britain had not deployed troops in Northern Ireland over the past decades, unchecked sectarian violence would have claimed thousands more lives.	The international community deploys peacekeeping forces only in the aftermath of violence. Even peacekeeping forces have violated individual rights and resorted to violence.
The nations that are party to international human rights conventions have a responsibility to see that other countries accept these noble ideals.	Guns and unstable peace are a volatile combination; in these situations even the smallest incident can lead to human rights violations.
"Force" does not necessarily involve the military. Diplomatic pressure, including sanctions, can force oppressive regimes to respect human rights.	Sanctions harm diplomatic relations well before they effect any change. No substantial evidence has been offered on the efficacy of sanctions. International sanctions against Iraq, for example, have not led to improved human rights. Instead, they have increased the suffering of the civilian population.
A nation can overthrow a cruel regime only with international support.	Nations do not need outside intervention to remove an oppressive dictator. In 2000, for example, Vojislav Kostunice won the presidential elections that helped oust Serbian dictator Slobodan Milosevic, in part, because he did not side with Western powers. Had the West intervened more forcefully to oust Milosevic, he might have clung to power longer.
Force is the only way to send a clear message that those who infringe on human rights are in the wrong.	Military intervention never provides a lasting solution to human rights abuses.

Sample Motions:
  This House would use force to uphold human rights.

Web Links:
  • Amnesty International. <http://amnesty.org>
  Information on Amnesty International and its campaigns for human rights as well as current news on potential human rights violations.
  • Human Rights Watch. <http://www.igc.org/hrw>
  Information on human rights by issue and geographical area.
  • United Nations Office of the High Commissioner for Human Rights (OHCHR). <http://www.unhchr.ch>
  Information on the operations of the OHCHR and its campaigns for children's rights, women's rights, and general human rights. Includes links to information on key human rights issues.

Further Reading:
  Forsythe, David. *Human Rights in International Relations*. Cambridge University Press, 2000.
  Gray, Christine. *International Law and the Use of Force*. Oxford University Press, 2001.
  Koh, Harold, and Ronald C. Slye, eds. *Deliberative Democracy and Human Rights*. Yale University Press, 1999.
  Robertson, Geoffrey. *Crimes Against Humanity: The Struggle for Global Justice*. New Press, 2000.

CRð℘

IMMIGRATION, RESTRICTIONS ON

In the last half of the twentieth century, the world saw dramatic population movements. Many people emigrated to escape war or religious persecution, but a large proportion moved from developing countries to Western nations for economic reasons. Some were actively recruited as cheap labor. Immigration policies vary from country to country, but no nation's door is completely open. Should immigration be restricted, and if so, to what extent; and do the industrialized nations have a moral obligation to the people of developing nations?

PROS

Labor is increasingly mobile in this age of globalization. People looking for work naturally move from areas of underemployment and poverty to regions with higher standards of living where workers are in demand.

The higher real wages that migrant workers earn abroad and send to their families at home are gains for a migrant's home country. In some countries these remittances are a significant part of the nation's income.

Many economists agree that immigration can be the "magic bullet" that will overcome the anticipated shortage of workers caused by the aging of populations in Europe. "Replacement migration," as it is called, could also help developing countries, whose populations are growing rapidly. If the European Union closes its doors, these people will still come to its shores, but they will come illegally. Individuals with no legal status have much less to lose than those who are in a country legally; thus enforcing a host country's laws becomes that much more difficult.

International migration can bring necessary knowledge and technologies to countries. For instance, the huge migration from Europe to the United States in the late nineteenth century contributed to American growth and development. Not only America, but also Australia and New Zealand emerged out of immigrant flow.

CONS

Economic migrants leave developing countries not because they cannot find jobs but because they want higher incomes. This can cause a brain drain that has a negative effect on development.

Workers move with their families, so there is no benefit to the home country. Often the worker's children and old parents become a burden on the host country's taxpayers. Frequently these workers are illegal. Their willingness to work for low wages lowers the wages of local workers and contributes to unemployment in the host country.

Thinking that immigration can miraculously solve labor problems for the European Union is far too simplistic. Once immigrants are settled, they tend to adopt the fertility patterns of the country in which they are living. They decide not to have many children, and they get old too!

Immigrants boosted the American economy only because the United States had a huge open market in which opportunity abounded. However, economic realities have changed since the nineteenth century. Today, opportunity is limited by intense global competition. Furthermore, the immigrants that now come to the United States and Western Europe do not try to integrate into their host culture, as they did in the past.

Sample Motions:
This House believes that rich countries should enforce immigration legislation.
The House believes that international immigration is beneficial to all concerned.

Web Links:
• World Immigration and Deportation. <http://www.world-immigration.com>
Broad site dealing with a variety of issues associated with international immigration.
• Immigration Issues. <http://immigration.about.com>

In-depth guide to immigration worldwide. Includes information on the current controversy as well as links to groups opposing mass immigration.

Further Reading:
Brettell, Caroline, and James Frank Hollifield, eds. *Migration Theory: Talking Across the Disciplines.* Routledge, 2000.
Martinez, Ruben. *Crossing Over: A Mexican Family on the Migrant Trail.* Metropolitan Books, 2001.
Stalker, Peter. *Workers Without Frontiers: The Impact of Globalization on International Migration.* Lynne Rienner, 1999.

⋘⋙

INTERNATIONAL CRIMINAL COURT

In 1998, the Rome Statute established the International Criminal Court (ICC) with jurisdiction over genocide, crimes against humanity, war crimes, and aggression. US President Bill Clinton authorized the signing of the statute in December 2000 but said the treaty was "significantly flawed" and recommended that the US Senate not ratify it. Congress and the Bush Administration have been even more hostile. In November 2001, President George W. Bush signed into law an act prohibiting the use of funds of several federal agencies, including the Departments of State, Commerce, and Justice, for cooperation with the ICC. Congress passed a bill restricting use of Defense Department funds the following month.

PROS

The ICC will lead to political prosecution. It will subject American service members and senior military and political strategists to criminal charges for military actions that are legitimate and necessary. Any nation can ask the ICC prosecutor to investigate an issue, and the prosecutor has the power to investigate *ex proprio motu.* The UN Security Council cannot override or veto his actions or decisions. Political prosecution is evident in the preliminary investigation by the International Criminal Tribunal for the Former Yugoslavia (ICTY) into the NATO bombing of Kosovo and the Federal Republic of Yugoslavia. The prosecutor chose to investigate a campaign that had been undertaken with clinical precision, that had received the support of the Security Council (although after the fact), and that had been directed against a military carrying out a brutal policy of genocide. This grim precedent suggests that a prosecutor will not hesitate to investigate other good faith and successful military actions across the globe.

The US holds a unique position in maintaining international peace and security. It might be appropriate for other countries to consent to the jurisdiction of the ICC because they do not have the same responsibilities and risks. US armed forces have responded to many more "situations" during the 1990s than during the whole of the Cold War. More than ever, the world looks to the US to ensure peace and safety. US military dominance increases the likelihood of prosecution. When

CONS

The US should have nothing to fear if it behaves lawfully. Moreover, determining if a violation of international law (by the US or any other nation) has taken place should be easy as the ICC prosecutor concerns himself only with the gravest offenses. The US certainly would not approve a strategy of genocide or systematic mass violations of human rights that would come under the jurisdiction of the ICC. The prosecutor's power is also limited by the requirement that he obtain the approval of three judges before issuing an arrest warrant or initiating proceedings. A preliminary investigation could benefit the US because it would end doubts about the justifiability of its actions. The US accepted the jurisdiction of the ICTY prosecutor because it did not expect its forces to commit the crimes they were deployed to prevent.

The very preeminence of the US demands that it adhere to the rule of international law. A nation can commit war crimes while conducting a military campaign to protect human rights and save lives. The ICC can demand that the US, or any other state, pursue its lawful ends by lawful means. Moreover, victims of gross human rights violations do not care who the perpetrator is. Other nations with significant military commitments overseas, such as the UK and France, have rati-

rogue regimes are incapable of defeating the US militarily, they are likely to challenge the US in the ICC. This will damage US interests far more than any conventional military action and will result in US reluctance to intervene in the future. The indispensable nation must be permitted to dispense with the ICC.

The Rome Statute has created the novel crime of "aggression," which increases the likelihood of political prosecution. One state could accuse another of aggression for intervening to protect human rights. Governments carrying out a policy of genocide could request that a nation be prosecuted for successfully preventing genocide. Moreover, by a quirk of the statute, a state that refuses to accept ICC jurisdiction can nevertheless request the prosecution of foreign nationals for crimes allegedly committed in its territory. Thus Yugoslav President Slobodan Milosevic could have demanded the investigation of NATO forces for activities during Operation Allied Force but could have prevented an investigation of the Bosnian Serb army in the same territory.

The ICC will not deter war crimes or genocide. The Third Reich accelerated its campaign to exterminate Jews when it became clear that the Allies would be victorious. Similarly, Milosevic and the Bosnian Serb army conducted a campaign of genocide in Kosovo while the ICTY was sitting in The Hague. War criminals do not commit gross human rights violations based on reason. The existence of a court, however well intentioned, will have no effect on those states that would commit such crimes.

ICC expenses will be crippling. Cautious estimates suggest an operating budget of $100US million per year. The costs of the ICTY and the international criminal tribunal for Rwanda spiraled out of control, and the latter left a legacy of misadministration and internal corruption.

fied the Rome Statute without hesitation. These states accept the principle that nations intervening in another state to uphold or establish human rights must respect those same human rights.

This objection to the ICC is purely hypothetical because the ICC has not yet defined "aggression." In addition, the "crime" of aggression is not novel. Intervening in the domestic affairs of a sovereign state is contrary to norms of conventional and customary law. The UN Charter prohibits both the unauthorized use of force against another state and intervention in its domestic jurisdiction. The US should ratify the Rome Statute so that its negotiators can play an active role in the Assembly of State Parties, which is currently working on drafting a definition of this crime.

You cannot claim that the ICC will not deter atrocities when such an institution has never before existed. Moreover, the offenders must be apprehended, tried, and punished. Retribution and protection of society are objectives not only for domestic criminal justice systems but also for the new international system.

The ICC's budget might seem excessive, but no price should be put on justice for thousands of victims of heinous crimes.

Sample Motions:
This House believes that the United States should not support the International Criminal Court.
This House believes that the creation of the ICC is a crime.

Web Links:
• The Coalition for an ICC. <http://www.iccnow.org/index.html>
Country-by-country report on the status of the Rome Statute.
• Crimes of War Project. <http://www.crimesofwar.org/>
Provides up-to-date information on possible violations of human rights and war crimes as well as the status of humanitarian law and justice.
• ICC Resources at the University of Chicago Library. <http://www.lib.uchicago.edu/~llou/icc.html>

Bibliography of Web and print resources on the ICC.
• International Committee of the Red Cross: International Criminal Court and Ad Hoc Tribunals. <http://www.icrc.org/
icrceng.nsf/813bf8350951d3bbc12564670032d7f3/49f216e46af8b377412565cb00486041?OpenDocument>
Links to information on the ICC and ad hoc international criminal tribunals for Yugoslavia and Rwanda.

Further Reading:
Goldstone, Richard J. *For Humanity: Reflections of a War Crime Investigator.* Yale University Press, 2000.
Gutman, Roy. *Crimes of War: What the Public Should Know.* Norton, 1999.
Schabas, William A. *An Introduction to the International Criminal Court.* Cambridge University Press, 2001.

CRID

INTERNET CENSORSHIP

The Internet (World Wide Web) is the fastest growing and largest tool for mass communication and information distribution in the world. In the last 10 years concern has increased about the Internet disseminating content that is violent and sexual, that gives bomb-making instructions, that abets terrorist activity, and that makes available child pornography. In response, some have called for censorship. But even if censorship of the Internet can be morally justified, practical problems with regulation arise.

PROS

Although democratic nations value freedom of speech, all put some restrictions on the right. Such restrictions usually surround hard-core and child pornography, but some nations restrict hate speech as well. The Internet should be no exception to these basic standards. Truly offensive material is no different because it is published on the Web.

Censorship is tailored to the power of the medium. Accordingly, a higher level of censorship is attached to television, films, and video than to newspapers and books: We recognize that moving pictures and sound are more graphic and powerful than text, photographs, or illustrations. Videos are normally more regulated than films seen in theaters because the viewer of a video has control of the medium—the power to rewind, view again, and distribute more widely. The Internet, which increasingly uses video and sound, should be regulated accordingly.

The Internet would be hard to control, but we must not use that as an excuse not to try. Preventing the sale of snuff movies or hard-core pornography is extremely difficult, but some governments do so because they

CONS

Censorship is usually evil. Governments should avoid it wherever possible. Child pornography is an extreme example; sufficient legislation is already in place to handle those who attempt to produce, distribute, or view such material. Other forms of speech may well be offensive, but the only way a society can counter such speech is to be exposed to it and have it out in the open. Without such freedom, these groups are driven underground and can take on the aspect of martyrs.

The distinction between censorship of print and broadcast media is becoming increasingly irrelevant. Print media are comparatively unregulated because they are the primary means of distributing information in society. In the near future, the Internet may become this prime disseminator. Thus the Internet must be allowed the same protections now enjoyed by print media. When English philosopher John Stuart Mill considered freedom of speech and the Founding Fathers of the United States spoke in the Constitution of freedom of the press they were concerned about the primary and most powerful organ of information distribution at that time, the print press. Nowadays they would more likely be concerned with preventing censorship of the broadcast media and the Internet.

Even allowing for the extreme problems surrounding curtailment of freedom of speech, Internet censorship would be more or less impossible. Governments can attempt to regulate what is produced in their own

deem it important. A more intractable issue is the anonymity that the Internet provides pornographers and criminals. Asian countries have experimented with requiring citizens to provide identification before posting content on the Web. If universally adopted, such a requirement could be a relatively simple way of enforcing laws against truly offensive and harmful content.

In many countries producing libelous material or material that incites racial hatred incurs multiple liability. Where the author or publisher cannot be traced or is insolvent, the printers can often be sued or prosecuted. The relatively small number of Internet service providers (ISPs) should be made liable if they assist in the provision of dangerous or harmful information.

The issues at stake in this debate—protection of children, terrorist activity, crime, racial hatred, etc. are all international problems. If a global solution is required, it can be achieved by international cooperation and treaties. All societies consider censorship justified where harm is caused to others by the speech, words, or art. All the examples cited above are clearly causing harm to various groups in society. By a combination of the initiatives listed above, we could limit that harm.

countries but regulating material originating outside national borders would be impossible. What is the point in the US removing all domestic links to hardcore pornography when such material from the UK or Sweden could be readily accessed and downloaded? Individuals could also produce banned material and store it in an overseas domain. True freedom of speech requires anonymity in some cases to protect the author. Governments that have introduced ID requirements for Internet use also deny many basic rights to their citizens. The Internet allows citizens to criticize their government and distribute news and information without reprisal from the state. These freedoms clearly could not survive Internet ID requirements.

Internet service providers (ISP) are certainly the wrong people to decide what can and cannot be placed on the Internet. Big business already controls far too much of this new technology without also making it judge and jury of all Internet content. In any case, the sheer bulk of information ISPs allow to be published is such that reviewing it all would be impossible. Were ISPs to be held liable for allowing such material to be displayed, they would inevitably err on the side of caution to protect their financial interests. This would result in a much more heavily censored Internet.

Many ISPs have shown themselves to be responsible in immediately removing truly offensive content where they have been alerted to it. What is required is self-regulation by the industry, not the imposition of arbitrary and draconian restrictions on Internet content and use. Parents can install software that will filter out offensive sites and sites inappropriate for children.

Sample Motions:
    This House would censor the Internet.
    This House calls for Net filters.
    This House would limit freedom of speech.

Web Links:
    • ACLU (American Civil Liberties Union): CyberLiberties. <http://www.aclu.org/issues/cyber/hmcl.html>
    Provides links to resources and information on campaigns against Internet censorship.
    • Electronic Frontier Foundation. <http://www.eff.org/blueribbon.html>
    Offers summaries of issues involving Internet censorship as well as information on fair use and privacy on the Net.

Further reading:
    Peck, Robert. *Libraries, the First Amendment and Cyberspace: What You Need to Know.* American Library Association, 1999.
    Wallace, Jonathan, and Mark Mangan. *Sex, Laws, and Cyberspace: Freedom and Censorship on the Frontiers of the Online Revolution.* Holt, 1997.

IRAQ, INVASION OF

Iraq invaded its neighbor, Kuwait, in 1990, provoking the 1991 Persian Gulf War. Although a United Nations coalition quickly defeated Iraq, it stopped short of removing Iraqi president Saddam Hussein from power. Fearing that he possessed, or was developing, chemical, biological, and nuclear weapons, one of the UN's peace conditions was that a Special Commission (UNSCOM) should investigate Iraqi weapons programs and shut them down. The UN also imposed sanctions to ensure compliance. UNSCOM withdrew from Iraq in 1998 after reporting that Iraq had refused to cooperate with its work. Early in 2002 US president George W. Bush singled out Iraq, Iran, and North Korea as an "axis of evil" rogue states intent on acquiring weapons of mass destruction. Since then the Bush administration has indicated that it is willing to invade Iraq to remove Saddam Hussein.

PROS

Saddam Hussein is developing weapons of mass destruction. During the 1990s UNSCOM uncovered nuclear, chemical, and biological weapons plants and programs but was unable to shut them down. Since UNSCOM left in 1998, stores of these kinds of weapons have been increasing rapidly according to recent Iraqi defectors. Because sanctions failed to force Iraq to cooperate with the UN, we have no alternative but to overthrow such a dangerous regime before it uses such terrible weapons.

Because Hussein has engaged in wars of aggression against Iran and Kuwait, and used chemical weapons against both Iran and the Kurdish minority within Iraq, we have good reason to believe he will use any weapons of mass destruction available to him. He may not be deterred by the threat of destruction. A brutal dictator, Hussein has shown no concern for the Iraqi people and may be prepared to take them all with him if his own position is threatened.

Hussein's regime is a sponsor of a number of international terrorist groups. Possible links to the Al Qaeda terrorist network may implicate Iraq in the September 11 attacks. Iraq was the only country not to condemn these attacks, and one of its agents twice met Mohammed Atta, a leading hijacker. At the very least, the regime provides encouragement, funding, and logistical support for groups that are intent on killing civilians and overthrowing legitimate governments. Might it not also give these groups access to weapons of mass destruction?

Overthrowing the present Iraqi regime and removing Hussein would relieve the terrible suffering of the Iraqi people. Hussein's regime is a dictatorship that uses brutal methods to silence dissent and maintain its hold

CONS

Where is the evidence that Saddam Hussein is close to possessing weapons of mass destruction? There is none. Recent defectors have been telling the United States what they know it wants to hear. Meanwhile US demands about inspections effectively require Iraq to prove a negative—that it is not producing the weapons that UNSCOM failed to find in seven years of intrusive searching. The weapons argument appears to be an excuse to overthrow a regime America, and the Bush family in particular, hates.

Iraq is not a serious threat. Its military never recovered from the Gulf War and is in no shape to fight wars of aggression. The Kurds in northern Iraq and the Marsh Arabs in the south are protected by US- policed no-fly zones. Evidence also shows that Hussein can be deterred; he heeded Israel's threat of "massive retaliation" in the Gulf War and did not use the chemical weapons he did possess. The greatest risk is that Hussein, if provoked by a US attack aimed at removing him from power, might use any weapons at his disposal.

The evidence for any link to September 11 is very tenuous. Iraq's secular regime has little in common with the fundamentalist members of Al Qaeda. The US State Department lists other countries as sponsors of terror, so why is Iraq being singled out as a target for invasion? Most of the groups Iraq is said to back are violently opposed to Israel, but many in the Middle East would see them as freedom fighters rather than terrorists. In this context, ending any Iraqi support for terrorists would have little or no impact on terrorist operations.

What guarantee do we have that any successor regime would be better? Should an invasion provoke a military coup, power would continue to be held by the same military and political groups that have served Hussein

on power. UN sanctions excepted food and medicine, but Hussein has deliberately withheld these from his people to score propaganda points. His attacks on the Kurds of northern Iraq and the Marsh Arabs and Shiite Muslims of southern Iraq have amounted to genocide.

so brutally. The United States has been backing the Iraqi National Congress, but this loose collection of exile groups is united only in its dislike for the present regime. It includes figures with dubious democratic credentials, including former military leaders who are implicated in brutal acts of their own, and enjoys no legitimacy within Iraq. The very real prospect of a post-Hussein civil war would make the lives of ordinary Iraqis even worse.

The present Iraqi regime is a great threat to regional stability. In the past it has begun wars against two of its immediate neighbors (Iran and Kuwait), threatened a third (Saudi Arabia), launched unprovoked missile attacks against Israel, and called upon the people of the Arab world to rise up against their own governments. It may again seek to divert its people's attention from their sufferings by starting another war. Because of the strategic and economic importance of the Middle East, regional instability is a direct threat to global security. Clearly a lasting and workable peace settlement between Israel and the Palestinians is impossible while Iraq remains a threat. Fear of Iraq also blights reform efforts in countries like Iran and Saudi Arabia.

The greatest threat to regional stability is the likelihood that Iraq might break up should the present regime be overthrown. Neighboring nations would be drawn into an Iraqi civil war in support or opposition to particular factions (e.g., Iran in support of Shiite Muslims, Turkey against the creation of an independent Kurdish state) or in an attempt to control Iraq's oil wealth. Outrage in the Arab world against US imperialism might also destabilize a number of fragile regimes in the Middle East, further threatening the region and making peace between Israel and the Palestinians even harder to achieve.

Overthrowing the Iraqi regime is feasible and need not result in large numbers of casualties. Sanctions prevented the Iraqi military from rebuilding after its destruction in the Gulf War. The defections of many senior army officers brought valuable intelligence to Western military planners. The regime, like the Taliban in Afghanistan, is likely to prove to be very brittle once subject to a forceful attack, collapsing through lack of military and popular support.

Invading Iraq would be a military gamble. If the regime did not fall through a coup in the early days of the attack, an invading force would have to commit ground forces for a long campaign; there are no domestic rebels to act as a proxy army (as was the case in Afghanistan). Iraqi soldiers may not be highly skilled or well equipped, but neither were the Vietcong. In addition, the elite Republican Guard, fiercely loyal to Hussein and 100,000 strong, would be a formidable force, especially in house-to-house fighting for control of the major towns and cities. Given Hussein's use of civilians as "human shields" in the past, casualties could be very high.

Overthrowing Hussein would deter other rogue states from attempting to acquire weapons of mass destruction and supporting terrorism. Failure to act decisively now will send a message that the international community is too weak and divided to take a stand against aggression. All present and future treaties designed to limit weapons of mass destruction will be worthless because there is no credible enforcement.

Given that the United States is friendly with some other nations that have ignored international arms control treaties, the invasion of Iraq would not send a clear message. Instead, an invasion is likely to make the United States, and the West in general, even more hated and generate more terrorist outrages. The greatest global danger is that the international coalition against terror will fall apart as a result of an invasion that so many other nations openly oppose.

Sample Motions:
   This House would invade Iraq.
   This House would overthrow Saddam.
   This House would extend the war on terror.

Web Links:
   • "The Case for Tough Action Against Iraq." <http://www.observer.co.uk/international/story/0,6903,610552,00.html>
   Article in the British *Observer* supporting the overthrow of Saddam Hussein by military means if necessary.
   • Iraqi National Congress. <http://www.inc.org.uk/>
   Web site maintained by loose coalition of exile groups opposed to Saddam Hussein.
   • Iraq Update. <http://usinfo.state.gov/regional/nea/iraq/>
   US State Department site presenting current information on US policy on Iraq.
   • "Should We Go to War with Saddam?" <http://www.observer.co.uk/worldview/story/0,11581,669024,00.html>
   Article in the British *Observer* summarizing the debate.

Further Reading:
   Butler, Richard. *The Greatest Threat: Iraq, Weapons of Mass Destruction, and the Crisis of Global Security.* Public Affairs, 2001.
   Farouk-Sluglett, Marion, and Peter Sluglett. *Iraq Since 1958: From Revolution to Dictatorship.* I. B. Tauris, 2001.
   MacKey, Sandra. *The Reckoning: Iraq and the Legacy of Saddam Hussein.* Norton, 2002.

CREO

IVORY TRADING

The African elephant population decreased from about 1.2 million in 1979 to approximately 600,000 in 1989, in part as a result of intense poaching to supply the international ivory trade. In 1989 the United Nations Convention on International Trade in Endangered Species (CITES) banned ivory trading. This resulted in population increases in some countries. In 1997 the ban was eased for Botswana, Zimbabwe, and Namibia, giving them a one-time opportunity to sell their stockpiled ivory to Japan, the center of ivory demand. The ivory was sold in 1999; in 2000, African nations agreed to a two-year freeze on sales, but in 2002, South Africa announced that it would apply for permission to sell its stockpiles beginning in 2003.

PROS

The elephant populations of southern African states are growing rapidly, placing a strain upon the national parks in which they live. This has necessitated government culls that have resulted in large stockpiles of ivory (also acquired from animals that died naturally) that these nations are currently unable to sell. Relaxing the CITES ban on trading ivory, subject to careful regulation, would bring much-needed cash to the environmental programs of these impoverished countries, helping them to safeguard the long-term survival of African elephants.

A trading ban does not choke off demand for ivory. Instead, it raises the price to exorbitant levels, encouraging poaching. Japan is emerging from the economic problems that depressed demand during the 1990s, and China's growing prosperity is creating a new market. Consequently the illegal trade will generate higher profits in the future. Legitimate, regulated sales would undercut the illegal market and drive the poachers out

CONS

Elephants are highly intelligent animals; to kill them for their ivory is unethical. Lifting the ban would legitimize the view that humankind can exploit them in any way convenient.

At present demand for ivory is low and shrinking; prices are actually lower than before 1989. Lifting the trading ban would renew interest in ivory artifacts and increase the size of the market, thus raising their price. Higher prices present a long-term threat to elephants and encourage continued poaching. In any case, poverty in Africa is so severe that even a drop in price will not stop the poachers.

of business.

Poaching has been effectively eliminated in southern Africa through effective management of game parks. The development of ecotourism also gives local peoples an incentive to protect wildlife as a long-term economic resource. To sustain this approach, parks must generate greater income from their elephant populations. Realistically, states can do this only by selling stockpiled ivory. If other countries have a poaching problem, they should follow the example of South Africa and Botswana rather than seek to harm the successful conservancy programs in these states.

Ivory is expensive to obtain (through culls or monitoring of very elderly animals) and store. It also degrades over time. Therefore, common sense tells us to allow its sale on a permanent, controlled basis, rather than through one-off schemes such as the sale to Japan.

According to the South African government proposal to lift the ban in 2000, "The experimental export of raw ivory in 1999 from Botswana, Namibia and Zimbabwe (conducted under rigorous CITES supervision) was successful in all respects and took place under intense international scrutiny. It can categorically be stated that no ivory, other than the registered stocks, was exported to Japan."

Although elephant populations in southern Africa are viable and increasing, this is not the case elsewhere in Africa. Nor is it true of the wild Asian elephant populations of South Asia. Testing cannot reveal where carved ivory originated or the subspecies from which it came. Consequently, lifting the trading ban would enable poachers to sell ivory more easily, thus increasing their profits and their motivation to kill more elephants. The widespread corruption in Africa and parts of Asia allows poachers to mask the illegal origins of their ivory, which they pass off as legally obtained.

Storage costs and depreciation are problems only if ivory is stored in the hope of eventual sale. Kenya's game conservancy burns the ivory it obtains from culls or confiscates from poachers, avoiding both of these problems and showing its commitment to ending all possibility of renewed trade.

The relaxation of CITES controls coincided with a fivefold upsurge in poaching in Kenya and a similar increase in India because criminals assumed that the ban would soon be lifted.

Sample Motions:
> This House would allow trade in ivory.
> This House would save the elephants.
> This House believes conservation must justify itself economically.

Web Links:
> • Convention on International Trade in Endangered Species of Wild Fauna and Flora (CITIES). <http://www.cites.org/>
> Provides information on CITES and CITES programs, the text of the CITES convention, and links to resources on endangered species.
> • International Fund for Animal Welfare. <http://www.ifaw.org/page.asp?id=672&p=elephants>
> Links to information on the status of elephants and projects to save them.

Further Reading:
> Pearce, David, ed. *Elephants, Economics and Ivory.* Earthscan, 1991.
> Snugg, Ike. *Elephants and Ivory: Lessons from the Trade Ban.* Institute of Economic Affairs, 1994.

ᩚᩚ

MANDATORY SENTENCING: THREE STRIKES

Early in the 1980s, national legislators became concerned that the criminal justice system had become inconsistent across the country. Similar crimes were being punished with dramatically different sentences, even though the same laws applied. Accordingly, Congress began to craft rules for mandatory prison sentences in federal cases; these rules were intended to ensure that similar crimes would be punished in similar ways, no matter where these cases were tried. Many state legislatures drafted parallel rules for lower courts. Over time, mandatory sentences in state courts evolved to include "three-strikes" rules: If a newly convicted felon had a criminal record of two prior felony convictions, the judge was obligated to impose the maximum sentence for the third crime. (There are some variations in the laws from state to state.) There has been growing concern, however, that the punishments imposed by three-strikes laws are not simply too severe, but also unconstitutional. In November 2002, the U.S. Supreme Court agreed to hear a constitutional challenge to the three-strikes law adopted in California in 1994.

PROS

One of the fundamental principles of criminal justice is that the punishment should fit the crime. That principle is abrogated when a life sentence is automatically imposed for a third felony—whether that felony is serious and violent, or minor and non-violent. Because there is only one sentence possible for many kinds of crimes, it follows that the sentence does not necessarily correspond to the gravity of the offense.

It often happens that the third felony—that is, the one that triggers the automatic sentence—is relatively minor. For example, a life sentence has been imposed on someone for the attempted shoplifting of video-tapes. A life sentence for such a crime is "cruel and unusual," and, as such, is forbidden by the Eighth Amendment to the Constitution.

Historically, judges have had discretionary powers when sentencing criminals; this practice recognizes that sentencing should take into account the circumstances of the crime, the character of the criminal, and the amount of harm caused by the crime. Mandatory sentences rob judges of those discretionary powers that are properly theirs. Indeed, mandatory sentences are imposed, in effect, by the legislative branch—thus violating the independence of the judiciary and the separation of powers outlined in the Constitution.

Defenders of the three-strikes laws claim that these laws have a powerful deterrent effect, and reduce the occurrence of crime. Statistics show, however, that recidivism has not been reduced by the presence of such laws, and the general reduction in crime, when and where it has occurred, is due to effective policing, rather than to harsh sentencing.

The three-strikes laws are, in effect, ex post facto laws:

CONS

It is a primary obligation of the criminal justice system to establish clear and certain penalties for crime. The three-strikes laws offer such clarity, and their mandatory nature makes punishment certain. These laws prevent inconsistency in the criminal justice system.

Historically, judges have abused the discretion that they have been given by the criminal justice system. Too often, judges have imposed light sentences on criminals, even when those criminals have been repeat offenders. The mandatory sentences imposed by three-strikes laws ensure that recidivists are punished appropriately.

The fundamental purpose of the criminal justice system is to protect the rights and the safety of law-abiding citizens. But these citizens are not protected by "revolving door justice," which allows criminals back on the street after repeat offenses. Three-strikes laws remove repeat offenders from society, and prevent them from committing further crimes.

Since three-strikes laws have been introduced across the nation, crime has dropped dramatically. The reason for this decline is obvious: Convicted recidivists are not free to commit more crimes, and felons with one or two strikes on their records are deterred by the punishment that they know will follow a third offense.

Opponents of three-strikes laws claim that these laws

that is, criminal sentences can take into account—as first and second strikes—crimes that were committed before the law was passed. Moreover, the imposition of mandatory maximum sentences because of past history constitutes "double jeopardy": Criminals are being punished again for crimes for which they already served time.

give criminals no chance to rehabilitate and redeem themselves. But studies have shown that rehabilitation is highly unlikely for recidivists. Someone who has committed three felonies is not likely to reform; rather, it is the destiny of the recidivist to keep committing crimes.

Sample Motions:
This House would restore discretion in sentencing to the judiciary.
This House would make the punishment fit the crime.

Web Links:
• Families Against Mandatory Minimums
http://www.famm.org/index2.htm
Website of an advocacy group that opposes a wide range of mandatory sentences, not just the three-strikes laws. Includes reviews of litigation and briefs written for Supreme Court.
• Families Against California's Three-Strikes
http://www.facts1.com/
Website of an advocacy group that focuses specifically on California laws. Includes history and links to key texts and other websites.
• Lungren, Dan. "Three Cheers for Three Strikes: California enjoys a record drop in crime"
http://www.policyreview.org/nov96/backup/lungren.html
Dan Lungren was attorney general of the state of California when he wrote this essay in defense of the state's three strikes law.

Further Reading:
Reynolds, Mike, Bill Jones and Dan Evans . *Three Strikes and You're Out: A Promise to Kimber: The Chronicle of America's Toughest Anti-Crime Law.* Quill Driver Books, 1996.
Shichor, David (editor), and Dale K. Sechrest, *Three Strikes and You're Out: Vengeance As Public Policy.* Sage Press, 1996.
Zimring, Franklin E., Sam Kamin and Gordon Hawkins. *Crime and Punishment in California: The Impact of Three Strikes and You're Out.* Institute of Governmental Studies Press, 1999.

CRSO

MARIJUANA, LEGALIZATION OF

The debate about the legalization of drugs, particularly that of soft drugs like marijuana, could be characterized as pitting freedom of the individual against a paternalistic state. Advocates of legalization argue that marijuana is not only less harmful than legal substances like alcohol and tobacco, but also has been proven to possess certain medicinal properties. Those opposed argue that the legalization of marijuana will act as a precursor to increased addiction to hard drugs and will necessarily lead to an increase in the crime rate.

PROS
Although marijuana does have some harmful effects, it is no more harmful than legal substances like alcohol and tobacco. Research by the British Medical Association shows that nicotine is far more addictive than marijuana. Furthermore, the consumption of alcohol and cigarette smoking cause more deaths per year than does marijuana. The legalization of marijuana will remove an

CONS
Unlike alcohol and tobacco, marijuana has an inherently dangerous hallucinatory effect on the mind. Furthermore, many individuals addicted to marijuana resort to crime to fund their addiction. The legalization of marijuana will lead to the drug becoming more readily available, which in turn will mean that many more people will gain access to it and become addicted.

anomaly in the law whereby substances that are more dangerous than marijuana are legal, while the possession and use of marijuana remains unlawful.

The crime rate will inevitably rise. Data from the Netherlands show that the decriminalization and eventual legalization of marijuana did lead to an increase in crime.

In recent years, scientists and medical researchers have discovered that marijuana possesses certain beneficial medicinal qualities. For instance, marijuana helps to relieve the suffering of patients with multiple sclerosis. The latest research that was conducted by the Complutense University in Madrid indicates that marijuana has the potential to kill some cancerous cells. Governments should acknowledge such findings and legalize marijuana.

The US has supported scientific research into the medical benefits of marijuana. Although evidence may show that marijuana may have some medicinal benefits, we should exercise caution about legalizing it because its use also has harmful side effects. More important, the legalization of marijuana will give rise to a host of social problems. The negatives of legalization far outweigh its benefits. We can thus safely say that the present approach represents the most sensible and evenhanded response to the issue at hand.

Individuals should be given the freedom to lead their lives as they choose. Of course, such freedom is not absolute, and laws should intervene to limit this freedom, especially when the rights of others are infringed. In the case of the use of marijuana, it is a victimless crime—only the user experiences the effects of the substance. The state should not act paternalistically by legislating against something that harms only the actual user.

The state is justified in introducing legislation to prevent individuals from causing harm to themselves. For instance, many countries have laws requiring the wearing of seatbelts in cars. Moreover, the use of marijuana does lead to medically and socially harmful outcomes that affect other members of society.

Where is the empirical evidence that the use of marijuana will certainly lead users into more dangerous narcotic substances? There is none. Undeniably, a large number of people use the drug despite it being illegal. Rather than turn away from this problem, the government should face reality. The legalization of marijuana will enable the government to regulate its use, thereby protecting its many users from harmful abuse of the substance.

The legalization of marijuana will lead to users moving on to harder drugs like morphine and cocaine. This would ultimately bring about an increase in social ills as well as the need to spend more government funds on rehabilitation programs.

Presently, organized crime sells marijuana. The legalization of marijuana will help facilitate the sale of the drug in establishments like Amsterdam's "coffee houses." This will shift the sale of marijuana away from the criminal underworld. Severing the "criminal link" will ensure that the users no longer need to come into contact with organized crime.

The same criminal elements that now sell marijuana might, when the drug is legalized, diversify and set up "coffee houses" themselves. Legalization will do nothing to separate the sale of marijuana from the criminal underworld. Conversely, it will give criminals a legitimate base from which to continue their activities.

Sample Motions:
This House believes that marijuana should be legalized.
This House supports the legalization of drugs.
This House advocates change in our present drug policy.

Web Links:
• Office of National Drug Control Policy. <http://www.whitehousedrugpolicy.gov>

Provides information on US government drug policy, statistics on drug use, news stories and publications from an anti-legalization perspective.
• Legalise Cannabis Alliance. <http://www.lca-uk.org>
Organization supporting the legalization of marijuana in Great Britain.
• National Organization for the Reform of Marijuana Laws. <http://www.norml.org/>
Information on marijuana facts, laws, and medical use from the oldest US organization supporting legalization.

Further Reading:
Brown, David. *Cannabis: The Genus Cannabis.* Taylor and Francis, 1998.
Matthews, Patrick. *Cannabis Culture: A Journey through Disputed Territory.* Trafalgar Square, 2000.

CR&SO

MIDDLE EASTERN POLICY, US

Since it was founded in 1948, the state of Israel has been in conflict with the Arab nations that surround it, and with the Arab people living within its own borders—and the United States has been part of that conflict. The United States was one of the first countries to recognize the legitimacy of the Israeli government, and for more than 50 years it has supported Israel militarily, economically, and diplomatically. The US has also been instrumental in negotiating diplomatic agreements between Israel and the Arab world. The central issue in the conflict today is the creation of a Palestinian state that would give autonomy to the Arabs living under Israeli rule (primarily on the West Bank of the Jordan River). Israel has been reluctant to create this state, which Palestinians regard as their right. Although the US has voiced support for a Palestinian state, many observers feel that the United States should do more to make such a state a reality.

PROS

US policy in the Middle East has been consistently on the side of Israel and has ignored the rights of other peoples. Although the US recognized the need for a Jewish homeland, it has not made a commitment to recognizing that Palestinians need a homeland as well.

American policy in the Middle East has been guided by politics, not principles. On the one hand, presidents have responded to the pressure from Jewish voters to support Israel. On the other, policy toward Arab states has been shaped largely by economic needs: The US has been friendly to countries with large oil reserves, e.g., Saudi Arabia, but has ignored poorer Arabs, e.g., the Palestinians.

American policy toward the militarization of the Middle East has been inconsistent and unfair. Although the US has taken a strong stance against the development of weapons in Arab nations, it has sold weapons to Israel and condoned Israel's development of nuclear capability.

The US has claimed that it supports Israel because

CONS

Do not forget that for most of its history, Israel's neighbors said that Israel had no right to exist. and must be destroyed. US support has been critical to Israel's survival.

Throughout the world, the United States is committed to the development of open, democratic societies. Israel is the only functioning democracy in the Middle East and shares many of America's political values. It deserves American support.

A distinction must be made between military defenses and military aggression. The US has provided military assistance to Israel so that Israel can defend itself against countries that have openly declared their hostile intentions. The US must, however, oppose the development of weapons in countries with a history of aggression—for example, Iraq, which launched an unprovoked attack on Kuwait.

The US has always acted as an impartial broker, seek-

PROS	CONS
it is the only democracy in the region—but such support of democracy has not been a firmly held principle and not acted on in other parts of the world. The US has knowingly supported corrupt and unjust authoritarian regimes in Arab countries when their oil policies favored America.	ing concessions from both sides. The US has used its influence to have Israel consider Arab demands and to have Arab nations and negotiators consider Israel's demands.
The US has been inconsistent in the application of its moral principles. It has routinely condemned Palestinians and other Arabs for terrorist actions, but it granted immediate recognition to the founders of Israel, who were engaged in a terrorist campaign against the British.	The US has acted in good faith with the Palestinian people, but negotiations have faltered because their leader, Yassir Arafat, is corrupt, duplicitous, and unstable.

Sample Motions:
This House supports US sponsorship of a Palestinian state.
This House would value democracy more than votes and oil.

Web Links:
- Great Decisions Guides: Middle East. <http://www.fpa.org/content2525/content.htm?section=research&attrib_id=2331&frame_id=2490>
The Web site of the Foreign Policy Association provides dozens of documents and links relating to issues that have shaped US policy.
- Israel and Palestine. <http://www.foreignpolicy-nfocus.org/briefs/vol6/v6n04israel.html>
Web site of a think tank without walls is highly critical of US policy.
- Israel/Mideast Briefings: Five Basic Talking Points on Israel.
<http://www.ajc.org/Israel/IsraelMideastBriefingsDetail.asp?did=208&pid=1436>
The Web site of the American Jewish Committee offers a pro-Israeli perspective that is largely supportive of US policy.

Further Reading:
Friedman, Thomas L. *From Beirut to Jerusalem.* Anchor, 1990.
Peters, Joan. *From Time Immemorial. The Origins of the Arab-Jewish Conflict over Palestine.* JKAP Publishers, 2001.
Said, Edward W. *The End of the Peace Process: Oslo and After.* Knopf, 2001.

CRSO

MINORITY LANGUAGES

Throughout human history, numerous languages have lived and died with their speakers. With the rise of nation-state ideology, centralized governments, unified education, and mass media, languages are becoming extinct at a much faster pace than before. Arguments for preserving linguistic diversity as part of the global human heritage and culture seem to be inherently in conflict with efforts to build unified states and with increased globalization. Many of the languages that are considered "oppressively imposed" majority languages in certain countries are themselves a minority language when viewed from an international perspective, their own existence threatened by global languages.

PROS

Any language is a reflection of human culture and is an invaluable cultural artifact. Humanity suffers a great loss when languages become extinct. Linguistic diversity deserves no less protection and care than does racial diversity or biodiversity.

CONS

In the course of human progress languages naturally disappear; it is normal. History is replete with examples of even the greatest languages dying out and new ones coming to prominence; this evolution has nothing tragic about it. English, the predominant international language, may itself break apart into several languages just as Latin did.

Currently about 100 languages enjoy the status of official or state languages, promoted through national education systems. This is very disadvantageous for minority languages. Minority languages deserve official protection. No language should be a victim in the name of statehood.

Existence of many languages within one state is destructive and hinders its development. A healthy state and national ideology are impossible without a single language. Support of minority languages is potentially dangerous because of the threat posed to national unity. Only through one lingua franca were modern industrial states able to reach their level of economic development. Unity means progress.

The spread and domination of "global" languages are the legacy of colonialism; these languages are an example of cultural imperialism. Depriving minorities of their linguistic rights is denying their right to an identity.

Other than the mother tongue, the speaker has a choice and a right to speak the language he pleases. Globalization supports multilingualism. As in any evolutionary process, humans discard languages that are no longer useful and adopt those that are most practical for them.

The death of minority languages negatively reflects on the intellectual linguistic capacity of humans. Because language is the means of developing the intellect, less linguistic diversity equals less intellectual diversity. Moreover, each extinct language contained irrecoverable information that could have greatly contributed to human knowledge had it survived.

The adoption of widespread languages brings many economic gains and results in more efficient communication and education programs. Historically, those nations that were able to unify their language were also able to reach the greatest level of development.

Sample Motions:
    This House supports protection of minority languages.
    This House would not give special status to minority languages.
    This House agrees that there should be only one official language.

Web Links:
    • Language Rights. <www.linguistic-declaration.org>
    Universal Declaration of Linguistic Rights represents a movement for equal rights for all language communities.
    • Multilingualism. <http://www.linguasphere.org>
    A research network devoted to the study of multilingualism.
    • U.S. English. <http://www.us-english.org>
    American nongovernmental organization lobbying to make English the official language of the United States.
    • World Languages. <http://www.ethnologue.com>
    A comprehensive resource on languages of the world, with a database of 6,500 languages.

Further Reading:
    Crowley, Terry. *An Introduction to Historical Linguistics.* Oxford University Press, 1998.
    Crystal, David. *Language Death.* Cambridge University Press, 2000.
    Pennycook, Alastair. *The Cultural Politics of English As an International Language.* Addison-Wesley, 1996.
    Skutnabb-Kangas, Tove, Robert Phillipson, and Mart Rannut, eds. *Linguistic Human Rights: Overcoming Linguistic Discrimination.* Mouton de Gruyter, 1995.

CRSO

MONARCHY, ABOLITION OF

Although the United Kingdom (UK) has perhaps the best-known monarchy in the world, it is far from unique. Denmark, Sweden, Norway, the Netherlands, Belgium, and Spain also function as constitutional monarchies, as do Japan and Thailand. Hereditary rulers in Africa and the Middle East (e.g., Morocco, Jordan, Lesotho, Kuwait, Saudi Arabia) still retain a great deal of real power. Are these heads of state anachronisms who should be swept away in the spirit of true democracy, or do they have much to commend them at a time when the leaders of many new republics still struggle to find popular legitimacy?

PROS

The concept of monarchy is undemocratic. If the monarch retains any significant political powers, these are unjustifiable. Why should the opinion of one person, in office by accident of birth, be able to influence the outcome of elections or of political decision making? Monarchy may also be used to prop up other unjustifiable elements within government, for example the House of Lords in the UK.

The concept of monarchy is also inegalitarian. Even if the monarchy retains little or no political power, its presence sustains the traditional class system, sending a message that the class you are born into matters more than what you make of yourself. This can stifle aspirations and lead to a culture of deference that does not value the entrepreneur or individual ability and initiative. A system of royal honors may be used to tie achievers into the traditional social structures, making radical social and political change less possible.

The costs of monarchy are unjustifiable. Typically monarchs and their immediate family receive substantial amounts of money from the state to maintain luxurious lifestyles. The state also spends a great deal to maintain and run palaces and other royal residences, which are seldom accessible to the general public that supports them through taxes. Security costs are also very high.

Royal families have become national embarrassments. In an age of mass media, monarchies are no longer able to maintain the mystique that once set them apart from the common folk. Instead kings, queens, princes, and princesses are revealed to be mortal, fallible, and sometimes foolish. As their wardrobes, squabbles, and failing marriages have become constant sources of media scru-

CONS

Constitutional monarchy is a very effective political system. A hereditary head of state acts as an important element of continuity within a democratic system. The real powers of European monarchs are negligible. (In theory a British ruler can veto an act of Parliament, but none has done so since the early eighteenth century.) As figures above the political conflicts of the day, monarchs retain an important symbolic role as a focus for national unity. In Britain their right "to advise, encourage and warn" the prime minister has acted as a check against overly radical policies. In Spain, King Juan Carlos actually faced down a military coup in the 1980s.

Monarchy acts as a guardian of a nation's heritage, a living reminder of the events and personalities that have shaped it. As such it is a powerful focus for loyalty and a source of strength in times of crisis, as well as a reminder of enduring values and traditions. Separating the positions of head of state and head of government also makes great practical sense: The monarch undertakes much of the ceremonial work at home and abroad, leaving the prime minister free to focus more on governing.

Monarchy is highly cost-effective when compared to the expense of maintaining a president with a large staff and equally stringent security requirements. Royal residences are held in trust for the nation and would incur the same upkeep costs whether a monarch inhabited them or not. Monarchy more than pays its way through its generation of tourist revenue as millions visit sites associated with royalty and through its role in promoting trade and industry abroad on royal visits.

Monarchy is preferable to an elected presidency. Presidents inevitably are associated with partisan politics and thus cannot represent the nation as monarchs can. Public trust of politicians is sinking to new lows in all countries, another reason why an elected president fails to provide a focus for national feeling. Constitutional monarchy is also a more effective system of government

tiny, any remaining respect for monarchy as an institution has waned. How many people traveling abroad like to find their head of state, and by extension their whole country, a source of amusement?

Monarchs no longer claim divine right to rule. For centuries the main justification of royal authority was a religious one. Roman Catholic rulers had their legitimacy supported by the Pope; Protestant rulers often headed their own state churches. In both cases the monarch's rightful authority was preached in church every Sunday, while the ruler in turn protected a single national church. Today societies include many faiths, and many people have no religion at all. Hardly anyone believes the monarch has a spiritual right to exercise authority. Indeed, those whose religion differs from that of the monarch (often ethnic minorities) may be alienated by the privileges granted a particular faith.

because it vests real power clearly in the hands of democratically accountable leaders with a mandate to govern but avoids all the dangers of political gridlock that can result from conflict between elected branches of government.

Monarchs can both form and lead public opinion. Although above party politics, modern monarchs have proved able to raise important and sometimes unpopular issues that would otherwise have been ignored. For example, in the UK Prince Charles has legitimized discussion of environmental issues and stimulated a lively debate about the purpose of architecture, while Princess Diana's work with AIDS sufferers helped shift public opinion.

Sample Motions:
This House would abolish the monarchy.
This House would storm the palace.
This House would rather be free citizens than loyal subjects.

Web Links:
• Australians for Constitutional Monarchy. <http://www.norepublic.com.au/>
Australian organization opposing the creation of a republic and supporting the continuation of a constitutional monarchy.
• The Centre for Republican Democracy. <http://www.centreforcitizenship.org>
Articles in support of a British republic from a radical point of view.
• Future of the Monarchy. <http://www.guardianunlimited.co.uk/monarchy/>
Special report by *The Guardian* on the contemporary British monarchy.
• Republic. <http://www.republic.org.uk/>
Offers policy statements and articles in support of an elected head of state for Great Britain.

Further Reading:
Freedland, Jonathan. *Bring Home the Revolution: The Case for a British Republic.* Fourth Estate, 1999.
Winterton, George. *Monarchy to Republic: Australian Republican Government.* Oxford University Press, 1995.

CℜℰƆ

NATIONAL TESTING

Responding to mounting concerns that the American educational system was failing its students, Congress passed the No Child Left Behind Act (2001), which mandates that states develop annual assessments (tests) of learning and skills mastered. The scores on these state tests are then compared with those from a sampling of state students who have taken the National Assessment of Educational Progress (NAEP). The intent is to use the results of these tests to chart national academic progress and provide extra help for schools and students who are falling behind. Education in the United States has historically been the responsibility of states and localities; this measure vastly expands federal oversight of education. Many advocates believe this approach to improving the nation's schools is wrong and will not accomplish its objective. Others argue that the only way to know how schools and students are performing is to measure them against other schools and other students in other states.

PROS

A national curriculum for most core subjects already exists without school boards and local communities even realizing it. Most high school students are preparing for standardized college entrance exams and therefore study what is needed to do well on these tests. Also, only a few textbook companies produce texts for high school students. When localities select one of these textbooks, they are, in effect, agreeing to what amounts to a national curriculum. Besides, students across the country should learn the same skills.

As long as school boards and localities follow the national curriculum, student success on the test will follow. Drilling and "teaching to the test" occur only when schools make a decision to test without altering their curriculums. Students undeniably need to have certain basic skills and subject mastery when they graduate. The National Assessment of Educational Progress and the state-developed assessments will test those; the school day affords plenty of time for students to learn the basics and still participate in additional activities and attend classes that go beyond the basics.

The entire reason that public education in America was founded was to develop a more productive workforce. Although education by itself is a worthy goal, ultimately what we want for our children is for them to be successful individuals who are able to earn a living when they graduate from high school or college. Focusing on word choices that may also be used in the business world is just a distracter, used by opponents of national testing to shift the debate away from what really needs to happen in our nation's schools.

In a society where education is so important to success, we must make sure our schools are performing for our nation's children. The primary reason for national standards and assessment is to make schools and teachers accountable for what goes on in the classroom. If schools and teachers are doing a good job, they have nothing to fear as we move to a national system of accountability through assessment.

Developing acceptable national standards is not easy, but other countries have demonstrated that creating good standard tests that motivate students and teachers is possible. Excellence is created by bringing together the right people, examining textbooks, and looking at standards already put in place by many national teach-

CONS

The mandate for a national test makes every locality teach the same curriculum. Each state and locality should be able to determine its own curriculum as schools across the country are very different and should be able to make decisions at the local level on what will be taught within their classrooms. Requiring national testing removes the traditional rights of localities to adapt to community standards and desires when making curriculum decisions.

Mandating a national test will result in teachers "teaching to the tests." Students will face days of learning how to take tests at the expense of learning skills and knowledge that will help them become good citizens and contribute in meaningful ways to society. They will become good test takers but will miss out on the joy of learning for learning's sake. Subjects like art and music that are not covered on the standardized tests could be cut. Our children's education would become narrowly focused on a yearly test.

Using a national test to determine if schools and students are working oversimplifies education. Advocates of national testing use terms that are more specific to business, as if children are simply widgets coming out at the end of an assembly line. Proponents of national testing use terms like "setting objectives," "getting results," and "the bottom line" when talking about our nation's children. We cannot let the unethical, corrupt, and profit-driven world of business encroach into our nation's classrooms.

Using a national test to determine if students are mastering material is unfair and will drive good teachers out of our classrooms, making existing problems worse. A better alternative is a broad-based assessment, which looks at multiple measures of what a student has learned. Instead of testing a student on one day, a multiple-measure assessment uses teacher evaluations, teacher-created tests, and student demonstrations that occur over the entire school year. This would especially benefit students who are not good test takers.

The idea of national standards may seem like a good one until you start to actually try to create the standards that teachers must teach to. Agreeing what must be taught is difficult enough in a local setting; nationally such agreement is probably not achievable. Which historic figures should all students learn about? What

er's associations. In the United States, the quality of education that students receive depends on what state, county, and town they live in and even in what part of town they reside. This violates the principle of equality that is fundamental to the values of our country. If all teachers are expected to achieve the same standards, the quality of education for all children can go up.

parts of history are most important? Also, good standards are difficult to craft. Standards are either too vague so the test makers and teachers do not know what material to focus on, or they are too detailed so that teachers and students are overwhelmed by the sheer number of subjects that must be mastered.

Sample Motions:

This House would ban national testing.

This House believes that national standards are more valuable than locally developed curriculums.

This House believes that national standards will have a detrimental effect on education.

This House believes that national standards promote equality in education.

Web Links:

• Education Commission of the States (ECS). <http://www.ecs.org/ecsmain.asp?page=/html/issues.asp?am=1>
Offers a wealth of information about the practical implications of national testing.

• National Education Association (NEA). <http://www.nea.org/accountability>
Site maintained by the major national organization that opposed national standards; currently focuses on the implementation of the initiative.

• PBS Frontline: Testing Our Schools. <http://www.pbs.org/wgbh/pages/frontline/shows/schools>
This companion Web site to the PBS show *Frontline* presents a balanced overview of the issue of national testing.

Further Reading:

Ohanian, Susan. *One Size Fits Few: The Folly of Educational Standards.* Heinemann, 1999.

Orfield, Gary, and Mindy Kornhaber, eds. *Raising Standards or Raising Barriers?: Inequality and High Stakes Testing in Public Education.* Century Foundation Press, 2001.

Tucker, Marc S., and Judy B. Codding. *Standards for Our Schools: How to Set Them, Measure Them, and Reach Them.* Jossey-Bass, 1998.

CRSO

NATION-STATES

The question of whether the nation-state has a viable future in the world of globalization becomes especially important with a growing number of challenges to the very idea of sovereignty. As such, the question is not simply "globalization: good or evil?", but whether the current international order (largely based on a nation-state framework dating to the Treaty of Westphalia of 1648) can survive in a globalized world. In this debate, the nation-state is defined as a stable entity with inviolable borders that encompass its culture and economy and contains a population that has a sense of national identity. It has an equal standing to all nation-states before international law regardless of its size and power.

PROS

Perceiving the world as a collection of distinct nation-states is still viable as a construct of the world order. Nation-states remain formidable and will be able to resist the tide of globalization for centuries. Human nature wants to remain separate and equal, maintaining an identity and marking and defending certain territory. No amount of internationalization can destroy the system that has worked successfully for almost 400 years.

CONS

In the near future the present framework of nation-states will be replaced by loose federations of countries, regional organizations, enormous transnational corporations, and international organizations. Politics based on national identity will die when technology and cultural and economic advances create global social and cultural cohesion. Globalization is too strong to resist, and any nation that tries to do so will be pushed to the margins of the world order.

PROS	CONS
What we are seeing is not globalization but growing regionalism, which people fear may challenge the nation-state.	Globalization is getting stronger. In fact, the domination of the world order by one superpower threatens the nation-state.
No viable alternative to the current order exists. The nation-state is the best system available for preserving cultures and institutions. Depriving people of their national identity for the sake of globalization is a violation of human rights.	Growing federalism and regionalism in areas like Europe have proved that humans can overcome their parochial concerns This combination of federalism and regional government is likely to be replaced by global government in the future.
Ongoing secessionist movements are evidence that no amount of unification can keep transnational "countries" intact. Numerous ethnic and national groups are fighting for their own nation-states, and this trend will continue.	The system of nation-states is outdated. It generates conflict and cannot guarantee global order. The ideology of the nation-state justifies violence in the name of the nation and thus runs counter to humanity's goals of global peace and security. Forcing people to remain loyal to their nations often results in human rights violations.

Sample Motions:
This House believes that the nation-state system does not describe the current international order.
This House should endorse nation-states against globalization.
This House holds that nation-states have no future.

Web Links:
• Advanced Research on the Europeanisation of the Nation-State. <http://www.arena.uio.no>
Provides links as well as an annotated list of journal articles and books on nationalism.
• The Globalist. <http://www.theglobalist.com>
Daily online magazine on key issues before the global community.
• The Nationalism Project. <http://www.nationalismproject.org>
Provides essays, articles, bibliographies, book abstracts and reviews, and links to nationalism-related information.
• Nations, States and Politics. <http://www.scholiast.org/nations>
Research program on the changes in Europe with a primary focus on the role of the nation-state.
• UN Report on Globalization and Nation-State. <http://www.un.org/Depts/dda/speech/07apr2001.hrm>
A page devoted to political theory as it applies to nations and states.

Further Reading:
Friedman, Thomas L. *The Lexus and the Olive Tree: Understanding Globalization.* Farrar, Straus & Giroux, 2000.
Gould, Carol, and Pasquale Paquino, eds. *Cultural Identity and the Nation-State.* Rowman and Littlefield, 2001.
Holton, R. J. *Globalization and the Nation-State.* Macmillan, 1998.
Huntington, Samuel P. *The Clash of Civilizations and the Remaking of World Order.* Simon and Schuster, 1996.
Soros, George. *George Soros on Globalization.* Public Affairs, 2002.

CR8O

NAZI WAR CRIMINALS, PROSECUTION OF

Following World War II, many of those responsible for war crimes escaped arrest and prosecution; the evidence against them was often subsequently lost or destroyed. Since the collapse of the Soviet bloc after the Cold War, much of this evidence has been rediscovered, and many criminals identified and prosecuted. These trials frequently raise the question of whether men in their 80s should be tried for crimes committed over 50 years ago.

PROS

No matter how long ago these crimes were committed, their horrific nature can leave no doubt that their perpetrators must be hunted to the ends of the Earth. That time has elapsed is not a legal defense. They would have been prosecuted if evidence had been available at the end of the war. We must mete out equal justice to all war criminals. The statute of limitations never runs out on murder.

We owe it to those who perished to fight on in their name against bigotry, and to prosecute those responsible for their deaths. If we do not, then they died in vain.

Holocaust survivors are among those most in favor of prosecution, and we should not make assumptions on their behalf. Nor should we insult them by publicly exculpating their torturers and refusing to prosecute them.

With the terrible genocide and "ethnic cleansing" of recent times, we need to send a signal to criminals that they will pay for their crimes. Otherwise leaders will continue to implement such policies, believing themselves safe from retribution.

Trials will remind the world of the terrible event and promote greater peace.

CONS

At some point prosecution of crimes committed so long ago serves no purpose. The people uncovered now were usually very young and of low rank. Frequently they are not German and cooperated with the Nazis out of fear. Most of the major figures responsible for atrocities are now dead, and their crimes are remembered in many Holocaust museums. Prosecuting in these circumstances, and after such a long time, serves no purpose.

Although prosecuting the architects of the "Final Solution," who are all dead now, might have made sense, such reasoning is less relevant to the low-level participants we are dealing with here. These people were merely following orders and did not necessarily believe in the cause that they felt compelled to follow. On a more practical level, as experience has shown, such prosecutions are likely to fail, given the problems of identification and proof after so much time.

Trials like these are not in the best interest of the victims, who may suffer incredible trauma from being forced to testify (possibly against their will if they have been subpoenaed). We must not risk opening old wounds in the name of retributive justice.

Are genocides based on rational calculations? The diversion of German resources to the Final Solution was a major reason why Hitler lost the war. Legal threats are not likely to deter war criminals, who are driven by fanatical hatred.

In fact, prosecuting such elderly people is likely to provoke sympathy for them, possibly leading to a resurgence of activity by the far right.

Sample Motions:
    This House would prosecute war criminals.
    This House would hunt them down.

Web Links:
    • Holocaust Study Resources. <http://www.hum.huji.ac.il/Dinur/internetresources/holocauststudies.htm>
    Extensive site with links to information on historical and educational resources, photo archives, museums and memorials,

and survivors.
- The Holocaust Teacher Resource Center. <http://www.holocaust-trc.org/>
Provides teachers, students, and the general public lesson plans, book reviews, bibliographies, exhibits, and lectures on the Holocaust.
- The Jewish Resources Site. <http://www.us-israel.org/jsource/holo.html>
Links to resources on the Holocaust and the international response to it.

Further Reading:
Rosenbaum, Alan. *Prosecuting Nazi War Criminals*. Westview, 1997.
Wiesenthal, Simon. *The Sunflower: On the Possibilities and Limits of Forgiveness*. Schocken, 1998.

CRSO

NUCLEAR VS. RENEWABLE ENERGY

Since the mid-1980s, nuclear power has been a major source of electricity in the United States, second only to coal. Yet the future of nuclear power in the US and the rest of the world is uncertain. The US Department of Energy predicts that the use of nuclear fuel will have dropped dramatically by 2020, by which time over 40% of capacity will have been retired. Currently, there are no plans to build further reactors in the US. Yet the use of nuclear energy continues to engender contentious debate, as experts predict that we may be running out of fossil fuels. There is much public fear about nuclear energy, fueled by accidents such as Chernobyl and Three Mile Island, and concern about disposal of nuclear fuel. But are there viable alternatives?

PROS

Currently, the majority of the world's electricity is generated using fossil fuels. Although estimates vary greatly about the world's supply of fossil fuels, some estimates suggest that oil could be exhausted within 50 years and coal within 25 years. Thus we must find a new source of energy. We must start to convert to nuclear energy now so there is not a major crisis when fossil fuels do run out.

Nuclear energy is clean. It does not produce gaseous emissions that harm the environment. Granted, it does produce radioactive waste, but because this is a solid it can be handled easily and stored away from population centers. Burning fossil fuels causes far more environmental damage than using nuclear reactors, even if we factor in the Chernobyl catastrophe. Consequently, nuclear energy is preferable to fossil fuels. Furthermore, as new technologies, such as fast breeder reactors, become available, they will produce less nuclear waste. With more investment, science can solve the problems associated with nuclear energy, making it even more desirable.

Unfortunately, the nuclear industry has a bad reputation for safety that is not entirely deserved. The overwhelming majority of nuclear reactors have functioned

CONS

Estimates of how long fossil fuel resources will last have remained unchanged for the last few decades. Predicting when these fuels will be depleted is virtually impossible because new deposits may be discovered and because the rate of use cannot be predicted accurately. In addition some experts estimate that the world has 350 years of natural gas. We have no current need to search for a new power source. Money spent on such exploration would be better spent on creating technology to clean the output from power stations.

Even apart from the safety issues, nuclear power presents a number of problems. First, it is expensive and relatively inefficient. The cost of building reactors is enormous and the price of subsequently decommissioning them is also huge. Then there is the problem of waste. Nuclear waste can remain radioactive for thousands of years. It must be stored for this time away from water (into which it can dissolve) and far from any tectonic activity. Such storage is virtually impossible and serious concerns have arisen over the state of waste discarded even a few decades ago.

The nuclear industry has a shameful safety record. At Three Mile Island we were minutes away from a meltdown, and at Chernobyl the unthinkable actually hap-

safely and effectively. The two major nuclear accidents, Three Mile Island and Chernobyl, were both in old style reactors, exacerbated in the latter case by lax Soviet safety standards. We are advocating new reactors, built to the highest safety standards. Such reactors have an impeccable safety record. Perhaps the best guarantee of safety in the nuclear industry is the increasing transparency within the industry. Many of the early problems were caused by excessive control due to the origin of nuclear energy from military applications. As a civilian nuclear industry develops, it becomes more accountable.

We must examine the alternatives to nuclear energy. For the reasons explained above, we can rule out fossil fuels immediately. We also see enormous problems with other forms of energy. The most efficient source of renewable energy has been hydroelectric power. However, this usually creates more problems than it solves. Building a large dam necessarily floods an enormous region behind the dam, displacing tens of thousands of people. Dams also cause enormous damage to the ecology and incur enormous social and cultural costs. Solar energy has never lived up to expectations because it is hugely inefficient. Wind energy is only marginally better, with an unsightly wind farm the size of Texas needed to provide the energy for Texas alone. The great irony is that not only are most renewable sources inefficient but many are also ecologically unsound! The opposition to building wind farms in certain areas has been just as strong as the opposition to nuclear power because wind farms destroy the scenery.

The nuclear industry is a major employer. It creates numerous jobs and, with investment, will create even more.

pened. The effects on the local people and the environment were devastating. The fallout from Chernobyl can still be detected in our atmosphere. True, modern nuclear reactors are safer, but they are not perfectly safe. Disaster is always possible. Nuclear power stations have had a number of "minor" accidents. The industry has told us that these problems will not happen again, but time and time again they recur. We have to conclude that the industry is too dominated by the profit motive to really care about safety and too shrouded in secrecy to be accountable. In addition, the nuclear industry has had a terrible impact on those living around power plants. The rate of occurrence of certain types of cancer, such as leukemia, is much higher in the population around nuclear plants.

Although alternative energy is not efficient enough to serve the energy needs of the world's population today, it could, with investment in all these methods, be made efficient enough to serve humankind. We are not advocating a blanket solution to every problem. Many dam projects could have been replaced by solar power had the technology been available. In addition, most countries usually have at least one renewable resource that they can use: tides for islands, the sun for equatorial countries, hot rocks for volcanic regions, etc. Consequently, any country can, in principle, become energy self-sufficient with renewable energy. The global distribution of uranium is hugely uneven (much more so than for fossil fuels); accordingly, the use of nuclear power gives countries with uranium deposits disproportionate economic power. Uranium could conceivably become subject to the same kind of monopoly that the Organization of Petroleum Exporting Countries has for oil. This prevents countries from achieving self-sufficiency in energy production.

Suggesting that nuclear power is the only employment provider is completely fatuous. Energy production will always provide roughly the same number of jobs. If spending on the nuclear industry were redirected to renewable energy, then jobs would simply move from the one to the other.

Sample Motions:
This House would look to the atom.
This House would go nuclear.

Web Links:
• Greenpeace International: Nuclear. <http://www.greenpeace.org/~nuclear/>
Information on the organization's campaigns against nuclear fuels and weapons.

Further Reading:

Berinstein, Paula. *Alternative Energy: Facts, Statistics, and Issues.* Oryx Press, 2001.

Blair, Cornelia, Nancy R. Jacobs, and Jacquelyn F. Quiram. *Energy: An Issue of the 90s.* Information Plus, 1999.

Makhijani, Arjun, and Scott Saleska. *The Nuclear Power Deception: U.S. Nuclear Mythology from Electricity "Too Cheap to Meter" to "Inherently Safe" Reactors.* Apex, 1999.

CRATED

NUCLEAR WEAPONS

The nuclear bombs dropped on Hiroshima and Nagasaki, Japan, in 1945 forever changed the face of war, and the half-century of Cold War that followed was dominated, above all, by the threat of nuclear destruction. The Soviet Union and the United States raced to produce increasingly powerful arsenals, eventually resulting in their ability to destroy the world several times over. This nuclear arms race led to the concept of "Mutually Assured Destruction," a stalemate in which both sides knew that the use of their weapons would totally annihilate one another and potentially the whole world. The end of the Cold War changed the global situation substantially. The fear of nuclear war between superpowers was replaced by the fear of nuclear proliferation, particularly by rogue states and terrorist groups.

PROS

Nuclear weapons are morally repugnant. Over the past 50 years, we have seen a movement toward limited warfare and precision weapons that minimize the impact on civilians. Nuclear weapons have massive, indiscriminate destructive power. They can kill tens of thousands and cause catastrophic harm to the world environment.

The idea of a so-called "nuclear deterrent" no longer applies. During the Cold War, peace was maintained only by a balance of power; neither superpower had an advantage large enough to be confident of victory. However, a balance of power no longer exists. With the proliferation of nuclear weapons, some rogue states may develop the ability to strike at nations that have no nuclear weapons. Would the major nuclear powers then strike back at the aggressor? The answer is unknown. In addition, most of the emerging nuclear threats would not come from legitimate governments but from dictators and terrorist groups. Would killing thousands of civilians ever be acceptable in retaliation for the actions of extremists?

By maintaining a strategic deterrent, the current nuclear powers encourage the proliferation of weapons of mass destruction. Countries believe that being a member of the "nuclear club" increases their international status. Also, nations at odds with a country with nuclear capability feel that they must develop their own capability to protect themselves. Therefore, nuclear powers must take the lead in disarmament as an example for the rest

CONS

The use of nuclear weapons would indeed be a great tragedy; but so, to a greater or lesser extent, is any war. The reason for maintaining an effective nuclear arsenal is to prevent war. The catastrophic results of using nuclear weapons discourage conflict. The Cold War was one of the most peaceful times in history, largely because of the nuclear deterrents of the two superpowers.

The deterrent principle still stands. During the Persian Gulf War, for example, the fear of US nuclear retaliation was one of the factors that prevented Iraq from using chemical weapons against Israel. A similar fear may prevent rogue states from using nuclear weapons. Moreover, although the citizens of the current nuclear powers may oppose the use of force against civilians, their opinions would rapidly change if they found weapons of mass destruction used against them.

The nuclear genie is out of the bottle and cannot be put back in. The ideal of global nuclear disarmament is fine in theory but it will not work in practice. Nations will not disarm if they fear a rogue state has secret nuclear capability. Without the threat of a retaliatory strike, a rogue nuclear state could attack others at will.

of the world.

PROS	CONS
Nuclear weapons can fall into the wrong hands. This is particularly true in Russia, which controls the former Soviet arsenal. The military is disastrously underfunded; nuclear experts and officers accustomed to a high standard of living are now finding themselves without pay, sometimes for years. At the same time, other nations and extremist groups are willing to pay substantial sums for their services and for access to nuclear weapons. Only destroying the weapons will end the danger of someone stealing a weapon or extremists taking over a nuclear base.	While nuclear weapons can be dismantled, they cannot be easily destroyed. Special facilities are needed for storage. In addition, dismantling missiles does not destroy the weapons-grade plutonium that forms their warheads. Plutonium is the most valuable part of the missile, hence the risk of theft does not decrease and may, in fact, increase. Security at plutonium storage facilities is often inadequate; moreover, stealing a relatively small quantity of plutonium is relatively easy.

Sample Motions:
    This House would abolish nuclear weapons.
    This House would ban the bomb.

Web Links:
    • Abolition 2000. <http://www.abolition2000.org/>
    Links to sites offering general information in support of global elimination of nuclear weapons.
    • Federation of American Scientists: Nuclear Forces. <http://www.fas.org/nuke/guide/index.html>
    Maintained by an organization of scientists advocating elimination of nuclear weapons, the site offers in-depth information on the status of nuclear proliferation, terrorism, and weapons of mass destruction.

Further Reading:
    Athanasopulos, Haralambos. *Nuclear Disarmament in International Law.* McFarland, 2000

ᎤᏁᎤ

NUCLEAR WEAPONS TESTING

Efforts to stop the testing of nuclear weapons have been made for nearly as long as nuclear technology has existed. The 1963 Limited Test Ban Treaty banned tests in the atmosphere, outer space, and beneath the sea. While the 1968 Nuclear Non-Proliferation Treaty included a statement of intent to work toward the total ending of nuclear testing, a complete moratorium became feasible only when the Cold War ended. USSR president Mikhail Gorbachev in 1991 and US president George H. W. Bush in 1992 declared unilateral moratoriums on testing and were followed by other nuclear powers. The Comprehensive Test Ban Treaty (CTBT) of 1996, which ruled out any nuclear tests, has not been ratified by the 44 nations needed to put it into effect. Non-ratifiers include the United States, China, and India, although major nuclear powers like Russia and the United Kingdom have committed themselves to its strictures.

PROS

The CTBT is the best way to stop the development and proliferation of more, and more complex, nuclear weapons. The treaty not only limits the technical development of weapons but also reduces the extent to which they can be displayed, thus reducing their value as a bargaining chip and a symbol of power. The CTBT means fewer weapons in fewer countries and is therefore a valuable way of reducing nuclear tensions.

CONS

The CTBT is a misguided attempt to freeze the current nuclear power balance. It will only curtail those nations that present no real threat to global stability. In fact, by restricting these countries, the treaty can make the reality of Mutually Assured Destruction less clear and actually encourage recklessness by less stable nuclear powers.

PROS	CONS
Nuclear explosions have a massive environmental impact and cause massive harm. Large areas are irradiated by the blasts and the long-term effects of radioactive materials thrown into the atmosphere by the explosions are uncertain. Nuclear tests often involve moving people off their own lands (as with the French tests in Polynesia in 1995) and involve the destruction of habitats. Although information is scanty, the underground tests conducted in China are suspected to have caused earthquakes.	Overt testing by nuclear powers happens in only the most deserted and environmentally stable areas, for example, Siberia and the deserts of Nevada and western Australia. Thus, their environmental impact is not just minimal but much less than that of secret tests that might take place to circumvent the treaty.
The CTBT can be effective in stopping the testing of nuclear weapons. The treaty includes specific measures of redress and gives scope for wider action. Moreover, voluntary commitments to curtail nuclear testing do hold moral force. The French government waited for the end of a one-year moratorium before resuming testing in 1995.	The CTBT is toothless and unenforceable. Its only specific measure is expulsion from the treaty rights and obligations; it is likely to affect only stable nations whose nuclear armories pose the least threat. Effectively this treaty puts the tool of nuclear testing in the hands of the least scrupulous of the nuclear powers.
Verification of the test ban is now possible; the Comprehensive Test Ban Organization in Vienna is in charge of the international monitoring system, a network of stations throughout the world that can take seismic, hydro-acoustic, and infrasound measurements in all environments. These stations can also measure radionuclide levels in debris. The treaty also provides a right of inspection between signatories like those included in the US-USSR weapons reduction treaties.	Verification can never be perfect, thus uncertainty and mistrust will always be present. If nations perform covert tests, not only are they more likely to be conducted in a more dangerous environment, but such tests will also increase international tensions because of the uncertainty about the source of the resulting nuclear pollution. Further, the areas in which testing was banned by the Limited Test Ban Treaty are more likely to be used if tests are conducted secretly.
The CTBT does not threaten existing nuclear arsenals. Other aspects of nuclear weapons like guidance systems and missiles can still be tested; besides, computer modeling now does much of the work for "testing" explosions. Russia and Britain have both ratified the CTBT; neither has any intention of relinquishing its status as a nuclear power.	Computer modeling works only if it is based on data from real explosions. The less real data, the less reliable computer modeling. As new technologies develop, modeling will become increasingly unsatisfactory. Moreover, it is exactly the unexpected effects that are important in the tests. They not only allow us to ensure the weapons are working but also yield data that has been found highly useful in the peaceful nuclear industries that are specifically protected in the Non-Proliferation Treaty.
Voters in the United States, for example, overwhelmingly favor the CTBT; 73% to 16% say that the United States should ratify the treaty. World opinion in all but a few rogue states strongly favors banning nuclear testing, thus showing significant support and creating political impetus for signing the treaty.	The CTBT is a political dead duck. Political support is nonexistent (proved by the fact that many of the nations involved in its development have not ratified it). A treaty that has none of the support necessary to come into force is clearly not one worth committing time and energy to.

Sample Motions:
This House would ban nuclear testing.
This House would ratify the Comprehensive Nuclear Test Ban Treaty.
This House would ban the bomb.

Web Links:
- Coalition to Reduce Nuclear Dangers. <http://www.clw.org/coalition/index.html>
Provides information on a wide variety of issues involving nuclear weapons.
- Comprehensive Nuclear Test Ban Treaty Organization. <http://www.ctbto.org/>
Summarizes the current status of the CTBT.
- Physicians for Social Responsibility. <http://www.psr.org/ctbtpage.htm>
Offers detailed essay on the US response to the CTBT.
- US State Department Arms Control Bureau. <http://www.state.gov/t/ac/>
Information on current US policy and diplomatic negotiations on a variety of arms control issues.

Further Reading:
Arnett, Eric, ed. *Nuclear Weapons after the Comprehensive Test Ban: Implications for Modernization and Proliferation.* Oxford University Press, 1996.
Lambers, William K. *Nuclear Test Ban Treaty: A Better Shield Than Missile Defense.* Bill Lambers, 2001.
Pande, Savita. *CTBT: India and the Nuclear Test Ban.* South Asia Books, 1996.

CRSO

OLYMPIC DREAM, DEATH OF THE

The Olympic flame is still burning, but is it an illusion? The ancient Olympic Games had as their motto "faster, higher, stronger," but perhaps a new triad should replace it: "drugs, commercialization, corruption." The question is probably whether any of these has suffocated athletes' desire to compete "for the glory of sport."

PROS

The use of performance-enhancing drugs is widespread at the Olympics and makes the victories of those who take them meaningless. New drugs such as the growth hormone EPO are very difficult to detect, but the Olympic authorities are doing little to address the problem.

The man who revived the Olympics at the end of the nineteenth century, Baron de Coubertin, insisted that educating the public in the spirit of fair play and in the importance of taking part rather than winning were just as important as the Games themselves. Today, the Games are played by "Dream Teams" of highly trained athletes—individuals we can watch with awe but never hope to copy.

The massive commercialization of the Games erodes

CONS

We should have some sympathy for athletes. Very often, the team's coach compels them to take drugs. There are stories of Chinese swimmers eating steroid-laced noodles. The International Olympic Committee (IOC) Conference in February 1999 recommended that coaches take the Olympic oath as well as athletes. Olympic authorities are embracing new techniques to detect drugs. A new mass-spectroscopy unit was installed for the first time at the 1996 Atlanta Games. An Independent Anti-Doping Agency was established in Sydney in 2000 as was a testing technique that can detect if an athlete has taken growth hormones up to six months earlier. The battle is being won: 12 cases of doping in 1984; two in 1996. The IOC is coming down hard on those who take drugs: It has introduced a two-year ban for the first offense.

The Olympic movement gives considerable funding to community sports programs to teach fair play. Meanwhile, "Dream Teams" are essential to fulfilling the basic Olympic aims: faster, higher, stronger. Surely watching the Games can only be a good thing because the competition gives young athletes a goal toward which they can work.

The Olympics offer no monetary prizes, yet the Olym-

the idea of participation for its own sake. With so much prize money at stake, winning at all costs is the inevitable aim. The sponsors and their heavy hands, e.g., interrupting television coverage of an event for a commercial, seem more important than the sport. Corporate sponsorship concentrates on athletes from the richest countries. The US teams, for example, benefit from huge funding and can thus train to far higher levels than can those of developing countries. This prevents competition on an equal footing, one feature of the Olympic dream.

The Olympics have been hijacked so many times for political purposes that competition "for the glory of sport" cannot help but have been smothered. The 1972 Munich disaster is the most horrifying: Palestinian terrorists killed nine Israeli athletes. Yet the Games were only temporarily suspended. Are those who play the Games less important than the spectacle of the Games? When the US boycotted the 1980 Moscow Games to protest the Soviet invasion of Afghanistan, the idea of sport for its own sake was devalued still further.

The IOC and many national Olympic committees lack integrity. This kills the Games' spirit. For example, several of the judges who selected Nagano for the 1998 Winter Olympics, Sydney for the 2000 Olympics, and Salt Lake City for the 2002 Winter Olympics are known to have taken bribes from the winning cities and from some of the other competing cities as well.

pics are still "the" competition to win. A few commercial breaks in coverage is a small price to pay for billions of people to be able to see the Games. The sponsors do not have significant control over the Games. The IOC has the stronger hand and a wide choice of sponsors. Without any sponsorship, many poor countries could not send teams. Sponsorship is the key to beginning the process of putting all countries on an equal footing.

Why should we expect the Olympics to transcend the much graver matters of world politics? The Games may be an excellent way to bring athletes of different nationalities together, but the Olympics cannot do the work of the United Nations as well. A boycott was the only real option open to the US in 1980. The UN had condemned the USSR's invasion of Afghanistan, and approximately 80% of the American people were demanding a boycott.

Whatever goes on in the committees cannot affect the Olympic dream itself—that is carried on the shoulders of the athletes. It is possible to be faster, higher, and stronger wherever the Games are held, so money matters are detached from the Olympic dream.

Sample Motions:
This House believes that the Olympic dream is dead.
This House believes that the battle against doping in sport is being lost.
This House wants to win at all costs.

Web Links:
• International Olympic Committee. <http://www.olympic.org>
Official Web site of the Olympic Games provides information on the Games since 1896 and on future Games.

Further Reading:
Jennings, Andrew, and Clare Shambrook. *The Great Olympic Swindle: When the World Wanted Its Games Back.* Simon & Schuster, 2000.
Lensky, Helen, and Varda Burstyn. *Inside the Olympic Industry: Power, Politics and Activism.* State of New York University Press, 2000.
Schaffer, Kay, and Sidonie Smith, eds. *The Olympics at the Millennium: Power, Politics and the Games.* Rutgers University Press, 2000.

CR≋SO

OUTING GAY CELEBRITIES

"Outing" is the practice of making public a person's sexual orientation against his or her will. In a March 1990 article in Outweek, *Michelangelo Signorile named the millionaire Malcolm Forbes as gay, one month after his death. This article prompted a furious debate about the ethics of "outing." Signorile founded the activist group Queer Nation, which made headlines by distributing posters identifying celebrities, including Jodie Foster, as gay.*

PROS

The 1990s saw a welcome trend toward the full inclusion of gays and lesbians in society, but much work remains. Homophobia and discrimination are still linked to the perception that gays are a tiny minority of the population. That so many gays remain "in the closet" (pretending to be heterosexual) contributes to this misperception. Outing celebrities increases the number of gay role models and improves the public's perception of gays, making the process of coming out easier for all gay men and women.

Celebrities enter into an unspoken contract with their fans. In return for the vast amounts of adoration and money, they must surrender a good deal of their privacy. The public has the right to know about the people who profit immeasurably from its support.

Outing celebrities is particularly justifiable in the political world, where sexuality can be linked to legislation. Many politicians are responsible for laws that affect sexual practice, such as the age of consent. Closeted politicians are hypocrites if they win the support of homophobic voters on the basis of their "heterosexuality."

Outing can actually be beneficial in the long run. Most closeted gays and lesbians regret having to live a secret life and would prefer to be honest, but fear persuades them to remain silent. Ultimately, outing ends their fear and helps them lead honest lives.

CONS

The gay rights movement has made such progress that these radical tactics are unnecessary. Many celebrities are now openly gay and can be role models to young gays and lesbians. The "need" for outing is thus nonexistent. Everyone has a right to privacy, including sexual privacy.

The public's obsession with celebrities has gone too far. For many, sexuality is very private information and is not something that celebrities must share with their fans.

In a democracy politicians pander to majority opinion. If a society is homophobic, then the only way a gay politician can succeed is to remain in the closet. It is naïve to expect politicians to sacrifice their careers for the sake of sexual disclosure.

Many people still condemn homosexuality Thus coming out of the closet can bring shame and the destruction of relationships. When a homosexual decides to come out, then he is often fully prepared for the consequences. Thus coming out is a personal decision, and an individual should be allowed to do it in his own time, not at the time chosen by someone who may not understand his situation fully.

Sample Motions:
  This House would force celebrities out of the closet.
  This House would name (but not shame) gay celebrities.

Web Links:
  • Does Human Dignity Require Outing Homosexuals? <http://www.artsci.wustl.edu/~rjbroach/wsouting.html>
  Academic article evaluating outing from a philosophical standpoint.

Further Reading:

Gross, Larry. *Contested Closets: The Politics and Ethics of Outing.* University of Minnesota Press, 1993.
Johansson, Warren. *Outing: Shattering the Conspiracy of Silence.* Haworth, 1994.
Mohr, Richard. *Gay Ideas: Outing and Other Controversies.* Beacon, 1994.
Murphy, Timothy. *Gay Ethics: Controversies in Outing, Civil Rights, and Sexual Science.* Haworth, 1995.

CRISO

OVERPOPULATION AND CONTRACEPTION

Despite scientific advances, no amount of technological innovation will solve the problem that Earth has only finite resources. Attention has therefore turned to the question of population growth; preserving the environment would be far easier if natural resources were shared among fewer people. Environmental degradation will accelerate if the rate of global population increase is not slowed. Over the years, much debate has been heard about whether widespread use of contraception is the solution to the population explosion in the developing world.

PROS

Population is a major problem today; the world population of 6 billion is expected to reach 10.7 billion by 2050. Given the strain on global resources and the environment today, an environmental disaster is clearly waiting to happen as the population time bomb ticks away. While reproduction is a fundamental human right, rights come with responsibilities. We have a responsibility to future generations, and population control is one method of ensuring that natural resources will be available for our descendants.

Contraception is an easy and direct method of slowing population growth. The popularity and success of contraception in the developed world is testament to this.

Contraception can reduce family size. With smaller families, a greater proportion of resources can be allocated to each child, improving his or her opportunities for education, health care, and nutrition.

CONS

Many population forecasts are exaggerated and do not take into account the different phases of population growth. A nation's population may grow rapidly in the early stages of development, but with industrialization and rising levels of education, the population tends to stabilize at the replacement rate. Even if the quoted figure of 10.7 billion by 2050 is true, this is likely to remain steady thereafter, as the developing nations of today achieve maturity. Developed nations can use alternative methods to solve the environmental and social problems arising from overpopulation. All available options should be exhausted before making the drastic decision to curb reproductive rights.

Implementing widespread contraception presents technical difficulties. The cost can be prohibitive, especially when considered on a national scale. Large numbers of trained workers are required to educate the public on the correct use of contraceptives. Even with an investment in training, birth control methods may be used incorrectly, especially by the illiterate and uneducated.

Many agricultural families need to have as many children as possible. Children's farm work can contribute to the food the family eats or be a source of income. In an undeveloped nation without a good social welfare system, children are the only security for old age. Furthermore, having a large number of children usually ensures that some reach adulthood; child mortality is very high in the developing world. Until the child mortality rate is reduced, families will not use contraception.

PROS	CONS
Contraception empowers women by giving them reproductive control. Delaying pregnancy gives opportunities for education, employment, and social and political advancement. Birth control can therefore be a long-term investment in political reform and offers some protection of women's rights.	Women may not have the choice to use contraceptives. In many developing nations, males dominate in sexual relationships and make the decisions about family planning. Religious pressure to have as many children as possible may also be present. Birth control may not even be socially acceptable. Are women's rights advanced by contraception? We don't really know. In reality, contraception typically is one element of a national population control policy. Such policies (e.g., China's one-child policy), when considered as a whole, often violate women's rights.
Contraception can help save the lives of women in the developing world. The lack of obstetric care and the prevalence of disease and malnutrition contribute to a high rate of mortality among pregnant mothers and their newborn children. This risk can be over 100 times that of mothers in developed countries.	While birth control should be a priority of many developing nations, such nations often need to address other, more pressing, issues. Providing basic health care and proper sanitation can improve the health of an entire family, in addition to reducing child mortality (often a major reason for parents wanting to have a large number of children). Spending on such infrastructure and services is a far better long-term investment than providing contraception.
Supporting contraception is an easy way for the developed world to help the developing world cope with the population crisis and the consequent stifling of development. Contraceptives, compared to monetary aid, are less likely to be misdirected into the pockets of corrupt officials.	Contraception is a controversial issue in both developed and developing nations. Some religions prohibit it. This can reduce the success of birth control programs in the developing world and diminish the political appeal of (and thus funding for) pro-contraception policies in the developed world.

Sample Motions:
 This House supports contraception in developing nations.
 This House would cap population growth in the developing world.
 This House believes that there are too many people.
 This House believes that there isn't enough room.

Web Links:
 • Global Population Information. <http://www.popnet.org/>
 Provides a comprehensive directory of population-related resources.
 • OverPopulation.Com. <http://www.overpopulation.com/>
 Extensive site with information on a wide variety of population issues. Includes a good overview essay on the overpopulation controversy.
 • Paul Ehrlich and the Population Bomb. <http://www.pbs.org/kqed/population_bomb/>
 Site connected with a PBS show on Paul Ehrlich, who in 1968 wrote the influential book *The Population Bomb,* explaining how population growth damages the Earth's ability to sustain life.
 • The United Nations Population Information Network. <http://www.un.org/popin/>
 Offers links to population information on the UN systems Web sites.

Further Reading:
 Cohen, Joel. *How Many People Can the Earth Support?* Norton, 1995.
 Zuckerman, Ben, and David Jefferson, eds. *Human Population and the Environmental Crisis.* Jones and Bartlett, 1996.

CRULO

OVERSEAS MANUFACTURING

In the new era of globalization, American companies often locate their manufacturing operations in countries outside the United States. Many countries are eager to attract American industries and the employment they bring; overseas factories usually can be run at substantially lower costs largely because wages for foreign workers are much lower than wages for American workers. The treatment of these foreign employees has engendered many questions and raised many issues. Their working conditions may not be safe; they may be asked to work unreasonable hours; they may be paid less than a living wage. In some parts of the world, many factory workers are school-age children. Increasingly, the public is putting pressure on American corporations to improve the treatment of their foreign workers and to provide the same kind of safeguards that protect American workers.

PROS

Companies build factories overseas for one primary reason: Foreign workers are cheaper. When companies are driven by the profit motive, they have an incentive to pay as little as possible and to skimp on equipment and procedures that would provide comfort and safety to workers. Workers need to be protected from corporations that care more about profits than people.

Some foreign governments are so eager to attract American investment that they favor management over labor. They do not protect their own citizens with strong labor laws, and they do not guarantee workers the right to form unions. Workers are at the mercy of their employers.

American companies located in foreign countries have no incentive for making commitments to the local community. If the workers become too expensive, or if the companies are forced to spend money to improve conditions, they simply pull out and move to another country with cheaper workers and lower standards.

Because they have no union protections, workers are often asked to work absurdly long hours, with no extra pay for overtime, and in dangerous conditions with hazardous materials. They fear that if they complain, or refuse to work when demanded, they will be fired and replaced by someone who is desperate for a job.

Child labor is condoned in many countries where American companies do business, but American companies should refuse to take part in this abuse. There is little hope for the future of countries where a child must provide manual labor, instead of getting an education.

CONS

Manufacturers know that mistreating workers does not pay in the long run. They know that a healthy and a happy workforce is going to be more productive and give their operation long-term stability. Certainly manufacturers care about the bottom line, and it is precisely that concern that motivates them to treat their workers well.

The presence of American companies has a direct benefit on the economies of their host countries. Workers are taught skills and exposed to new technology. Moreover, a strong industrial economy has been proved to be the best way to lift people out of poverty. In time, foreign workers will achieve wages and working conditions comparable to those enjoyed by American workers today.

Wages may be low compared to US standards; however, the cost of living in these countries is also low. It is absurd, therefore, to expect American companies to pay the standard minimum US wage in a country where that wage has 10 times the buying power that it has in America.

Activists like to say that factory jobs in foreign countries are intolerable and undesirable, but the facts do not support that assertion. People are eager to work in a factory, when their alternative is making less money for a full day of backbreaking agricultural work. To the workers, jobs in American factories represent opportunities to gain a higher standard of living.

The American objection to child labor is founded on the idealistic notion that children should be in school. But in many countries where the factories operate, universal schooling is nonexistent, and the child who is thrown out of a factory job goes back on the street. In many cases, the child who does not work in a factory will simply work someplace else; in poor families, it is expected that anyone who is able to work will earn a wage to support the family.

Sample Motions:
    This House will not buy materials made in foreign sweatshops.
    This House would force American companies to let foreign workers unionize.

Web Links:
    • Solutions for a Global Problem. <http://www.sweatshops.org/>
    This Web site is sponsored by the activist organization Co-op America. It discusses "sweatshop" conditions in foreign countries
    and encourages citizens to take action to eliminate them.
    • Sweatshops for the New World Order. <http://www.fee.org/vnews.php?nid=3639>
    This essay, from the Foundation for Economic Education, argues that American protests about foreign factories are ill informed.

Further Reading:
    Featherstone, Liza, et al. *Students Against Sweatshops: The Making of a Movement.* Verso Books, 2002.
    Moran, Theodore H. *Beyond Sweatshops: Foreign Direct Investment and Globalization in Developing Nations.* Brookings Institution, 2002.
    Varley, Pamela, and Carolyn Mathiasen, eds. *The Sweatshop Quandary: Corporate Responsibility on the Global Frontier.* Investor
    Responsibility Research Center, 1998.

CRBEO

PACIFISM

*Pacifism has a long history in the United States. Although their numbers have been small, pacifists have opposed
every American war from the Revolution to the Persian Gulf War. Occasionally their voices have contributed
to policy changes, as was the case in the Vietnam War. Although the American public overwhelmingly supports
military action against terrorists in Afghanistan, pacifists are currently urging a peaceful solution to the problem
of terrorism. The debate between nonviolent objection and the use of force to achieve a goal brings up issues like
morality vs. practicality: Is violence ever constructive; and, does pacifism in the face of a threat serve to increase or
diminish evil. The debate also contrasts the lives lost in war with the liberty that might be lost if war is avoided
and thus raises the difficult issue of sacrificing lives to preserve a principle.*

PROS

Violence is never justified under any circumstances. Life is sacred, and no cause or belief allows a person to take the life of another.

Neither side in a war emerges as a victor. War rarely settles issues. (For example, World War I created the conditions that led to World War II.) War always creates suffering on both sides. Often the innocent suffer, as in the case of the firebombing of Dresden or the dropping of the atomic bomb on Hiroshima during World War II.

Pacifists believe that violence begets violence. Pacifists do not have to retreat completely from world and domestic affairs; they are not cowards. During World War I, conscientious objectors stood up against the militarism and cynical diplomacy that had led to the conflict. In many countries they were executed for their

CONS

We are not arguing that violence is of itself a good thing. We are saying that when others are using violence to endanger principles as fundamental as human rights, people have a duty to stand up against them. Not to do so would merely allow evil to spread unchecked.

Disputes do sometimes persist after wars, but often wars can lead to the resolution of some issues. For example, World War II prevented fascism from taking over Europe, and the Gulf War led to Saddam Hussein's withdrawal from Kuwait. In these cases, the failure to act would have led to the oppression of millions and permitted an aggressor to triumph.

Pacifism is a luxury that some can practice because others fight. Pacifists claim moral superiority while enjoying the liberty for which others have died. We fought both world wars to combat aggression and maintain justice. We did our moral duty in resisting tyranny.

beliefs.

PROS	CONS
When war is inevitable, pacifists can protest the cruelties of war, such as torture, attacks on civilians, and other contraventions of the Geneva Convention, in an attempt to curb violence's excesses.	This type of protest is not true pacifism, which rejects war outright. By admitting that war is sometimes inevitable, you are acknowledging that sometimes people cannot sit by and do nothing.
Great religious leaders, such as Jesus and Gandhi, have always advocated pacifism. They believe that "He who lives by the sword dies by the sword." For thousands of years the wisest thinkers have believed that violence does not end suffering, but merely increases it.	In practice, most world religions have adopted violence, in the shape of crusades or holy wars, to serve their ends. And does not the Bible advocate "an eye for an eye"? When an aggressor endangers liberty and freedom, humanity must use violence to combat him.

Sample Motions:
   This House would be pacifist.
   This House rejects violence.
   This House would turn the other cheek.

Web Links:
   • The Good War and Those Who Refuse to Fight It. <http://www.pbs.org/itvs/thegoodwar/american_pacifism.html>
   PBS Web site providing overview of pacifism in American history.
   • Pacifism. <http://www.utm.edu/research/iep/p/pacifism.htm>
   Philosophical discussion of pacifism.
   • The Paradox of War and Pacifism. <http://www.leaderu.com/socialsciences/clark.html>
   Historical discussion of pacifism from a Christian point of view.

Further Reading:
   Cooper, Sandi. *Patriotic Pacifism: Waging War on War in Europe, 1815-1914.* Oxford University Press on Demand, 1991.
   McCarthy, Colman. *All of One Peace: Essays on Nonviolence.* Rutgers University Press, 1994.

CRSO

POLITICIANS AND SPECIAL INTERESTS

Political dialogue in America is frequently peppered with accusatory references to "special interests." These special interests are organized groups that play active political roles, either through making contributions to parties and candidates, or through lobbying government officials in an attempt to influence legislation and public policy. Some special interest groups act in their economic self-interest (e.g., manufacturers' associations, unions, farmers' groups); some special interest groups act on behalf of particular segments of society (e.g., National Organization for Women, National Association for the Advancement of Colored People, AARP [formerly known as the American Association of Retired Persons], American Indian Movement); some special interest groups are dedicated to public causes or policies (e.g., Sierra Club, National Rifle Association, American Civil Liberties Union, National Right to Life Committee). Many of these groups have millions of dollars at their disposal. The question is whether this money corrupts the political system, that is, are legislators more concerned with pleasing donors and lobbyists than they are with responding to the will of average citizens?

PROS
No person who is financially dependent on someone else is truly free to serve the public good in a disinterested way. When a politician depends on huge sums of

CONS
If a politician were dependent on only one source of funding, undue influence might be a possibility. But so many special interest groups are active in Washington

money contributed by an organization, his or her vote is inevitably influenced by the wishes of that organization rather than by what is best for the country.

The size of contributions has become so large that donors certainly expect some kind of payback. A manufacturers' association will not give $100,000 away just as a gesture of good will; it expects to see its concerns favorably addressed in legislation.

For generations, lawmakers have recognized that the power of special interests can lead to corruption; more than 50 years ago, for example, Congress forbade unions from acting to influence federal elections. But the creation of political action committees (PACs) and the proliferation of soft money have allowed special interest groups to violate the spirit of the law while obeying its letter.

Money purchases access to politicians, who are more willing to make time for donors than for average citizens. Access leads naturally to influence. The average citizen is shortchanged by the current system, which favors cash-rich organizations.

Organizations often spend hundreds of millions of dollars to lobby politicians. They would not spend such sums if they did not think such expenditures were effective in helping them get what they want. Again, money clearly is shaping legislation.

that politicians get contributions from dozens, if not hundreds, of them. The influence of any one group, therefore, is negligible; even a contribution of $10,000 is only a "drop in the bucket" when campaigns cost millions.

Accusations of undue influence are often vague and unsupported by facts. Watchdog organizations like to make statistical correlations between donations and votes, but that is not real evidence that votes have been "bought." Don't forget that actually buying votes is a crime and is vigorously prosecuted.

Special interests are condemned for having too much influence, but the causal logic of the accusers is fundamentally flawed. When the National Abortion and Reproductive Rights Action League (NARAL) makes contributions to politicians, it does not buy the votes of legislators who would have voted differently on reproductive issues. Rather, NARAL gives money to candidates who have already indicated their support for policies in line with NARAL's position.

People who want to kill special interest groups are usually thinking of groups that support a position they oppose. Special interest groups span the political spectrum and represent many points of view. Indeed, the variety of groups with competing interests is an indication of a healthy and vigorous political system.

Individuals should organize themselves into groups to represent themselves more effectively. Congress passes laws that affect the daily lives of teachers, for example; surely, teachers have the right to have their voices heard—through their unions—when those laws are drawn up.

Sample Motions:
This House would change campaign finance laws to allow contributions from individuals only.
This House would lobby Congress to advance its interests.

Web Links:
• Missing the Point on Campaign Finance. <http://www.claremont.org/writings/precepts/20020321ellmers.html>
An essay from the Claremont Institute for the Study of Statesmanship and Political Philosophy that argues that the fear of special interest groups has been exaggerated.
• Money and Politics: Who Owns Democracy? <http://www.network democracy.org/map/welcome.shtml>
A project of Information Renaissance and National Issues Forums Research, this Web page discusses the pros and cons of various proposals to change the role of money in politics.
• Your Guide to the Money in U.S. Elections. <http://www.opensecrets.org/index.asp>
Web site of the Center for Responsive Politics provides data about campaign contributions by donor and by recipient. "News alerts" flag instances where contributions may have influenced congressional voting.

Further Reading:
Drew, Elizabeth. *The Corruption of American Politics: What Went Wrong and Why.* Overlook Press, 2000.

Elder, Larry. *Showdown: Confronting Bias, Lies, and the Special Interests That Divide America.* St. Martin's Press, 2002.

Judis, John B. *The Paradox of American Democracy: Elites, Special Interests, and the Betrayal of the Public Trust.* Routledge, 2001.

Phillips, Kevin. *Wealth and Democracy: A Political History of the American Rich.* Broadway Books, 2002.

CRSO

PORNOGRAPHY, BANNING OF

Most adult pornography is legal in the United States, where it is protected by the First Amendment guarantee of freedom of speech. Nevertheless, many campaigns to restrict it have been mounted. Initially such suggested restrictions were based on moral grounds, but in recent years women's groups have urged a ban because some studies have shown that pornography contributes to violence against women.

PROS

Pornography debases human interactions by reducing love and all other emotions to the crudely sexual. Sex is an important element in relationships, but it is not the be all and end all of them. Pornography also debases the human body and exploits those lured into it. It also encourages unhealthy, objectifying attitudes toward the opposite sex. Pornography is not a victimless crime. The victim is the very fabric of society itself.

Pornography helps to reinforce the side of our sexual identity that sees people as objects and debases both their thoughts and bodies. We have seen evidence of this in the way pictures of seminaked women (hardly ever men) are used in advertising. Society's acceptance of pornography leads to the objectification of women and thus directly to sexual discrimination.

Society's apparent tolerance of legal pornography encourages illegal forms, such as child pornography. Are we to allow pedophiles the "legitimate sexual exploration" of their feelings? The opposition cannot let human impulses override societal rules that protect children.

Many rapists are obsessed with pornography. It encourages them to view women as objects and helps justify their contention that women are willing participants in the act. Indeed, feminists have proposed that pornography is rape because it exploits women's bodies. Pornography serves only to encourage brutal sex crimes.

CONS

Freedom of speech is one of our most cherished rights. Censorship might be justified when free speech becomes offensive to others, but this is not the case with pornography. It is filmed legally by consenting adults for consenting adults and thus offends no one. Pornography injures no one and is a legitimate tool to stimulate our feelings and emotions in much the same way as music, art, and literature do.

Pornography is a legitimate exploration of sexual fantasy, one of the most vital parts of human life. Psychologists have confirmed the important, if not driving, role that sexual impulses play in shaping our behavior. Repressing or denying this part of our personalities is both prudish and ignorant. Consequently, pornography should be available for adults to vary their sex lives. Indeed, far from "corroding the fabric of society," pornography can help maintain and strengthen marriages by letting couples fully explore their sexual feelings.

This is not true; no "slippery slope" scenario exists. People interested in child pornography will obtain it regardless of its legal status. Human sexuality is such that mere exposure to adult pornography does not encourage individuals to explore child pornography.

Sadly, rape will exist with or without pornography. Rapists may use pornography, but pornography does not create rapists. The claim that pornography is rape is invalid. Our legal system depends on the distinction between thought and act that this claim seeks to blur. Pornography is a legitimate form of expression and enjoyment. Government should not censor it in the interests of sexual repression and prudery.

Sample Motions:
    This House believes pornography does more harm than good.
    This House would ban pornography.
    This House believes that pornography is bad for women.

Web Links:
    • American Civil Liberties Union. <http://www.aclu.org/>
    Information on court challenges to censorship, including arguments in support of a broad understanding of freedom of speech.
    • Pornography as a Cause of Rape. <http://www.dianarussell.com/porntoc.html>
    Summary of scholarly book showing the relationship between pornography and violence against women.

Further Reading:
    Cornell, Drucilla. *Feminism and Pornography.* Oxford University Press, 2000.
    Juffer, Jane. *At Home With Pornography: Women, Sex and Everyday Life.* New York University, 1998.
    Strossen, Nadine. *Defending Pornography: Free Speech, Sex, and the Fight for Women's Rights.* New York University Press, 2000.

CRLSO

PRIESTLY CELIBACY, ABOLITION OF

One of the requirements set by the Roman Catholic church for priests is that they remain celibate. Celibacy is the renunciation of sex and marriage for the more perfect observance of chastity. This vow of celibacy has been propelled to the forefront of public discussion by the recent accusations that the church conspired to protect priests accused of child molestation. The vow of celibacy is seen by some as a cause of the pedophilia that seems to be rampant within the Catholic church in America. The Vatican has not changed its stance on celibacy in the wake of the controversy, but some within the church have called for the elimination of the vow of celibacy.

PROS

Until 1139, priests in the Western church were permitted to marry. The Bible does not mandate celibacy and, in fact, St. Peter, the first pope, was married. The true history and traditions of the Roman Catholic church include the option for priests to marry.

The number of priests in America is on the decline, and many parishes are without a priest. The prohibition on marriage pushes some men away from the priesthood. The requirement of celibacy drastically reduces the pool from which the church can select priests and means that the church is not always getting the "best and the brightest."

Protestant clergy successfully balance their work in the church and their families. Were priests permitted to marry and have families, their families could serve as examples to others. In addition, marriage can provide a priest with increased social support and intimacy.

CONS

The earliest church fathers, including St. Augustine, supported the celibate priesthood. In the fourth century, church councils enacted legislation forbidding married men who were ordained from having conjugal relations with their wives. We do not know if any of the apostles, other than Peter, were married, but we do know that they gave up everything to follow Jesus. More important, Jesus led a celibate life.

Protestant churches, which do not require celibacy, also are having problems recruiting clergy. Worldwide, the number of new priests is increasing. Only the developed world has seen a decline in priestly vocations. A recent study showed that vocations were on the rise in dioceses in the US that were loyal to the teachings of the church, including priestly celibacy.

A celibate priest can devote all his time to his parishioners. A married priest must spend time with his family. Protestant clergy have balanced their work for the church with their family responsibilities only with difficulty. Many wives and families of Protestant clergy report feeling second to the congregation.

PROS	CONS
Priestly celibacy is outdated. It sets the priest apart from the modern world and the experiences of his parishioners.	The priest is set apart from the world. He has a unique role: He represents Christ to his parishioners. Just as Jesus led a life of chastity dedicated to God, a priest must offer his life to God's people.
Celibate priests can never experience the intimate and complicated marital relationship. They lack credibility when conducting marital and family counseling. Married priests can better serve their parishioners because of their marital and family experiences.	The celibate priest has a unique understanding of the power of self-control and the giving of the self, which are key ideas in marriage. The priest is married to the church and can counsel couples and families using that knowledge.
The prospect of celibacy draws sexually dysfunctional men to the priesthood. They hope that by totally denying their sexuality, they will not engage in pedophilia, but unfortunately they often cannot overcome their deviant desires. Permitting priests to marry would bring men with healthy sexual desires to the priesthood.	Celibacy and pedophilia are not connected. Sexual abuse also occurs in religions where clergy are permitted to marry. Studies have shown that sexual abusers account for less than 2% of Roman Catholic clergy, a figure comparable to clergy in other denominations.

Sample Motions:
 This House would permit priests to marry.
 This House would have the Vatican stop requiring priestly celibacy.
 This House believes that a married priest is a better priest.

Web Links:
 • Celibacy of the Clergy. <http://www.newadvent.org/cathen/03481a.htm>
 Offers a detailed article on the history and theology of priestly celibacy.
 • How to Refute Arguments Against Priestly Celibacy. <http:::://www.catholicity.com/commentary/Hudson/celibacy.html>
 Clear presentation of arguments against celibacy, with refutations.
 • Let's Welcome Back Married Priests. <http://www.uscatholic.org/1999/02/sb9902.htm>
 Article, written by a married former priest, argues against priestly celibacy.

Further Reading:
 McGovern, Thomas. *Priestly Celibacy Today.* Four Courts Press, 1998.
 Schoenherr, Richard A. *Goodbye Father: The Celibate Male Priesthood and the Future of the Catholic Church.* Oxford University Press, 2002.
 Stickler, Alphonso M. *The Case of Clerical Celibacy: Its Historical Development and Theological Foundations.* Ignatius Press, 1995.
 Stravinska, M. J., ed. *Priestly Celibacy: Its Scriptural, Historical, Spiritual and Psychological Roots.* Newman House Press, 2001.

CR8D

PRIVACY *VS.* SECURITY

In the aftermath of the terrorist attacks of September 2001, Congress passed the Patriot Act, which gave new rights and powers to law enforcement agencies. For example, the act gives the FBI greater latitude in wiretapping and in the surveillance of material transmitted over the Internet. Legislators have also proposed national identification cards, facial profiling systems, and tighter restrictions on immigration. All of these measures are aimed at protecting Americans from further terrorist attacks. But this increased security comes at a cost: The government will be able to gather more information about the private actions of individuals. To some observers, this invasion of privacy is unwarranted and represents an attack on fundamental freedoms guaranteed in the Constitution.

PROS

The primary function of government is to "secure the general welfare" of its citizens. Security is a common good that is promised to all Americans, and it must take primacy over individual concerns about privacy.

Electronic surveillance—of financial transactions, for example—is an essential tool for tracking the actions of terrorists when they are planning attacks. The government cannot stand by and wait until criminal acts are committed; it must stop attacks before they happen.

Tighter security controls at airports and borders will help prevent damage and loss of life. In addition to their deterrent effect, they will enable officials to stop attacks as they are happening.

Tighter immigration laws and more rigorous identification procedures for foreigners entering the country will reduce the possibility of terrorists entering the country.

The right to privacy is by no means absolute, and Americans already allow the government to control some of their private actions. (The government can require drivers to wear safety belts, for example.) Any intrusions on privacy for the sake of security would be minimal, and fundamental rights would still be respected.

CONS

The right to privacy underlies the Fourth Amendment to the Constitution, which prohibits unreasonable "search and seizure." When the government collects and shares information about its citizens, it is conducting an electronic version of such prohibited searches.

Any proposal that increases the power of government agencies should be dismissed. Historically, government agencies (e.g., the IRS) have abused their power over citizens. Increased power means a greater potential for abuse.

Tighter security controls can be used to target specific ethnic and religious groups in a way that is unfair and discriminatory.

Preventive measures affect the innocent as well as the guilty. This is especially true in the case of foreign nationals: Tighter immigration controls may exclude foreigners whose presence in America would be beneficial to the country.

History has shown that the invocation of national security has often led to the restriction of fundamental rights. For example, Japanese-American citizens were interned during World War II to increase security. We should not allow the government to take even small steps in a direction that can lead to something worse.

Sample Motions:

This House supports the creation of a national identity card.
This House would give the government more power in time of war.

Web Links:

• Privacilla.org. <http://www.privacilla.org>
A Web site devoted to gathering information on privacy issues and links to privacy Web sites.
• Privacy vs. Security: A Bogus Debate? <http://www.businessweek.com/technology/content/jun2002/tc2002065_6863.htm>

In an interview for *Business Week*, David Brin, author of *The Transparent Society*, argues that the conflict between privacy and security is a false dichotomy.
• Privacy vs. Security in the Aftermath of the September 11 Terrorist Attacks. <http://www.scu.edu/ethics/publications/briefings/privacy.html>
• From the Markkula Center for Applied Ethics at Santa Clara University, this Web site offers a framework for assessing the conflict between privacy and security. Includes links to other sites.

Further Reading:

Alderman, Ellen, and Caroline Kennedy. *The Right to Privacy.* Vintage, 1997.
Brin, David. *The Transparent Society: Will Technology Force Us to Choose between Privacy and Freedom?* Perseus Publishing, 1999.
Etzioni, Amitai. *The Limits of Privacy.* Basic Books, 2000

CRSO

PRIVATE LIVES OF PUBLIC FIGURES, REVEALING

The extent to which the media should be free to publish the details of the private lives of public figures is debated whenever the press gives extensive coverage to the misdeeds of stars or politicians. Many nations have strict laws protecting personal privacy, but in the United States the press is usually free to publish what it wants unless the article is libelous. The arguments below apply primarily to public officials, but are also applicable to celebrities like film stars and sport figures.

PROS

The people have a right to know about those in power. Their salaries are paid for by the people, whether through taxes, in the case of politicians and civil servants, or by revenue generated by films, CDs, TV, etc., in the case of celebrities. The decisions of politicians affect many aspects of people's lives; in exchange, the people have the right to make informed judgments about the kind of leaders they want. Any attempt to restrict what may be reported about public figures could easily become a conspiracy to manipulate voters or to keep them in the dark.

All elections are to a greater or lesser extent about the character of politicians. Unless the voters know about politicians' private lives, they will not be able to make informed decisions at the polling booth. For example, many would think that a politician who betrayed his wife by having an affair was equally capable of breaking his promises and lying to his country.

If investigative journalists are prevented from scrutinizing the private lives of public figures, then corruption and crime will be much easier to hide.

Where is the dividing line between public and private behavior? Drawing up rules to limit the press will mean

CONS

People will always be fascinated about intimate details of the powerful and famous. Nevertheless, public figures have the same right to privacy that the rest of us enjoy. Nor should public figures be held to higher standards of personal behavior than the rest of society by a sensationalist press. If the press focused on the policies and public actions of politicians, rather than their personal foibles, democracy would be better served.

Private morality and eccentricities are not automatically related to someone's ability to do a job well. Many great political leaders have had messy personal lives, while others, with blameless private lives, have been judged failures. If modern standards of press intrusion and sensationalism had been applied in the past, how many respected leaders would have reached or survived in office?

Such close press scrutiny actually places public figures under considerable strain, making both poor performance in office and personal problems more likely.

Continual probing into the private lives of public figures actually harms democracy. Very few potential can-

that some questionable behavior may never be reported. For example, President François Mitterrand of France hid his cancer from the French electorate for years. Was this a public or a private matter? He also had a mistress and illegitimate daughter, who secretly accompanied him on some of his foreign visits at state expense. Again, was this a private or a public matter?

Many politicians point out their family values and publicize aspects of their private lives when it is to their advantage. If the public image they seek to create is at variance with their own practice, such hypocrisy deserves to be exposed.

Public figures seek election or fame knowing that it will bring attention to their private lives. Constant scrutiny is the price of fame. Many celebrities actively seek media exposure to advance their careers. Once success has been bought in such a fashion, complaining of press intrusion into those few aspects the star would prefer to remain hidden is hypocritical.

didates have spotless private lives. The prospect of fierce and unforgiving press scrutiny will deter many from seeking public office and deny the public their talents. Those who do run for office will tend to be unrepresentative individuals of a puritanical nature, whose views on sex, family life, drugs, etc., may be skewed and intolerant.

When politicians use their personal morality and family lives to win elections, they have chosen to make them a public issue. This does not justify intrusion into the privacy of those politicians who do not parade their personal lives in a campaign.

Many public figures achieve celebrity status largely by accident; it is a by-product of their pursuit of success in their particular field. They do not wish to be role models and claim no special moral status, so why should their private lives be subjected to public scrutiny?

Sample Motions:
This House believes that public figures have no right to private lives.
This House demands the right to know.
This House celebrates the power of the press.

Further Reading:
Collins, Gail. *Scorpion Tongues: Gossip, Celebrity, and American Politics.* Morrow, 1998.
Wacks, Raymond. *Privacy and Press Freedom.* Gaunt, 1995.

CRNECD

PROSTITUTION, LEGALIZATION OF

Prostitution has long been opposed on moral grounds, but recently concerns about sexually transmitted diseases, particularly AIDS, and about the violence that surrounds prostitution have contributed to renewed demands to stop the selling of sex. Criminalizing prostitution has not worked, and some nations have moved to regulate or legalize it to protect prostitutes and monitor the conditions under which they work. In Singapore and Denmark, selling sex is legal; the Dutch city of Amsterdam and the Australian state of New South Wales have no laws for or against prostitution. Nevada has made prostitution lawful in a limited number of licensed brothels. This arrangement also has enjoyed notable success in the Australian state of Victoria.

PROS

Prostitution is an issue of individual liberty. The control of one's own body is the most basic of human rights. We do not impose legal penalties on men and women who choose to be promiscuous. Why should the exchange of money suddenly make consensual sex

CONS

Prostitutes do not have a genuine choice. They are often encouraged or forced to work in the sex industry before they are old enough to make a reasoned decision. Many have their reasoning impaired by an unhappy family background, previous sexual abuse, or drugs. They may

illegal?

be compelled to enter prostitution by circumstances beyond their control, such as substance addiction or the necessity to provide for a family.

Prostitution has existed in all cultures throughout history. Governments should recognize that they cannot eradicate it. Consequently they should pass legislation that makes prostitution safer, rather than persist with futile and dangerous prohibition.

Governments have a duty to protect the moral and physical health of their citizens. Legalizing prostitution would implicitly approve a dangerous and immoral practice. Prostitution is never a legitimate choice for a young girl.

Prostitutes have performed a valid social function for thousands of years. Prostitution actually helps maintain marriages and relationships. A purely physical, commercial transaction does not jeopardize the emotional stability of a relationship. In Italy, for example, visiting a prostitute does not violate the law against adultery.

Prostitution harms the fabric of society. Sexual intercourse outside of marriage or a relationship of love shows disregard for the sanctity of the sexual act and for the other partner in a relationship. Emotional commitment is inextricably linked to physical commitment.

Many libertarian feminists believe that prostitution reflects the independence and dominance of modern women. The majority of prostitutes are women. Once the danger of abuse from male clients and pimps is removed, the capacity of women to control men's sexual responses in a financially beneficial relationship is liberating. Furthermore, many campaigners for the rights of prostitutes note that the hours are relatively short and the work well paid. Prostitutes are paid for services other women must provide without charge.

Feminists overwhelmingly oppose prostitution. The radical feminist school that emerged in the 1990s supports the idea that prostitution leads to the objectification of women. Men who use women's bodies solely for sexual gratification do not treat them as people. This lack of respect dehumanizes both the prostitute and the client and does not represent a victory for either sex.

Some studies suggest that prostitution lowers the incidence of sex crimes.

How can you prove that some individuals who visit prostitutes would otherwise have committed violent offenses? Psychological therapies that recommended the use of prostitutes have been widely discredited. The number of reported attacks on prostitutes and the considerably greater number of such crimes that go unreported suggest that prostitutes are the victims of the most serious crimes. In Victoria, where prostitution is legal, two rapes of prostitutes are reported each week.

Legalization would improve the sexual health of prostitutes and, as a result, that of their clients. The sexual transaction would occur in a clean and safe environment rather than on the street. In areas where prostitution is legal, prostitutes have regular health checks as a condition of working in the brothels. Furthermore, the use of contraception is compulsory and condoms are freely available.

More sexual health problems are inevitable. When prostitution is lawful and socially acceptable, a greater number of men will use prostitutes. Medical studies show that the condom is only 99% effective. Moreover, during the period between each health check, a prostitute could contract and transmit a sexually transmitted disease. Consequently, the legalization of prostitution will result in the transmission of more potentially fatal diseases.

Legalizing prostitution would break the link between prostitutes and pimps. Pimps physically abuse prostitutes and often threaten greater violence; they confis-

The legalization of the Bunny Ranch in Nevada did not prevent the majority of prostitutes from continuing to work outside of the licensed brothel and remain

PROS

cate part, if not all, of their earnings, and often encourage the women to become addicted to drugs. Providing a secure environment in which to work frees men and women of pimps.

Licensed brothels will improve the quality of life for people who live and work in areas currently frequented by prostitutes. Regulations can require brothels to locate in areas away from homes and schools.

Existing legal prohibitions against soliciting and prostitution do not work. Prostitutes are regularly arrested and fined. To pay the fines, they must prostitute themselves. The laws banning prostitution are counterproductive.

Legalizing prostitution would give governments economic benefits. A tax on the fee charged by a prostitute and the imposition of income tax on the earnings of prostitutes would generate revenue.

The problem of a high concentration of "sex tourists" in a small number of destinations will disappear once a larger number of countries legalize prostitution. Supporting this motion, therefore, will reduce the problem of sex tourism.

CONS

dependent on pimps. Licensed brothels are expensive for prostitutes to work in and for clients to visit. A legal business has to pay for rent, health checks and security; prostitutes working outside the "system" need not worry about such expenses. Some prostitutes use private apartments, while others work on the street. Legalizing prostitution will not remove the street market or the dangers associated with it. The dangerous street environment is a consequence of economics, not legal controls.

Prostitutes will continue to work on the streets and are unlikely to work near the competition offered by the licensed brothels. Furthermore, will local governments want to create "ghettos" of prostitution in certain areas?

Merely because some individuals break a law does not mean that the law itself is at fault or that it should be abolished. The ease with which prostitutes can return to work suggests that penal sanctions should be more severe rather than removed altogether.

An economic benefit cannot offset social harms that result from the legalization of certain prohibited activities. Otherwise we would encourage governments to become involved in other unlawful trades including trafficking in drugs. Moreover, sex workers are unlikely to declare their true earnings from what is a confidential relationship between the worker and client. Thus the amount of revenue generated is likely to be slight.

Legalizing prostitution would render the country in question a destination for sex tourists. Relaxed legal controls on prostitution in Thailand, the Philippines, and in the Netherlands have made these countries attractive to these undesirable individuals.

Sample Motions:
This House would have lots more sex.
This House would legalize brothels.
This House would decriminalize prostitution.

Further Reading:
Chapkis, Wendy, Jill Poesner, and Annie Sprinkle. *Live Sex Act: Women Performing Erotic Labor.* Routledge, 1997.
Ivison, Irene. *Fiona's Story.* Little Brown, 1997.

CREO

REFERENDA

In contemporary democracies decisions are made by elected representatives. If governments or citizens believe that an issue should have a fuller demonstration of public will, they call or petition for a referendum. Referenda are questions put to a popular vote. They can have the full force of law or they can be advisory. The frequency with which governments use them varies from nation to nation. There have been approximately 1,000 referenda in history; half of them in Switzerland. The United States has never had a national referendum, but some states, e.g., California, use them frequently.

PROS

In a democracy the people should have their say as often as possible. Referenda were uncommon in the past because they were difficult to organize. Now that technology (i.e., the Internet) makes this task easier, we should utilize it to further the spirit of democracy and increase the involvement of the people. Switzerland is an example of a nation that uses frequent referenda efficiently.

Freakish results can be avoided by requiring a certain percentage (say 30%) of the electorate to cast a vote for a referendum to be valid.

People are apathetic about politics because their voice is heard only at the voting booth. Frequent referenda would stimulate interest in politics because people would actually get a say in decisions.

In many cases legislatures decide on the wording of a referendum, but countries could establish an independent body that would take over this task and oversee the process. It could be done by the body that oversees general elections. In most democracies these authorities are acknowledged as fair and unbiased.

Many countries have party systems with little difference between parties. Consequently, large sectors of the public find their views unrepresented. Referenda would be a remedy.

CONS

Governing involves establishing long-term goals. Once the people elect their representatives, the voters should permit them to enact their platforms. Often legislation is unpopular initially but becomes acceptable, even popular, in the long run. Such legislation would never survive a referendum. If people don't like what their government is doing, they can vote the politicians out of office. Government's job is to lead, not to follow, especially on social legislation that initially may have limited support. We've seen dramatic examples of this during the 1950s and 1960s, when the US federal government forced desegregation in opposition to southern white opinion.

Freakish results can occur if no turnout threshold is required for a referendum to be valid. If the threshold is too high, no referendum will ever be valid!

People are currently bored with politics. The last thing they want is to vote more often. This will lead only to greater apathy and even lower turnouts. California is a classic example of frequent referenda failing to draw noticeable interest.

Referenda are very artificial. The government can control the timing, which is a key factor in deciding the outcome. The media, by playing an irresponsible role, can further distort the result. Furthermore, how should the all-important wording of the question be decided? Referenda waste a huge amount of money.

If none of the parties support a policy, it is because it has no significant support among the people!

Sample Motions:
This House calls for the increased use of referenda.
This House would vote on it.
This House would give power back to the people.

CRSO

RELIGION: SOURCE OF CONFLICT OR PEACE?

Religion has always been one of the most influential forces in the world. It has been a force for peace, but it also has served as a cause, if not a genuine reason, for some of the greatest wars. Today, with the growth of Muslim fundamentalism in Islamic areas, the Western world views religious extremism as the great threat. The events of September 11, 2001, proved that such concerns were justified; however, the war on terror led by the West caused resentment among those for whom Islam was a peaceful source of spiritual stability. So what is religion today? Is it harmful or good? If it can be a source of conflict, can it serve as an instrument of resolution as well?

PROS

Religion is a stronger force than any material incentives. It is far better at directing behavior toward social betterment than either laws or physical force. For example, both Gandhi and Martin Luther King, Jr., conducted nonviolent protests based on religious values.

The very existence of theocratic states, e.g., Iran, proves that religion can be a legitimate source of political power. Governments in theocratic states are much more stable than in secular countries because leaders are viewed as appointed by God. Political stability, in its turn, leads to economic welfare.

Biblical commandments are the basis of Western ethical and legal systems. Religion teaches us tolerance for people of other races and religions. Usually believers are more peaceful and tolerant than nonbelievers.

In the states where religion develops freely and people have free access to places of worship, churches have always served as a shelter for the poor. Some of the greatest works of art were created in the name of God. Furthermore, Woodrow Wilson suggested that a strong affinity exists between religious commitment and patriotism. Love of country, just like love of God, certainly inspires good deeds.

Most wars are not started by religion, although religion

CONS

Religion is extremely dangerous because it can be used to justify brutal actions. The Inquisition carried out its torture in the name of God. Hitler's followers, among them the so-called German Christians, were also believers in their Führer. Religion should never be involved in politics because it can be used as an instrument of control or to achieve a ruler's aims.

Theocratic states become totalitarian regimes because they are based on obedience to a ruler who is seen as God's representative rather than on a democratic constitution.

Religions like Islam justify "holy" wars against the "unfaithful," meaning people of other religions. Religious convictions like these paved the way for the terrorist attacks of September 11.

Religion has led to the creation of great art but it has also led to its destruction. Remember the Taliban's destruction of the great Buddhas in Afghanistan? Still worse, religion can be a source of extreme nationalism. In Islam, Christianity, and Judaism, God is described as "mighty warrior," "just king," or "righteous judge." He punishes the unjust, the unrighteous, and the disobedient. The idea that a nation is the instrument of God's will has led to war and the subjugation of people viewed as ungodly.

Whether religion is a genuine reason for war or only its

PROS	CONS
often serves to justify them. Most wars are started for economic reasons or for territorial gain.	pretext is not important. What is vital is that religion can be and is often used to make people fight in the name of high ideals to further aims of hatred. Thus, religion causes more harm than good.
Western states grew as a result of religion and religious philosophy. Western European and North American societies are still based on Protestant ideals of diligence, thrift, and moderation.	North American nations emerged only because of economic factors: the existence of famine and overpopulation in Europe on the one hand, and the free markets of the United States on the other. The realities of capitalism, not the tenets of religious faith, prompt people to be diligent and thrifty.

Sample Motions:
This House believes that religion is a positive influence on people.
This House believes that church and state must be kept separate.

Web Links:
• United States Institute of Peace. <http://www.usip.org/religion/religion.htm>
Site reports on the Institute's Religion and Peacemaking Initiative and presents reports on peacemaking efforts in religious wars.
• Ontario Consultants on Religious Tolerance. <http://www.religioustolerance.org>
Presents information on various aspects of religion and includes an extensive table of all contemporary religious wars with a brief description of each.

Further Reading:
Gopin, Marc. *Holy War, Holy Peace: How Religion Can Bring Peace to the Middle East.* Oxford University Press, April 2002.
Hunter, Shireen T., and Marc Gopin. *The Future of Islam and the West: Clash of Civilizations or Peaceful Coexistence?* Praeger, 1998.
Kepel, Gilles. *Jihad: The Trail of Political Islam. Translated by Anthony Roberts.* Harvard University Press, 2002.
Smock, David R. *Religious Perspectives on War: Christian, Muslim, and Jewish Attitudes.* Rev. ed. United States Institute of Peace Press, 2002.

CR8O

RELIGIOUS BELIEF: RATIONAL OR IRRATIONAL?

The majority of the world's population is at least nominally committed to some religion. Despite the perception in some parts of the Western world that religious belief is in terminal decline, or that economic and social development go hand-in-hand with secularization, in many parts of the world religious belief is firmly entrenched, including in the United States, arguably the most "developed" nation on Earth. Religion offers a fascinating topic for debate: the question of the existence of God; the social, moral, and political questions about the effects of religious belief on individuals and communities both now and in the past.

PROS

Religious belief is completely irrational. God exists? Where's the proof? There is none. Reported miracles, healings, etc., are never reliably proved. In any case everyone's religious experiences are different and show the psychological differences between human beings rather than proving any objective divine reality. Belief in God is simply wish fulfillment. A loving all-powerful being

CONS

Evidence that God is a reality is good. That we live in a beautiful, orderly universe in which human beings exist and have special moral and spiritual awareness points clearly to the existence of a divine creator of the universe. Billions of people have had religious experiences, all of them revealing the existence of divine reality.

watching over us would be nice, but there isn't any.

The world is full of the suffering and pain of the innocent. If God is good and all powerful then why is such suffering permitted? Either God does not exist or he is not worth believing in because he does not care about human suffering.

Most suffering and pain can be accounted for by the free will that humans exercise. God made us free, and we use that freedom for evil as well as for good. As for illness and disease, it is hard for us to know the mind of God, but it may be that these trials are a necessary part of a world in which free and spiritual human beings can evolve and develop.

Modern science has shown religious belief to be wrong. From Galileo to Darwin to the modern day, scientists have continually uncovered the true natural mechanisms behind the beginning and evolution of the universe. These leave no gaps for God to act in; science has revealed a closed natural order governed by natural laws. Science has also proved that there is not a "soul," but that all our mental states are simply caused by brain activity. Accordingly, there is no reason to believe in life after death, one of the main tenets of religious belief.

What an inaccurate caricature of the relationship between science and religion. In fact, most of the great scientists of history have been religious believers. The more we learn about the physical world, the more it seems that an intelligent God designed it to produce human life. The physical side of reality does not, in any case, preclude a spiritual dimension. Nor does the fact that the mind and brain are closely correlated mean that they are the same thing.

Religions through the ages, and still today, have been agents of repression, sexism, elitism, homophobia, conflict, war, and racial hatred. The evils for which religion is responsible in the social and political worlds easily outweigh whatever small psychological comfort religious belief may give.

Religion may have been the occasion for various social and political wrongs, but it is not the cause. You can be sure that if you took away all the world's religions people would still identify themselves with national and political groups and go to war over territory, etc. Equally, elitism and bigotry are, sadly, parts of human nature with or without religion. Serious and sincere religious belief is a force for good in the world, promoting humility, morality, wisdom, equality, and social justice. Social justice is at the heart of the Christian gospel.

Religious traditions and the irrational fervor with which people adhere to them divide humanity. They provide a proliferation of incompatible and contradictory moral codes and values. The only prospect for a global morality is a secular one based on rational consensual views and positions rather than on partisan, local, irrational prejudices. In the interest of global harmony, we should discard religious beliefs.

We need religious traditions to provide us with morals and values in a rapidly secularizing age. Scientists and politicians cannot tell us how to distinguish right from wrong. We need the moral insight of religious traditions, which are repositories of many generations of spiritual wisdom, to guide us in ethical matters.

Sample Motions:
This House rejoices that God is dead.
This House does not believe.
This House believes that religion has done more harm than good.

Web Links:
• Counterbalance. <http://www.counterbalance.org>
A "science and religion" site sympathetic to Christianity.
• The Secular Web. <http://www.infidels.org/>
Contains essays and articles supporting a metaphysical philosophy of naturalism that denies the existence of God.

• Theism, Atheism, and Rationality. <http://www.leaderu.com/truth/3truth02.html>
Philosophical essay in support of a theistic world view.

CREO

REPARATIONS FOR SLAVERY

Reparations are compensation given to make amends for previous wrongs. In the United States, some people believe that the descendants of slaves should be compensated for the wrongs of slavery. The historical facts behind the argument are universally agreed on. Europeans shipped millions of Africans as slaves to North and South America. Once there, the slaves' labor developed the colonial economies. The profits from the slave trade and from the produce cultivated by slaves greatly improved the material well-being of the colonies and sponsor states involved. Historians have debated the economic impact of the complex system, although a broad outline is now apparent. The transatlantic slavery system brought huge economic privilege to the slaveholders in the Americas and to maritime Europe. Africa was left with the loss of millions of people, the residue of violence, and the commodification of life that made the slave trade possible. The severity of the consequences is now impossible to calibrate. Several legal decisions are pending on reparations.

PROS

The legal precedent behind African-American demands for slavery reparations originates from US Army Field Order 15 issued by Gen. William Tecumseh Sherman in 1865. It stated that each "freedman" should receive 40 acres of land and a draft animal to work the land as compensation for their enslavement. Bitterness over the government's failure to honor that order exists in black culture and contributes to racial hostility. Reparations could possibly reduce some of that hostility and lead to better race relations in America.

Historical precedents for reparations to African-American descendants of slaves are the payment by Germany to Israel for the Nazi Holocaust and the payments made by the US federal government for its internment of Japanese Americans during World War II. In addition, historical precedent for reparations exists in the ongoing provision of social services to Native American populations in North America.

CONS

Reparations are not historically justified. The call for reparations is merely the merging of demagogic appeals to populism by African-American leaders and the overly litigious nature of American culture. General Sherman would have given property and tangible goods. Cash payments and property transfer are no longer justified. If the government wants to help descendants of slaves, it should offer opportunities for economic development and education. Furthermore, should reparations be decided on, how would they be determined? How much is an 1865 mule worth in today's dollars? Should the government execute the order or adjust it based on cost-of-living changes and economic changes? Calls for reparations entrench perceptions of African Americans as victims, a sure road to learned helplessness.

Who should receive the payments? African Americans or Africans or both? The historical precedents cited are invalid. Germany was forced to make reparations to Israel because Germany had committed a crime against humanity, genocide, against the Jewish people of Europe. Genocide is different from slavery. Economically, slavery mandates better treatment because the slaves possessed value on the open market. The Japanese Americans in concentration camps were treated horribly by the US government. However, they were also a very easily defined and tracked group of individuals who could be monetarily compensated. The African-American slaves are many generations away from their ancestors who were actually slaves. Tracking down who is descended from whom would be a huge, if not impossible, task. Native Americans receive payments and social services based on their treaties with the United States government and the governments of the Indian tribes. The descendants of African slaves have no nation-state or treaties with the government.

Slavery was deemed a crime against humanity in the summer of 2001 at the United Nations World Conference Against Racism in South Africa. The designation has legal implications. Most important, there is no statute of limitations for crimes against humanity, meaning US institutions could be held liable for transgressions dating to the first instance of slave trade in the Americas in 1619 in Jamestown, Virginia.

The US government is not affected by this designation. The Rome Statute of the International Criminal Court has not been ratified by the US. In addition, the US has sovereign immunity and could not be sued by its own citizens in American courts. The first case seeking reparations, *Cato v. the United States* (1995), was dismissed citing US sovereign immunity.

Africans should be paid reparations for slavery. Slavery entrenched a violent and corrupt political system and fostered a culture that accepted the commodification of human life. The harms inflicted by slavery hindered Africa's development, thus Africans should receive compensation and reparations.

Allowing some harmed groups to receive reparations from the government will encourage other transgressed groups to produce and present their own claims for reparations. Reparations claims could conceivably bankrupt our government and torpedo our economy. Why should the US government provide reparations? Many other nations participated in the slave trade, including African nations. Many Arab nations also benefited from the institution of slavery. Saudi Arabia traded and used slaves for development extensively many decades after the institution of slavery had been abolished in the Western Hemisphere.

Private corporations should pay reparations to descendants of slaves. Many private corporations held slaves or sold slaves and profited greatly from their participation in chattel slavery. In March of 2002, lawyers for Deadria Farmer-Paellman filed a class-action reparations lawsuit in Brooklyn federal court against FleetBoston Financial Corp., Aetna Inc., and CSX Corp. seeking $1.4 trillion for 37 million Americans of African descent. In July 1998, Volkswagen AG admitted to using the forced and unpaid (slave) labor of 15,000 Eastern Europeans during World War II and announced plans to set up a fund to compensate these workers.

Private corporate liability lawsuits should be avoided. Mergers and acquisitions make the financial liability too complicated to trace, thus only obvious and financially important corporations would be caught up in this folly. Think on this also: One unfavorable and half-thought-out court ruling could derail the many serious efforts to bring this issue to public attention and discussion in the United States.

Sample Motions:
   This House would give reparations to the descendants of slaves.
   This House believes that the United States federal government should provide reparations for its part in the transatlantic slave trade.
   This House believes that moral and/or financial atonement for the racial sins of this country's fathers is desirable.

Web Links:
   • All the Current Slavery Reparations News. <http://slaveryreparations.newstrove.com>
   Impartial site offers scores of links to other Web pages and full text of newspaper and magazine articles about slavery reparations.
   • Millions For Reparations. <http://www.millionsforreparations.com>
   This Web site, maintained by an organization in favor of reparations, has some news and magazine literature and some personal

thoughts about reparations.
• We Won't Pay. <http://www.wewontpay.com>
This Web site has the personal testimony of more than 100 Internet visitors who all sound off about racism. Some of the participants are qualified and cite sources; others do not. This is a great Web site for teaching about source qualifications and logical fallacies in argument.

Further Reading:
Horowitz, David. *Uncivil Wars: The Controversy over Reparations for Slavery.* Encounter, 2001.
Robinson, Randall. *The Debt: What America Owes to Blacks.* Plume, 2001.
Winbush, Raymond A., ed. *Should America Pay: Slavery and the Raging Debate over Reparations.* Amistad, 2003.

CRSO

RUSSIAN-AMERICAN COOPERATION: TEMPORARY OR LONG-TERM

War creates unexpected alliances, and the war on terrorism provided a good opportunity for improved cooperation between the United States and Russia. These two former enemies now have a chance to forge deep strategic, economic, and cultural ties. For the first time since the end of World War II, Russia and the United States have a common enemy: international terrorism. Moreover, both countries are interested in broader economic cooperation and in reducing nuclear weapons stockpiles. But differences remain. Russia worries about American efforts to build new defense systems, while the United States points to Russian cooperation with Iran, one of the "rogue" states, as an example of its untrustworthiness.

PROS

The Cold War ended more than a decade ago. Now, the two most powerful countries in the world find it natural and necessary to cooperate to fight terrorism and in other arenas. Both countries have elected new presidents who quickly established friendly, even personal, relations. Good relations between leaders often improve relations between countries.

Good relations between two superpowers make the world much safer. Because of its location, Russia is vital to fighting international terrorism. Russia's intelligence services have monitored the activities of Islamic fundamentalist groups on its borders for years.

Economic cooperation between Russia and the United States can be nothing but positive. Russia desperately needs investment and technology to modernize, which the United States can supply. The United States, in turn, can buy oil from Russia, thus reducing its reliance on Saudi Arabia.

CONS

Russia's desire to regain its status as a superpower, not solidarity with the United States, is the real reason for cooperation. Russia has been dissatisfied with its role in international affairs since the collapse of the Soviet Union.

Such an alliance does not permanently make the world any safer; this alliance is just a convenience for the period of the war on terrorism.

Good economic relations are possible only as long as the United States believes Russia is genuinely trying to bring its economy into line with the Western world. If Russia does not conform to American expectations, investment will stop. The people who control Russia's energy assets are resisting the changes needed to facilitate foreign investment because they fear loss of control. We must also remember that Russia's economic interests are often at odds with American foreign policy goals. For example, Russia benefits from exporting weapons to China and Iran, which the United States opposes.

<table>
<tr><td>

Russia and the United States must jointly face a host of problems, from environmental degradation to the growth of ethnic violence and the challenges posed by globalization. Addressing these problems will forge a close relationship between the two nations.

</td><td>

Accordingly, close, long-term cooperation between two states with very different goals is improbable.

Russian and US interests will always clash. While politically the two countries need each other to face global challenges—assuming their interests do not conflict—militarily they will remain strategic enemies. US strategic nuclear planning will always assume Russia is a potential nuclear threat. Likewise, Russian planners will not rule out a US attack on Russian targets.

</td></tr>
</table>

Sample Motions:
   This House believes that long-term cooperation between Russia and the United States is possible.
   This House believes that today's warming US-Russia relations are just a temporary alliance to face global challenges, primarily the war on international terrorism.

Web Links:
   • Carnegie Endowment for International Peace. <http://www.ceip.org/programs/ruseuras/usrus/contents.htm>
   Presents a detailed report on US-Russia relations by the Carnegie Endowment for International Peace (Washington) and the Council on Foreign and Defense Policy (Moscow).
   • Center for Defense Information: Views from Moscow. <http://www.cdi.org/moscow/zolotarev0202-pr.cfm>
   Provides an article by the former deputy chief of staff of the Russian Defense Council outlining a possible new framework for relations between Russia and the United States.
   • Radio Free Europe. <http://www.rferl.org/nca/special/RUvsUS/default.asp>
   Includes an archive of all the recent articles concerning US-Russian relations.

Further Reading:
   Ellis, Jason D. *Defense by Other Means: The Politics of US-NIS Threat Reduction and Nuclear Security Cooperation.* Praeger, 2001.
   Pikayev, Alexander. *Russia, the U.S. and the Missile Technology Control Regime.* Oxford University Press, 1998.

ଓଃ୨୦

SCHOOL UNIFORMS

Traditionally, students in American parochial schools and some private schools have worn uniforms. Only a smattering of public schools had uniform policies until the mid-1990s, when Long Beach, California, mandated uniforms in an effort to stop school crime. The apparent success of the measure combined with studies indicating that students in many schools with uniform policies performed better academically than those without, opened a floodgate of uniform adoption. President Bill Clinton even promoted uniforms in his 1996 State of the Union message. To avoid legal challenges, school districts now make provision for students who cannot afford uniforms or for parents to opt out of the uniform requirement.

PROS

Uniforms help create a strong sense of community, thus promoting discipline and helping raise academic standards. This is why educators frequently adopt them when trying to revive failing schools.

CONS

Uniforms suppress individualism and discourage students from accepting responsibility for aspects of their own lives. They encourage teachers to view students as a group rather than as individuals with different characters and abilities. Uniforms were better suited to an age of rote learning and military-style discipline. They do not belong in modern education, which encourages the imagination and intellectual exploration that is becoming increasingly important in the wider economy. Many schools, indeed many countries, manage to maintain high standards of discipline, community, and academic performance without adopting uniforms.

Wearing uniforms acts as a social leveler; all students are equal in the eyes of the school and of each other. In institutions without uniforms students are often competitive in dress and worry endlessly about their appearance. Pupils without expensive, trendy clothes may become social outcasts. Many parents prefer uniforms because they save money.

Students always find ways to tease or bully others regardless of what clothes are worn. The fashion-conscious will own the same number of outfits regardless of whether or not they can wear them to school; they will change the minute classes are over. Parents often find some uniform items, such as jackets, very expensive and complain that they can never be worn outside the school.

Uniforms have practical benefits outside the school building. If students are identified with a particular institution, they may be more aware of their behavior. They may act more considerately of others while traveling to and from the school. On organized trips, teachers find keeping track and monitoring behavior of students easier.

Uniforms make students very identifiable. They emphasize the divisions between schools, increasing the possibility of bullying and fights between students from rival institutions.

Uniforms prepare students for life after graduation, when businesses will expect them to adhere to corporate dress codes.

The business world is increasingly relaxed about dress codes, making the schools that insist on uniforms anachronistic. Adults who attended schools without uniforms do not appear to struggle in the workplace.

Uniforms make it easy for teachers to monitor dress codes fairly. School administrators and students constantly battle about what clothing is appropriate in schools without uniforms.

Often it is the uniform that is inappropriate—not warm enough in winter or too hot in summer—largely because it is badly designed and cheaply produced. Girls complain about being forced to wear skirts even in the coldest months. Some groups, such as conservative Muslims, may oppose specific uniform styles for cultural reasons. Students will always attempt to subvert dress codes, so the staff will have to be vigilant in any case.

Sample Motions:
This House would introduce school uniforms.
This House would create a stronger school ethos.
This House believes successful education rests on firm discipline.

Web Links:
• American Civil Liberties Union (ACLU): All Dressed Up and Nowhere to Go: Students and Their Parents Fight School Uniform Policies. <http://www.aclu.org/features/f110499a.html>
Site summarizing one campaign against school uniforms with links to information on other protests and ACLU legal action.
• ACLU: Philly Adopts School Uniform Policy. <http://www.aclu.org/news/2000/w050800a.html>
2000 press release presenting opposing viewpoints on Philadelphia's adoption of school uniforms.
• ACLU: Litigation Resulting from Mandatory School Uniform Policies. <http://www.gate.net/~rwms/UniformLinksLitigation.html>
Links to information on ACLU challenges to dress codes as well as summaries of ACLU stands on the issue.

• U.S. Department of Education: Manual on Uniforms. <http://www.ed.gov/updates/uniforms.html>
1996 summary of arguments in support of school uniforms, guide to adopting uniforms, and sample school district policies on uniforms.

CR8O

SCHOOL VOUCHERS

Over the past decades, Americans have been increasingly concerned about the quality of public education, particularly in inner-city neighborhoods, where many public schools are failing. One of the most controversial suggestions for improving education for all children is to establish school voucher programs. Although the specifics of these programs vary with locality, all would distribute monetary vouchers to parents who could then use them to help pay the cost of private, including parochial (religious), schools. Critics fear that vouchers would further damage public schools and argue that they subvert the separation of church and state. Supporters say they will help the children most in need.

PROS

The current public education system is failing countless students, particularly in inner-city neighborhoods. In an era where education is the key to success, these children are not being provided with the chance to develop the skills necessary to compete in the modern world. Vouchers give poor parents the ability to send their children to better schools. These children should not be sacrificed while we wait for public school reform.

The competition for students will force all schools to improve. They will have to use their resources to educate their students rather than squander them on bureaucracies as many do today. Eventually, the unsalvageable schools will close and the others will grow stronger, producing an overall better learning environment. The market will regulate the education produced.

The money would help some families, and that is worth the risks. Not all students in nonperforming schools will be able to attend a private school. However, after the students who can afford such an opportunity leave nonperforming schools, more resources will be available at those nonperforming schools to educate the remaining students. Private schools would have no reason to change admission standards or tuition, nor is there reason to think that a great swell in private school enrollment would result.

Vouchers will eventually lead to a school system that

CONS

The American public education system has been central to American democracy. It has provided education for all children regardless of their ethnic background, their religion, their academic talents, or their ability to pay. It has helped millions of immigrants assimilate and provided the civic education necessary for future citizens to understand American values. Establishing a voucher system is saying that we are giving up on public education. Instead of giving up, we should put our efforts into reforming the system.

The competition for students would destroy inner-city public schools. Much of their student body would flee to "better" private schools, leaving inner-city schools with little to no funding. Most states' funding of public schools is determined by number of students enrolled. If enrollment lags, then the school is not as well funded as it was the previous year. If enrollment booms, then funding increases. Thus, even if urban schools are motivated to improve they will lack the resources to do so.

The government vouchers are not monetarily substantial enough to give true financial aid to students. They are not large enough to help poor students go to private schools. The vouchers make private education more affordable for people who could already afford it. In addition, private schools may not be willing to accept all students with vouchers. They could always raise tuition or standards for admission, neutralizing any impact vouchers would have.

Voucher programs would set up a school system that

is liberated from bureaucrats and politicians, enabling educators and parents to determine how best to educate children.

is not accountable to the public. Investigations of current programs in Milwaukee, Wisconsin, and Cleveland, Ohio, have found unlawful admissions requirements, illegally imposed fees, and even fraud.

No violation of the separation of church and state would occur. No student would be forced to enter a religious school. Only families and students interested in a private or religious education would use the vouchers. Any students who desired a more traditional curriculum would be allowed to study in public schools.

Vouchers involve the indirect giving of public funds to religious schools. This transfer of funds amounts to a violation of the doctrine of separation of church and state.

Sample Motions:
This House believes that the government should cease the use of school vouchers.
This House recommends that educational vouchers be used for private and parochial schools.
This House believes that the issuing of vouchers by the government is justified.

Web Links:
• School Vouchers: The Wrong Choice for Public Education. <http://www.adl.org/vouchers/vouchers_main.asp>
This is an anti-school voucher Web site containing a detailed report outlining many reasons why vouchers are a poor policy option.
• Vouchers and Educational Freedom: A Debate.
<http://www.cato.org/pubs/pas/pa-269es.html>
This Web page from the Cato Institute presents a debate on the issue of vouchers. Along with both sides of the argument, the site offers links and policy analysis.
• What Are the Issues: Vouchers? <http://www.pta.org/programs/ISSvouchers.htm>
The PTA Web site provides excellent background on the issue through various links and articles.

Further Reading:
Doerr, Edd, Albert J. Menendez, and John M. Swomley. *The Case Against School Vouchers.* Prometheus, 1996.
Kilpatrick, David W. *Choice in Schooling: A Case for Tuition Vouchers.* Loyola Press, 1990.
Kolbert, Kathryn, and Zak Mettger, eds. *Justice Talking: School Vouchers.* New Press, 2002.

CR&SO

SCIENCE: THREAT TO SOCIETY?

As the twenty-first century dawns, science is extending the boundaries of human knowledge and understanding further than many people feel comfortable with. Both cutting-edge technologies, such as cloning, and other more established procedures, such as in vitro fertilization, have sparked moral outrage and accusations of "playing God." The development of nuclear weapons is just one illustration of the possible danger introduced by scientific advances.

PROS

Science gives humans the ability to "play God" and to interfere in areas about which we know nothing. Scientists have already cloned animals, and recently some scientists announced that they will attempt to clone humans. Such irresponsible and potentially dangerous meddling is taking place in the name of scientific advancement.

CONS

Talk of "playing God!" Aside from assuming the existence of a deity that many do not believe in, the talk of playing God implies a violation of set boundaries. What boundaries? Set by whom? The proposition is simply afraid of things about which it knows nothing. The assertion that we are meddling in areas we do not understand should be replaced with a call for better regulation of scientific enquiry, not its abolition.

Science has greatly increased the capability of men and women to kill each other. Wars that used to be fought face-to-face on the battlefield, with comparatively few casualties, are now fought from miles away in anonymity. The buildup of nuclear arsenals during the Cold War gave humanity the capability of obliterating the entire world 10 times over. At certain times in history, such as the 1962 Cuban missile crisis, the world has stood on the brink of destruction.

Science does not kill; humans do. We cannot blame science for the flaws in human nature, and we cannot attribute suffering to science any more than to religion or philosophy, both of which have caused wars. The example given illustrates how science brings with it accompanying responsibility. Mutually assured destruction ensured that neither the United States nor the Soviet Union deployed nuclear weapons.

Science has perverted the fundamental basis of human relations. The word "society" itself comes from "socialization"—the idea of interaction and communication. With the Internet, television, and computer games, humans are communing with a lifeless collection of microchips, not each other.

Science has greatly increased the ability of people to communicate. Telephones and e-mail now enable people on opposite sides of the world to stay in touch. The Internet allows people unprecedented access to information, anything from sports scores to debating crib sheets. Any study of preindustrial society will show that computer games appear to have taken the place previously held by recreational violence.

Science is despoiling the natural world. Power grids ruin the countryside, acid rain from coal- and gas-fired power stations kills fish, and animals are cruelly experimented on to further research. Not only does science give us the potential to destroy each other, it also takes a massive toll on our natural surroundings.

Modern medicines have more than doubled our life expectancy and prevented fatal childhood diseases. The world's population could not be fed without fertilizers and pesticides to increase crop yields and machinery to harvest them efficiently. Science and technology are essential to modern existence. We must use them with care and not abuse them. But condemning science as a menace is ludicrous.

Sample Motions:

This House believes science is a threat to humanity.

This House fears science.

This House believes that scientists are dangerous.

Web Links:

• Institute of Scientists in Society (ISIS). <http://www.i-sis.org>

Maintained by ISIS, a nonprofit organization working for social responsibility in science, the site offers information on current issues in science.

• International Center for Technology Assessment. <http://www.icta.org>

Site provides information on the organization's initiatives to explore the economic, social, ethical, environmental, and political impacts of technology.

• Scientists for Global Responsibility. <http://www.sgr.org.uk>

UK-based organization promoting the ethical use of science provides news on scientific issues and information on its initiatives.

Further Reading:

Collins, H. M., and Trevor Pinch. *The Golem: What You Should Know About Science.* Cambridge University Press, 1998.

The Golem at Large: What You Should Know About Technology. Cambridge University Press, 1998.

Peacocke, Arthur. *Paths from Science Towards God.* One World Publications, 2001.

CRSO

SECURITY AND LIBERTY

The events of September 11, 2001, forced governments worldwide to take extraordinary measures to improve the security of their citizens. Measures included unparalleled searches of passengers and baggage at airports; more frequent searches of possessions when entering public places; tracking and monitoring of foreign nationals; and random searches of Internet content by intelligence officers. Most of these measures are associated with loss of privacy. Extraordinary security measures seem justified in response to the imminent and continuing threats of terrorists, who have become much more cunning and resourceful over the last decade. The introduction of these measures, however, comes at the expense of some of our most cherished civil liberties. No doubt, we must trade some liberty for security, but what is the ideal balance?

PROS

The current tension in the international arena is likely to increase, leading to greater dissatisfaction with American policies. This, in turn, may result in more terrorist attacks. Terrorists now use advanced technology and are organized in networks of hard-to-track cells. Addressing modern terrorism is impossible without curbing some rights.

Liberty depends on security. We must eliminate terrorism to protect our freedom. We need to update wiretapping laws to conform to changing technologies and give law enforcement agencies added powers of search and seizure.

Our immigration laws have been too lax, and the Immigration and Naturalization Service has failed in its job. The terrorists responsible for September 11 entered the United States legally, and undoubtedly others are still here in hiding. We need stricter immigration laws and better enforcement.

In any large-scale attempt to fight terrorism some abuses of rights are certain to occur. However, ending all security measures because they may violate rights is not a good idea. The majority of the measures are intended to safeguard civil liberties, not abuse them.

Security measures have not really limited freedom, and US measures are comparable with those of other developed countries.

Random searches at airports ensure against ethnic profiling. In many airports, the software that runs the airline reservation system, called Computer Assisted Passenger Prescreening System (CAPPS), selects passen-

CONS

We don't have enough evidence to show that terrorism is more of a threat than in past decades. Governments are likely to take advantage of the fear of terrorism and seize the moment to strengthen their regimes. Modern government agencies are sophisticated enough to counter terrorism without impinging on citizens' rights. What is not acceptable is to infringe on civil rights using the events of September 11 as an excuse.

The United States was founded on the principle of limited government and inalienable rights. The government can take steps to thwart terrorism without infringing on our rights. For example, instead of giving agencies broader rights of detention, the agencies could do better work in collecting evidence so that they can bring credible charges.

In the wake of September 11, the government detained over 1,000 non-U.S. nationals. Some remained in custody for months, deprived of basic rights guaranteed under international law. This is not appropriate for a nation that prides itself on its support of individual freedom.

Historically, many limitations on rights started with good intentions. Permitting violations of rights, even in a few cases, is the top of a slippery slope. The public will tolerate increased violation of rights, and eventually fundamental rights will be eroded.

If the United States loses its cherished liberties to terrorism, the terrorists win.

Fruitless random searches of elderly women, toddlers, and uniformed airline pilots have become standard at US airports as more and more innocent passengers are treated like suspects rather than customers. Some of

gers whose carry-on and checked bags will require additional security screening. CAPPS also chooses passengers at random for screening.

the red flags for CAPPS system are: person's last name; methods of payment (tickets paid in cash are highly suspect); or whether a rental car is waiting. These criteria are very vague and do not target real suspects.

Sample Motions:
    This House believes that security is the most important goal.
    This House would not trade liberty for security.

Web Links:
    • Amnesty International Concerns Regarding Post-September 11 Detentions in the U.S. <http://web.amnesty.org/ai.nsf/Index/AMR510442002?OpenDocument&of=COUNTRIES\USA>
    Report by international rights organization expressing concern about potential human rights violations in the national sweep for possible terrorists following September 11.
    • Balancing Security and Liberty. <http://www.heritage.org/views/2001/ed101101.html>
    Article in support of Bush administration anti-terrorism policies by the conservative Heritage Foundation.
    • Office of Homeland Security. <http://www.whitehouse.gov/homeland/>
    Bush administration site providing latest news on the domestic campaign against terrorism.
    • On Trading Security for Liberty.
     <http://www.objectivistcenter.org/articles/wthomas_trading-security-liberty.asp>
    Article by the Objectivist Center views Bush administration actions in response to terrorism as threats to liberties and recommends alternatives.

Further Reading:
    Chang, Nancy, and Howard Zinn. *Silencing Political Dissent: How Post-September 11 Anti-Terrorism Measures Threaten Our Civil Liberties.* Seven Stories Press, 2002.
    Dempsey, James X., and David Cole. *Terrorism & The Constitution, Sacrificing Civil Liberties in the Name of National Security.* First Amendment Foundation, 2002.
    Netanyahu, Benjamin. *Fighting Terrorism: How Democracies Can Defeat Domestic and International Terrorists.* Noonday Press, 1997.

CRSO

SELF-DETERMINATION AND NATIONALISM

Across the world nationalist movements like the Québecois in French-speaking Canada and the British Nationalists in Gibraltar, campaign to determine their own allegiances and government. Many of these movements are peaceful, but some have degenerated into violence. India and Pakistan are currently locked in conflict over the future of (predominantly Muslim) Kashmir (under the control of Hindu India); and the Arab-Israeli conflict continues to rage over the proposed establishment of a State of Palestine. On the one hand, self-determination reflects the democratic goal that a people choose their own government; on the other, self-determination and nationalism can generate dangerous conflict and fragmentation where identity generates exclusivity (e.g., Yugoslavia). Can minority rights can be successfully accommodated in a single homogeneous state?

PROS

Self-determination is a fundamental right that must be afforded to a native or national group. The UN General Assembly Resolution 1514 (The Declaration Granting Independence to Colonial Countries and Peoples), the Helsinki Act, and the African Charter of Human Rights all assert that self-determination is an important right.

CONS

Calls for independence destabilize countries, as seen in Northern Ireland, Kashmir, Palestine, the Basque areas of Spain, and Sri Lanka. Turmoil does not support human rights, it almost always abrogates them. If the minority is able to actively take part in a legitimate and representative government, then self-determination is viewed as an illegitimate claim in international law.

The UN General Assembly Resolution 2625 argues that territorial integrity and stability "trump" claims for self-determination.

Some claims for self-determination and independence were nourished in the soil of the ill-treatment of native peoples by colonial powers. The recognition of minority rights protects cultural identities that risk being diluted. The activities of terrorist groups should not undermine the political agendas of nationalist parties and the protests of minority groups.

The wrongs inflicted by the colonial powers are not the fault of the new governments. In the post-Cold War era we are moving away from nationalist ideology. Nationalism is about difference, which flies in the face of the idea of the global citizen. Nationalist causes are often pursued by violent terrorist organizations that should not be rewarded for their disregard of human life. By trying to recognize minority rights, governments run the risk of giving minorities preferential treatment at the expense of the majority. National borders are becoming less significant definers of identity; Irish Americans, British Muslims, Catholic Africans, and French-speaking Arabs are all coherent identities. Boundaries are not the solution to the fear of the threat of cultural dilution or oppression.

The state borders drawn (particularly in Africa) by colonial empires were completely artificial. Ethnic groups were split and divided. In the post-colonial environment, these borders are inappropriate and do not delineate "true" nations. Self-determination would allow borders to be redrawn realistically. Nations of the world can have self-determination only if they have statehood.

The redrawing of country boundaries is hardly the best way to promote stability in newly independent nations. In 1964 the Organization of African Unity stated in the Cairo Resolution that it would accept the boundaries drawn by colonial powers. Governments ought to concentrate on bolstering states with civic identities. Federalism is one government structure that can accommodate self-determination within national boundaries. For example, in Canada, Quebec has relative autonomy including some native courts.

Self-determination does not always mean independence; in Gibraltar in 2002 a referendum on rejoining Spain was voted down by residents. More than 99% chose to maintain historic and legal ties to Britain. Self-determination is about representation and identity and choice.

How to determine who has the right to choose? Who is a "native"? Should all of Spain have been allowed to vote on the fate of Gibraltar? Should residents of the British mainland have voted? The broader international context may mean that other interests or legal agreements must take precedence (e.g., returning Hong Kong to China after over 100 years under British rule).

Sample Motions:
This House believes in native rights.
This House believes self-determination is a human right.
This House believes that one man's terrorist is another man's freedom fighter.

Web Links:
• International Institute for Self-Determination. <http://www.selfdetermination.net/>
Site maintained by an organization promoting peaceful self-determination, contains a list of conflicts centered on the issue of self-determination, a bibliography of print resources on the subject, and a list of issues in self-determination.
• Michael Freeman, "National Self-Determination, Peace and Human Rights," *Peace Review,* vol. 10, no. 2.
<http://www.mtholyoke.edu/acad/intrel/freeman.htm>
Article providing an overview of nationalism in the 20th century and contemporary world.

• Self-Determination for Gibraltar Group. <http://www.self-determination.gi/>
Site illustrates the kinds of issues involved in a campaign for self-determination.

Further Reading:
Hobsbawm, Eric J. *Nations and Nationalism Since 1780: Programme, Myth, Reality.* Cambridge University Press, 1993.
Ignatieff, Michael. *Blood and Belonging: Journeys into the New Nationalism.* Noonday Press, 1995.
Ranger, Terence, ed. *The Invention of Tradition.* Cambridge University Press, 1992.

CRℰSo

SEX EDUCATION IN SCHOOLS

For years conservatives and liberals in the United States debated whether schools should teach sex education or whether this responsibility is that of the parents. With the rise of teenage pregnancies and sexually transmitted diseases, particularly AIDS, the focus has shifted to what should be taught, rather than where. Should schools advocate sexual abstinence (refraining from sexual activity until the age of consent or marriage), or should society assume that the students will be sexually active and therefore encourage teaching safe sex?

PROS

The primary cause of unwanted pregnancies and the spread of sexually transmitted diseases (STDs) is ignorance about safe sex. The AIDS crisis of the 1980s and 1990s has shown that sex education must be a vital part of the school curriculum and may be supplemented by frank discussion at home.

As the US Guidelines for Comprehensive Sexuality Education (1991) state, "all sexual decisions have effects or consequences" and "all persons have the . . . obligation to make responsible sexual choices." While Hollywood promotes casual, thoughtless sex as the norm, teacher-led discussions can encourage responsible attitudes about sexual relationships.

Abstinence is an outdated approach based on traditional religious teaching. Some young people may choose it, but we cannot expect it to be the norm. Teenagers express their sexuality as part of their development. Having sex is not the problem; having unsafe sex or hurting people through sexual choices is.

CONS

Judging by the number of teenage pregnancies and the continuing spread of STDs, teenagers are not getting the message. Sex education in schools can be counterproductive because teens find it fashionable to ignore what teachers advocate. The most effective channel for sex education is the media, particularly TV, films, and magazines.

This is the wrong approach. Sex education in the classroom encourages young teenagers to have sex before they are ready and adds to peer pressure to become sexually active. In addition, any class discussion may lead to ridicule, thus devaluing the message. Sexual responsibility should be discussed in a one-to-one context, either with older siblings or parents.

Classroom education should promote abstinence. Sex education encourages sexual promiscuity. Advocating both safe sex and restraint is self-contradictory. Children are at risk of severe psychological and physical harm from having sex too young and should be encouraged to abstain.

Sample Motions:
This House believes that sex education should take place at home.
This House would rather not discuss it with its parents.

Web Links:
• Avert: AIDS & Sex Education. <http://www.avert.org/educate.htm>
Information on sex education from a leading UK-based AIDS education and medical research group.
• Sex Education Forum. <http://www.ncb.org.uk/sexed.htm>
Part of the larger UK National Children's Bureau site promoting sex education and offering information on questions involving sex.

• Sex Education, Teenage Pregnancy, Sex and Marriage: An Islamic Perspective. <http://www.crescentlife.com/articles/sex_education.htm>
Essay advocating sex education in a religious context.

Further Reading:
Moran, Jeffrey P. *Teaching Sex: The Shaping of Adolescence in the 20th Century.* Harvard University Press, 2000.

CRISO

SEX OFFENDERS: PUBLICLY NAMING

During the 1990s the US Congress passed two laws designed to protect children from dangerous sex offenders released from prison. The first law, the 1994 Jacob Wetterling Act (named after a child abducted at gunpoint), requires states to register individuals who have been convicted of sex crimes against children. The second, Megan's Law (1996), compels states to make information on registered sex offenders available to the public but gives states discretion in establishing the criteria for disclosure. Megan's Law was named after Megan Kanka, a 7-year-old girl who was sexually assaulted and murdered by a paroled sex offender. States vary on how they have implemented this law. Many post the name and address of offenders on Web sites or offer the public this information on CD. Others permit law enforcement officials only to notify neighbors of the offender. Megan's Law has generated heated discussion. Those supporting it maintain that it will protect children; those opposing it say that it is ineffective and will force convicts who had served their sentences to wear a "badge of infamy" for the rest of their lives.

PROS

Sex offenders, even more so than other criminals, are prone to repeat their crimes. Making their names public enables parents to protect their children and reduce the rate of sexual crime by repeat offenders.

Crimes of a sexual nature are among the most abhorrent and damaging that exist; they can ruin a child's life. Those guilty of such crimes cannot be incarcerated forever, thus extra precautions must be taken on their release to ensure that they pose no threat to the public.

These laws help the police to track down re-offenders

CONS

This proposal is a fundamental violation of the principles of our penal system, which are based on serving a set prison term and then being freed. Registration imposes a new punishment for an old crime, and, inevitably, will lead to sex offenders being demonized by their neighbors. Offenders have been forced out of their homes or lost their jobs as a result of notification. Innocent people will also suffer. Families of offenders have been subject to threats, and inaccurate information made public by the police has led to the harassment of innocent people. Such a risk cannot be tolerated; we cannot as a society revert to mob rule in place of justice.

Psychological evaluations can determine accurately whether an offender is still a risk to society or not. Should the offender be found to still be a threat, he should remain in custody. If the tests indicate that the offender is no longer a threat, he should be freed and allowed to live a normal life. Megan's Law eliminates this distinction and stigmatizes those who have genuinely reformed. Our penal system is based on the principle of reforming offenders. Ignoring the possibility of change is both ludicrous and unfair.

Registering offenders with the police may help law

PROS	CONS
more quickly, thus they are also brought to justice more swiftly and surely. These laws and their strong and swift enforcement provide a strong deterrent against repeat offenses.	enforcement, but making public the offender's whereabouts adds no advantage and might be counterproductive. The abuse and harassment that offenders might suffer could drive them underground, making police monitoring more difficult.
We cannot know how many children were saved by these laws, but even one child saved from sexual assault justifies them.	What evidence do we have that these laws have been effective in protecting people and preventing crime? Very little. As a result of the law, many prosecutors are reluctant to charge juveniles as sex offenders because they do not want children stigmatized for life. These offenders are not getting treatment and could pose a future risk to the public.

Sample Motions:
This House supports a national register of sex offenders.
This House would name and shame.

Web Links:
• Megan's Law Legislation in All 50 States. <www.klaaskids.org/pg-lgmg.htm>
Offers background information on the Jacob Wetterling Act and Megan's Law as well as links to summaries of state notification laws.
• Revising Megan's Law and Sex Offender Registration.
<http://www.appa-net.org/revisitingmegan.pdf>
Detailed essay in opposition to Megan's Law.

Further Reading:
Pryor, Douglas W. *Unspeakable Acts: Why Men Sexually Abuse Children.* New York University Press, 1999.
Ryan, Gail, Sandy Lane, and Alan Rinzler, eds. *Juvenile Sex Offending: Causes, Consequences and Correction.* Jossey-Bass, 1997.
Sampson, Adam. *Acts of Abuse: Sex Offenders and The Criminal Justice System.* Routledge, 1994.

CRSO

SINGLE SUPERPOWER: BENEFICIAL?

When the Soviet Union collapsed, people talked about the end of the "bipolar" world dominated by the Soviet Union and the United States. Ever since, the United States has been viewed as the single superpower, dominating the world culturally, economically, and militarily. Many argue that a single dominant power is not good. Others say that US domination will bring stability and prosperity across the globe. This dispute is also part of the ongoing debate on whether the world is "multipolar," with numerous centers of power and influence, or "unipolar," with real power concentrated in the United States.

PROS

The world is safer with a single strong superpower than it was in the "bipolar" Cold War with competing global alliances. It is also far safer than it was during the first half of the twentieth century, when having a number of powers resulted in two world wars and many smaller conflicts. History shows that the world is best off dominated by a single democracy.

CONS

Without any other nation to check its power, the United States can operate as it wants in the world arena, ignoring the wishes of other countries in pursuit of its goals. At least the bipolar structure of the Cold War world kept the two superpowers in check.

The existence of a single democratic superpower promotes the spread of democracy. If there is to be only one superpower, let it be democratic since democracy is the most desirable form of government.

As September 11 demonstrated, many international actors are hostile to peace and security. The world needs a powerful leader to unify the global effort against terrorism and provide better security for all people. Without a single superpower coordinating global security measures, Earth is much more likely to be a troubled place in the near future.

While the United States extols democracy, it frequently dictates to or ignores the concerns of other nations and is willing to intervene in the domestic affairs of other nations for its own purposes. The United States definitely abuses its power in the international arena. Democracy abhors the one-sided vertical distribution of power. Democracy prospers best in a world in which power is divided among many players.

September 11 demonstrated that a single nation, no matter how powerful, cannot control world events. World domination by a single superpower destroys the concept of equal nation-states upon which global society is based. It is bound to lead the world into chaos.

Sample Motions:

This House agrees that the existence of a single superpower is beneficial.
This House supports a multipolar structure for the world.
This House condemns the single superpower.

Web Links:

- Carnegie Council on Ethics and International Affairs. <http://www.carnegiecouncil.org>
  US international relations think tank focusing on ethical aspects of foreign policy.
- Foreign Policy Association. <http://www.fpa.org/newsletter_info2454/newsletter_info.htm>
  Features a variety of links and resources on the US role in the world.
- Muslimedia.com. <http://www.muslimedia.com/>
  A collection of anti-American views, among them a few positions about US hegemony.

Further Reading:

Brilmayer, Lea. *American Hegemony: Political Morality in a One-Superpower World*. Yale University Press, 1994
Huntington, Samuel P. "The Lonely Superpower." *Foreign Affairs* 78, no. 2 (March/April 1999).
Kagan, Robert. "The Benevolent Empire." *Foreign Policy* (Summer 1998).

CRSO

SINGLE-SEX SCHOOLS

Studies have shown that boys gain more academically from studying in coeducational schools, but that single-sex schools promote greater achievement in girls. But academic results are not the only criterion on which to judge the success of the education system. In 1996, a long-standing controversy over the Virginia Military Institute's male-only policy resulted in a landmark US Supreme Court ruling that the Institute must admit women. However, the Court left room for private (i.e., not state-run) single-sex institutions and for the establishment of such schools where needed to redress discrimination.

PROS

Women benefit from a single-sex education. Research shows that girls in single-sex schools participate more in class, develop much higher self-esteem, score higher in aptitude tests, are more likely to choose "male" disci-

CONS

A 1998 survey by the American Association of University Women, a long-time advocate of single-sex education, admitted that girls from such schools did not show academic improvement. That women from sin-

plines such as science in college, and are more successful in their careers. In *Who's Who*, graduates of women's colleges outnumber all other women. The United States has only 83 women's colleges.

gle-sex schools are more inclined to study math and science is of questionable importance to society. As the report noted, "Boys and girls both thrive when the elements of good education are there, elements like smaller classes, focused academic curriculum and gender-fair instruction." These conditions can be present in coeducational schools.

Children in the formative years, between 7 and 15, gravitate to their own sex. They naturally tend toward behavior appropriate to their gender. Thus implementing an education strategy geared specifically toward one gender makes sense. Certain subjects, such as sex education or gender issues, are best taught in single-sex classrooms.

The formative years of children are the best time to expose them to the company of the other gender so that they learn each other's behavior and are better prepared for adult life. The number of subjects benefiting from single-sex discussion is so small that this could easily be organized within a coeducational system.

Boys and girls distract each other from their studies, especially in adolescence as sexual and emotional issues arise. Too much time can be spent attempting to impress or even sexually harass each other. Academic competition between the sexes is unhealthy and only adds to unhappiness and anxiety among weaker students.

In fact boys and girls are a good influence on each other, engendering good behavior and maturity; particularly as teenage girls usually exhibit greater responsibility than boys of the same age. Academic competition between the sexes is a spur to better performance at school.

Single-sex schools (such as the Virginia Military Institute) are a throwback to the patriarchal society of the past; historically in many cultures, only men were allowed an education of any sort. Such single-sex institutions both remind women of past subservience and continue to bar them from full social inclusion.

Single-sex schools for women are a natural extension of the feminist movement; men have had their own schools, why shouldn't women? If single-sex schools existed only for men, then that would be discriminatory; however, as long as both genders have the choice of attending a single-sex institution (or a coeducational one), you cannot call it discrimination.

Teachers themselves are often discriminated against in single-sex schools; a boys' school will usually have a largely male staff where women may feel uncomfortable or denied opportunity, and vice versa.

Teachers frequently favor their own gender when teaching coeducational classes; for example, male teachers can undermine the progress and confidence of girl students by refusing to call on them to answer questions.

Sample Motions:
> This House believes in single-sex education.

Web Links:
- Atlantic Monthly: The Trouble with Single-Sex Schools. <http://www.theatlantic.com/issues/98apr/singsex.htm>
Article opposing single-sex schools by a graduate of a women's college.
- Single-Sex Education: The Supreme Court Speaks. <http://www.taiga.ca/~balance/index002/rutgin.html>
Text of the Supreme Court decision requiring the Virginia Military Institute to admit women.

Further Reading:
Miller-Bernal, Leslie. *Separate by Degree: Women Students' Experiences in Single-Sex and Coeducational Colleges.* Peter Lang, 2000.
Ruhlman, Michael. *Boys Themselves: A Return to Single-Sex Education.* Holt, 1997.
Streitmatter, Janice. *For Girls Only: Making a Case for Single-Sex Schooling.* State University of New York Press, 1999.

SMOKING, FURTHER RESTRICTIONS ON

Although most countries put age restrictions on the purchase of tobacco, over a billion adults smoke legally every day. Supplying this demand is big business. By the 1990s major tobacco companies had been forced to admit that their products were addictive and had serious health consequences, both for the user and for those subject to second-hand smoke. In the developed world, public opinion shifted against smoking, Many governments substantially increased taxes on tobacco to discourage smoking and to help pay for the costs of smoking-related illness. Yet, while smoking has declined among some groups, it has increased among the young. Meanwhile tobacco companies look to developing nations for new markets.

PROS

Smoking is extremely harmful to the smoker's health. The American Cancer Society estimates that tobacco causes up to 400,000 deaths each year—more than AIDS, alcohol, drug abuse, car crashes, murders, suicides, and fires combined. Worldwide some 3 million people die from smoking each year, one every 10 seconds. Estimates suggest that this figure will rise to 10 million by 2020. Smokers are 22 times more likely to develop lung cancer than nonsmokers, and smoking can lead to a host of other health problems, including emphysema and heart disease. One of the main responsibilities of any government is to ensure the safety of its population; that is why taking hard drugs and breaking the speed limit are illegal. Putting a ban on smoking would therefore be reasonable.

Of course, personal freedom is important; we should act against the tobacco companies, not individuals. If a company produces food that is poisonous or a car that fails safety tests, the product is immediately taken off the market. All cigarettes and other tobacco products are potentially lethal and should be taken off the market. In short, smoking should be banned.

Smoking is not a choice because nicotine is an addictive drug. Evidence suggests that tobacco companies deliberately produce the most addictive cigarettes they can. Up to 90% of smokers begin when they are under age 18, often due to peer pressure. Once addicted, continuing to smoke is no longer an issue of free choice, but of chemical compulsion. The government should ban tobacco just as it does other addictive drugs like heroin and cocaine because it is the only way to force people to quit. Most smokers say that they want to kick the habit,

CONS

While a government has a responsibility to protect its population, it also has a responsibility to defend freedom of choice. The law prevents citizens from harming others. It should not stop people from behavior that threatens only themselves. Dangerous sports such as rock climbing and parachuting are legal. No laws have been passed against indulging in other health-threatening activities such as eating fatty foods or drinking too much alcohol. Banning smoking would be an unmerited intrusion into personal freedom.

Cigarettes are very different from dangerous cars or poisonous foods. Cigarettes are not dangerous because they are defective; they are only potentially harmful. People should still be permitted to smoke them. A better comparison is to unhealthy foods. Fatty foods can contribute to heart disease, obesity, and other conditions, but the government does not punish manufacturers of these products. Both cigarettes and fatty foods are sources of pleasure that, while having serious associated health risks, are fatal only after many decades. They are quite different from poisonous foods or unsafe cars, which pose high, immediate risks.

Comparing tobacco to hard drugs is inaccurate. Tobacco is not debilitating in the same way that many illegal narcotics are, it is not comparable to heroin in terms of addictiveness, and it is not a mind-altering substance that leads to irrational, violent, or criminal behavior. It is much less harmful than alcohol. Many other substances and activities can be addictive (e.g., coffee, physical exercise) but this is no reason to make them illegal. People are able to abstain—many give up smoking every year—if they choose to live a healthier life. Nev-

so this legislation would be doing them a favor.

ertheless, many enjoy smoking as part of their everyday life.

Most smokers are law-abiding citizens who would like to stop. They would not resort to criminal or black market activities if cigarettes were no longer legally available; they would just quit. Banning smoking would make them quit and massively lighten the burden on health resources.

Criminalizing an activity of about one-sixth of the world's population would be insane. As America's prohibition of alcohol during the 1920s showed, banning a popular recreational drug leads to crime. In addition, governments would lose the tax revenue from tobacco sales, which they could use to cover the costs of health care.

The effects of smoking are not restricted to smokers. Second-hand smoke jeopardizes the health of nonsmokers as well. Research suggests that nonsmoking partners of smokers have a greater chance of developing lung cancer than other nonsmokers. Beyond the health risks, smoke also can be extremely unpleasant in the workplace or in bars and restaurants. Smoking causes discomfort as well as harm to others and should be banned.

The evidence that passive smoking causes health problems is very slim. At most, those who live with heavy smokers for a long time may have a very slightly increased risk of cancer. Smoke-filled environments can be unpleasant for nonsmokers, but reasonable and responsible solutions can be found. Offices or airports could have designated smoking areas, and many restaurants offer patrons the choice of smoking and nonsmoking sections. Allowing people to make their own decisions is surely always the best option. Restricting smoking in public places may sometimes be appropriate; banning it would be lunacy.

At the very least all tobacco advertising should be banned and cigarette packs should have even more prominent and graphic health warnings.

Where is the evidence that either of these measures would affect the rate of tobacco consumption? Cigarette companies claim that advertisements merely persuade people to switch brands, not start smoking. People start smoking because of peer pressure. Indeed, forbidding cigarettes will make them more attractive to adolescents. As for health warnings, if the knowledge that cigarettes have serious health risks deterred people from smoking, then no one would smoke. People start and continue to smoke in the full knowledge of the health risks.

Sample Motions:
    This House would ban tobacco.
    This House would not smoke.
    This House would declare war on the tobacco industry.

Web Links:
    • Center for Disease Control and Prevention: Tobacco. <http://www.cdc.gov/tobacco/index.htm>
    Research, data, and reports relating to tobacco as well as tobacco industry documents and campaigns for tobacco control.
    • Phillip Morris. <http://www.philipmorrisusa.com/>
    Major tobacco company site offering government reports on tobacco as well as information on tobacco issues including the marketing of tobacco products.
    • Smoking From All Sides. <http://www.cs.brown.edu/~lsh/smoking.html>
    Links to statistics and hundreds of articles on both sides of the argument.
    • The Tobacco Homepage. <http://www.tobacco.org/>
    Provides recent information on tobacco-related issues as well as documents, timelines, and links to all aspects of the tobacco controversy.

• World Health Organization: Tobacco Free Initiative. <http://www.who.int/toh/>
Information on WHO's worldwide program to stop smoking, as well as background information on the economic, health, and
societal impact of tobacco and smoking.

Further Reading:

Whelan, Elizabeth. *Cigarettes: What the Warning Label Doesn't Tell You: The First Comprehensive Guide to the Health Consequences of Smoking.* Prometheus, 1997.

ભ્ર

SPACE EXPLORATION

The space programs of both the US and the USSR were, perhaps, the most important prestige projects of the Cold War. From the launch of Sputnik, the first artificial satellite, in 1957, through to the first human space flight by Yuri Gagarin in 1961, the first moon landing in 1969, and beyond, both superpowers invested huge amounts of money to outdo each other in the Space Race. Since the end of the Cold War, however, the future of space exploration has become less clear. Russia no longer has the resources to invest in a substantial space program, and the United States has also cut back. Near the end of the twentieth century, American emphasis was on unmanned missions that are "faster, better, cheaper." Expensive, complex projects such as the Voyager missions of the late 1970s seem unlikely to be repeated. In particular, the commitment to manned exploration of space has almost disappeared, although potential missions to Mars are planned for the middle of the twenty-first century.

PROS

Humankind always struggles to expand its horizons. The curiosity that constantly pushes at the boundaries of our understanding is one of our noblest characteristics. The exploration of the universe is a high ideal; space truly is the final frontier. The instinct to explore is fundamentally human; already some of our most amazing achievements have taken place in space. No one can deny the sense of wonder we felt when for the first time a new man-made star rose in the sky, or when Neil Armstrong first stepped onto the moon. Space exploration speaks to that part of us that rises above the everyday.

The exploration of space has changed our world. Satellites allow us to communicate instantaneously with people on different continents and to broadcast to people all over the world. The Global Positioning System allows us to pinpoint locations anywhere in the world. Weather satellites save lives by giving advance warning of adverse conditions; together with other scientific instruments in orbit they have helped us gain a better understanding of our world. Research into climate change, for example, would be almost impossible without the data provided by satellites.

Space exploration has had many indirect benefits. The

CONS

High ideals are all well and good, but not when they come at the expense of the present. Our world is marred by war, famine, and poverty, with billions of people struggling simply to live from day to day. Our dreams of exploring space are a luxury we cannot afford. Instead of wasting our time and effort on prestige projects like the space program, we must set ourselves new targets. Once we have addressed the problems we face on Earth, we will have time to explore the universe, but not before then. The money spent on probes to distant planets would be better invested in the people of our own planet. A world free from disease, a world where no one lives in hunger, would be a truly great achievement.

Satellite technology has benefited humankind. However, launching satellites into Earth orbit differs significantly from exploring space. Missions to other planets and into interstellar space do not contribute to life on our planet. Moreover, most satellites are commercial; they are launched and maintained by private companies. Space exploration requires huge government subsidies and will never be commercially viable. For example, the Voyager missions alone cost almost $1US billion. This money could be better spent elsewhere.

These auxiliary advantages could have come from any

space program has brought about great leaps in technology. The need to reduce weight on rockets led to the microchip and the modern computer. The need to produce safe but efficient power sources for the Apollo missions led to the development of practical fuel cells, which are now being explored as possible power sources for cleaner cars. The effects of zero gravity on astronauts have substantially added to our knowledge of the workings of the human body and the aging process. We can never know exactly which benefits will emerge from the space program in the future, but we do know that we will constantly meet new obstacles and in overcoming them will find new solutions to old problems.

Space exploration is an investment in the future. Our world is rapidly running out of resources. Overpopulation could become a serious worldwide threat. Consequently, ignoring the vast potential of our own solar system—mining resources on asteroids or other planets, or even colonizing other worlds—would be foolish. If we fail to develop the ability to take advantage of these possibilities, we may find it is too late.

project. They are a result of giving people huge amounts of money and manpower to solve problems, not a result of a specific program. For example, many of the advances in miniaturization were the result of trying to build better nuclear missiles; this is not a good reason to continue building nuclear weapons. Similar resources would be far better devoted to projects with worthier goals, for example, cancer research or research into renewable energy sources. These, too, could provide many side benefits, but would tackle real problems.

Space exploration is a waste of resources. If we want to tackle the problems of overpopulation or of the depletion of resources, we must address them on Earth instead of chasing an elusive dream. We can deal with the problems of our planet in practical ways, and we must tackle them with all the resources and all the political will we have.

Sample Motions:
This House would explore the universe.
This House would explore the Final Frontier.
This House would reach for the stars.

Web Links:
• European Space Agency (ESA). <http://www.esa.int/export/esaCP/index.html>Provides information on the missions of the European Space Agency and the earthly use of space.
• Jet Propulsion Laboratory (JPL). <http://www.jpl.nasa.gov/>
Describes the research conducted by the JPL and provides an extensive collection of images of Earth, the stars and galaxies, the solar system, and deep space.
• National Aeronautics and Space Administration (NASA). <http://www.nasa.gov/>
Vast site describing the US space program and the other NASA activities.

Further Reading:
Cooper, Gordon. *Leap of Faith: An Astronaut's Journey into the Unknown.* HarperCollins, 2000.
Launius, Roger, Bertram Ulrich, and John Glenn. *NASA and the Exploration of Space.* Stewart, Tabori & Chang, 1998.

CRSO

STEM CELL RESEARCH AND THERAPEUTIC CLONING

Stem cells are cells that give rise to specialized cells such as heart or brain cells, muscle tissue, or skin in a developing embryo. Researchers believe that these cells hold the promise of future cures for deseases—such as diabetes, Parkinson's disease, and Alzheimer's disease— caused by the disruption of cellular function. Ethical issues surround stem cell use because such cells are "harvested" from embryos created during in vitro fertilization. (Stem cells can also be derived from adults, but they may not be as useful as embryonic cells.) Extracting the cells destroys the embryo and thus ends future human life. In addition, fears have been expressed that humans will clone themselves (therapeutic cloning) to create embryos to mine for stem cells.

PROS

Although therapeutic cloning will involve the creation and destruction of thousands of embryos, the resulting benefits will be so great as to outweigh moral considerations. Once the research goals have been achieved, the use of embryo treatments can be greatly reduced. The likely result of curing people of fatal diseases is worth the cost.

We already accept the creation and destruction of "spare" embryos for cycles of in vitro fertilization (IVF). IVF facilitates the creation of human life. Stem cell treatments will save existing human lives. The infertile will still survive. The sufferers of Huntington's chorea or Alzheimer's will not. If we accept the morality of IVF, we must accept the morality of stem cell treatment.

The creation, storage, and destruction of embryos can be strictly controlled. There should be no fear of "Frankenstein science."

The moral status of the embryo is distinct from that of the fetus. What reason is there to assert that life begins at the stage of embryo creation? The accepted test for clinical death is an absence of brain stem activity. The fetus first acquires a functioning brain six weeks after the embryo has been created. We cannot condone the "wastage" of human embryos. However, we must be wary of regarding the loss of an embryo as the loss of human life.

We cannot equate human embryos with human beings just because they could develop into adults. Between 50% and 70% of embryos are lost naturally through failure to implant in the wall of the uterus. The poten-

CONS

Merely hoping for a good outcome does not make immoral actions acceptable. Medical research should be governed by moral and ethical concerns, specifically, the duty every human being owes to another. However much sympathy we feel for sufferers of terminal diseases, we cannot tolerate the use of human embryos as means to an end. Stem cell research is inherently contradictory: Lives would be created and then destroyed in order to save other lives.

The loss of embryos in IVF is a reason to condemn IVF treatment. It is not a reason for allowing another procedure that will sacrifice much more potential life.

Media fears of mad scientists free to manipulate and destroy human life may be overstated. However, research projects carry a significant risk of destroying thousands of embryos for little or no scientific gain.

The embryonic human should have the same moral status as the fetus or the child or the adult. At what physiological point do we declare an embryo "human."? Are we to base a declaration of being human on physical appearance? That the embryo looks different from the fetus and from the adult does not prove that the embryo is not a human being.

The proper test of humanity should be if the embryo has the potential to organize itself into a "living human whole." Every embryo has this capacity. The fact that embryos are lost naturally does not imply that the

tial of an embryo to develop does not of itself make the embryo human.

Further research requires the use of the stem cells found in embryos. Research done with adult cells has yielded very little progress because of the difficulty of "reprogramming" an adult cell to develop as the particular neuron or tissue cell required. The greater understanding of human cells that scientists will gain from research with embryo stem cells may increase the utility of adult cells in the future. For the present, resources should be concentrated on research with stem cells harvested from embryos.

destruction of embryos is morally acceptable.

Researchers have no need to use embryo stem cells. Research has continued for many years into the use of adult stem cells. These cells are replaceable and could be used for the purposes of treatment and research without the destruction of embryos.

Sample Motions:
This House would allow stem cell research.
This House supports therapeutic cloning.

Web Links:
• American Journal of Bioethics. <http://www.ajobonline.com/cloning.php>
Provides a wide variety of resources on the ethics of cloning and genetic research.
• Ethics of Cloning. <http://www.wits.ac.za/bioethics/genethics.htm>
Scholarly article that argues that no ethnical issues arise in reproductive and therapeutic cloning.
• ReligiousTolerance.org. <http://www.religioustolerance.org/clo_ther.htm>
Provides good explanation of cloning for the lay person.

Further Reading:
Harris, John. *Clones, Genes and Immortality: Ethics and the Genetic Revolution.* Oxford University Press, 1998.
Holland, Suzanne, Karen Lebacqz, and Laurie Zoloth, eds. *The Human Embryonic Stem Cell Debate: Science, Ethics, and Public Policy.* MIT Press, 2001.
Lauritzen, Paul, ed. *Cloning and the Future of Human Embryo Research.* Oxford University Press, 2001.

CREED

SURROGATE MOTHERS

For many people, the first time they heard about surrogate motherhood was with the Baby M case in the mid-1980s. In this case the surrogate (biological) mother changed her mind about the adoption and took the baby into hiding rather than give her to the biological father and his wife. Ultimately, the courts gave the surrogate mother parental rights but gave custody of the child to the biological father. Since then, states have passed differing laws regarding surrogacy, ranging from outlawing paid surrogacy to recognizing surrogacy. A veritable industry has sprung up around surrogacy in the states with more liberal laws, with agencies charging fees to find surrogates and match them with potential adoptive parents. Surrogacy can be an expensive endeavor for the prospective parents, costing as much as $35,000 (and higher). But for infertile couples the lure of having a child that can be genetically linked to at least one of the partners is often irresistible. For other couples, especially gay, male couples, surrogacy presents one of the only paths to parenthood. The moral, legal, and practical aspects of surrogate reproduction make it contentious in debate and in practice.

PROS

Adoptive parents can require psychological evaluations for their surrogates to ensure they will make sacrifices for the unborn child. In addition, most of the women who commit to being a surrogate mother do so because they have a caring attitude and want to help people. This attitude would likely contribute to their making the best decisions for the child before it is born.

If surrogacy is done correctly, the birth (surrogate) mother and birth father and partner or spouse understand the ramifications of their decision before the pregnancy is embarked upon. Although more expensive, agencies are a good option. The agency will do psychological screening of and counseling of the surrogate mother and will ensure that the legal documents are in order. In a recent study in Britain, 90% of surrogate mothers had no anxieties about handing the baby over to the adoptive parents after birth. Only the rare cases where there is a problem make the media. The many surrogacy success stories do not.

Surrogacy enables parents to have children who are genetically linked to them. The child can actually have the DNA of both the father and the mother, depending on what method is used. In this way, parents know the genetic background of their child and can interact with the child from birth.

Women who are doing surrogacy solely for the money are usually weeded out through psychological tests. Most women who become surrogates enjoyed being pregnant and love their children. They want others to enjoy parenting too. Many surrogates have seen people close to them deal with infertility and want to help others avoid the pain of wanting children and not being able to have them. The money paid to surrogates is to compensate them for the effort it takes to carry a child. Often the money is used to enable the surrogate to not have to work during the pregnancy, so she can concentrate on keeping as healthy as possible. Surrogates and adoptive parents are more concerned with finding people whom they want to have a special relationship with rather than selling services to the highest bidder.

A recent study showed that the adoptive parents of babies born to surrogate mothers have higher-than-average parenting skills. The surrogate-born babies had normal temperaments. Parents of children born to surrogates have worked hard to become parents, usually turning to surrogacy as a last resort. They truly have

CONS

Because surrogate mothers do not have to raise the children, they have no incentive to make sure the children they are carrying have the best possible start. They may take drugs or medicines that could harm the child or may make unhealthy lifestyle choices during the pregnancy. A mother who will raise the child to which she gives birth is more likely to give the fetus every possible advantage.

The breaking of surrogate agreements involves many more complications than the breaking of other kinds of contracts. Surrogacy should not be allowed because a child should not be knowingly conceived in a circumstance where he or she could be brought into the world with such controversy. Surrogacy gone bad, as has happened in many media-hyped cases, can result in children growing up with one set of parents and being ripped away from them via court order and given to another set. Entering into a surrogacy agreement entails risks that are too great.

Many children in the US and abroad do not have parents. These children could be adopted by couples who are instead using surrogacy to become parents. Some individuals want to raise a child from infancy; however, other adults could choose to adopt older children to make their family.

Surrogacy is fundamentally capitalism in action. Despite feel-good images and rhetoric, the surrogate mothers are simply renting their wombs to the highest bidder in exchange for a monetary reward. We do not permit people to buy organs, so why should we permit people to rent a womb? The ethics of growing a person in one's womb and then selling them are highly suspect. We do not permit the selling of children after they are born; so the selling of a child while it is in the womb should also be outlawed. Surrogacy violates our ethical standards.

Children of surrogate mothers must face the fact that at birth they were turned over to their adoptive parents for a fee. They must deal with the rejection of knowing that the person whose womb they grew in did not want them. The adoptive mother does not have the opportunity to bond with the baby in utero and does not have

a desire to be parents and ultimately are good parents to the children they adopt at birth. Often the adoptive parents will keep in touch with the surrogate mother and sometimes allow the surrogate to have a relationship with the child. This creates a situation where the child knows that he or she was born in a unique way, but if handled correctly, the child knows how much he or she was wanted.

the connection to the baby that the birth mother does. The adoptive mother cannot usually give the benefits of breastfeeding to the baby, and the baby may wonder about his or her birth mother as they get older if the adoptive parents do not continue the relationship with the surrogate. If the relationship is continued, the child must negotiate a relationship with both mothers. The relationship with the adoptive mother may suffer when a relationship with the surrogate mother is maintained or developed.

Surrogacy gives gay couples who would like to share their lives with children the chance to have a family. Studies have shown that the children of gay couples are well adjusted. What is important is that the children are born to adoptive parents who will love them and care for them. Gay men deserve to have the option to become fathers just as heterosexual men do. If a surrogate mother feels comfortable providing the gay couple with a child, the state should not attempt to regulate this private arrangement.

Gay male couples are major users of surrogate services. Because many states will not permit gay adoptions, surrogacy is the only way these couples can have children. Placing children in a situation where they do not have a male and female role model is not right. These children will always be a minority in society and will face hardships that other children do not have to face. These couples should simply remain childless.

Sample Motions:
This House would ban the use of surrogate mothers.
This House believes that the potential harms of surrogacy outweigh the benefits.
This House advocates a federal law protecting the right to surrogacy.
This House believes that surrogate motherhood is the moral equivalent of selling an organ.

Web Links:
• The American Surrogacy Center, Inc. <http://www.surrogacy.com>
The purpose of the site, which was founded by a woman who became a mother through surrogacy, is to disseminate information on the third-party reproductive options of surrogacy and egg donation.
• Surrogacy From a Feminist Perspective. <http://www.healthlibrary.com/reading/ethics/10_97/chap5.htm>
This article, which lays out many of the arguments opposing surrogacy, maintains that surrogacy is simply a function of the patriarchal system.
• Surrogate Mothers On-Line. <http://www.surromomsonline.com>
This Web site is run by women who are involved in the surrogacy process as adoptive parents or as surrogates. It contains personal stories, a classified section where you can find ads for surrogates and adoptive parents, and articles about surrogacy.

Further Reading:
Dutton, Gail. *A Matter of Trust: The Guide to Gestational Surrogacy.* Clouds Publishing, 1997.
MacKlin, Ruth. *Surrogates & Other Mothers: The Debates over Assisted Reproduction.* Temple University Press, 1994.
Saban, Cheryl. *Miracle Child: Genetic Mother, Surrogate Womb.* New Horizon, 1993.

CR8O

TERM LIMITS

For years, the president was one of the few US politicians subject to term limits. As disaffection with politics and politicians grew in the early 1990s, voters looked to term limits to reform the system. By the end of the decade, 18 states had passed laws automatically forcing long-term state legislators out of office, while many municipalities limited the terms of mayors and other elected officials. Congressional term limits were part of the Republicans' 1994 "Contract with America," but Congress twice failed to muster the votes necessary for the constitutional amendment needed to make the change. In the early years of the new century, term limits receded from the political agenda and some states moved to repeal them.

PROS

Term limits ensure that politicians do not become corrupted by power and lose touch with the people and principles that first got them elected. Representatives who spend too many years in office, living in the national capital far from their constituents and surrounded by lobbyists and fellow politicians, easily become part of a professional governing class, remote from the concerns of normal people. Term limits recreate a class of citizen-legislators who see political office as a brief chance to improve their country, rather than as a long-term, comfortable career.

Term limits will overcome the advantages that incumbents have in any re-election campaign. These advantages include name recognition and greater access to funding from special interests.

The regular need to wage costly re-election campaigns may damage elected representatives' judgment (and even their honesty). They must do what is popular rather than what is right, acting in the narrow interest of constituents rather than considering the general welfare of the entire country's population. In addition, politicians running for re-election must pander to special interests to secure funding.

Term limits would bring fresh faces, talents, and experiences to the political process. They would ensure that elected officials had experience in the "real world" outside party political machines and bring more first-hand knowledge of business and industry to government.

CONS

Experience counts in politics, where even the most able new officeholder will take many months or even years to fully grasp the job. Policy issues and legislative bills are complicated, and the public is best served by a system that allows the re-election of experienced politicians. If long-term officeholders become too divorced from the voters, they will lose the next election. The regular need to run for re-election ensures accountability and keeps politicians in touch with grass-roots opinion.

Term limits are an insult to the intelligence of voters, who in a democracy are at liberty to vote out an unsatisfactory incumbent. Preventing a popular incumbent from running simply removes the voters' right to make important political decisions. If incumbents seem to have an unfair advantage, it is because of other aspects of the political system, e.g., lack of controls on campaign financing.

Corruption is actually more likely to occur in a system with term limits because officeholders have no incentive to do their best for the voters, whom they will not face again. Indeed, less honest politicians may become more corrupt, seeing the need to profit from their position as quickly as possible. Alternatively, they may toady to big business in the hope of landing lucrative lobbying jobs once out of office.

Amateur politicians, thrown into legislatures by the enforced early retirement of more experienced politicians, are likely to be naïve and easily exploited by special interests. Term limits are also likely to affect the relationship between the legislative and executive branches of government, because legislators will not have the experience to deal effectively with the president.

Sample Motions:
   This House would impose term limits.
   This House would clean up politics.
   This House calls for the return of the citizen-legislator.
   This House believes a new broom sweeps clean.

Web Links:
   • Term Limits: Special Report.
   <http://www.washingtonpost.com/wp-srv/politics/special/termlimits/termlimits.htm>
   Washington Post article on the status of term limits at the end of the 1990s.
   • U.S. Congressional and State Term Limit Action Page. <http://www.termlimits.org/>
   Presents justifications for term limits as well as state-by-state information on the status of term limits and other resources on the topic.

Further Reading:
   Coyne, James. *Cleaning House: America's Campaign for Term Limits.* Regnery Publishing, 1992.
   Crane, Edward H., and Roger Pilon, eds. *The Politics and Law of Term Limits.* Cato Institute, 1994.
   Kamber, Victor. *Giving Up on Democracy: Why Term Limits Are Bad for Democracy.* Regnery Publishing, 1995.
   Will, George F. *Restoration: Congress, Term Limits and the Recovery of Deliberative Democracy.* Free Press, 1994.

CR80

TERRORISTS, NEGOTIATING WITH

The rash of suicide bombings in Israel during the spring of 2002 has once again brought the question of negotiating with terrorists to the fore. Over the past decade, violence has declined in some areas, Northern Ireland for example, where terrorists have come to the negotiating table. In South Africa, the African National Congress, once considered a terrorist group, helped bring democracy to that nation and is now its major political party. Yet most nations will not negotiate with terrorists, and, as events in the Middle East have shown, negotiation does not always bring an end to terrorist attacks.

PROS

One man's terrorist is another man's freedom fighter. Most terrorist organizations do not engage in violence simply for the joy of it or for personal gain. Instead, they stand for a particular political position and often for a group of people. Every conflict has at least two sides. Look at the African National Congress in South Africa. For many years the South African government—and many foreign governments—regarded it as an illegal terrorist organization. South Africa's black majority, on the other hand, viewed it as a champion of freedom. History will record that it was on the side of justice, and the apartheid government was in the wrong.

Any government's primary responsibility is to save lives. History has shown that military action has little chance of succeeding against terrorists. Defeating terrorist groups is almost impossible without unbearably restricting the freedoms of the innocent. In the case of prolonged internal campaigns of terrorism, the promise of negotiations will almost always lead to a ceasefire.

CONS

The example of South Africa is an isolated one. In many cases, the political situation in regions where terrorists operate is far more complex, and it is far less clear who is in the right and who is in the wrong. Bottom line: Killing people is immoral. By accepting violence as a political tool, these groups become no more than murderers and should be treated as such.

Giving in to terrorists may save lives in the short term but is harmful in the longer term. Many terrorist groups resort to violence because they have not been able to achieve their goals through democratic means. By making concessions, the legitimate government sets a dangerous precedent and basically says that groups who use violence are more likely to get their way than

In the case of more isolated incidents, such as hostage-taking, making concessions usually saves lives.	those that use peaceful methods. Governments must demand that groups abandon violence and cease acts of terrorism before negotiations can even be considered.
Many terrorist campaigns are the result of long-standing political disagreements. Terrorism is often fueled by a long history of hatred and distrust. In such situations, the government must take the first steps because it is always the more powerful side in the conflict and can more readily make concessions. Only by taking the lead will the government be able to end the killing.	In fact, terrorists' willingness to use violence gives them undue power at the negotiating table; they can insist that all their demands be met or they will resume targeted and random murder. In Northern Ireland, Spain, and Israel negotiations have encountered this same stumbling block again and again. Terrorists cannot be trusted.
Refusing to talk to terrorists can cloud the issues surrounding their activities. Public sympathy for their cause may be aroused because they appear to be fighting an unresponsive, even oppressive, government. By negotiating, a government denies them the opportunity to present themselves as martyrs and permits public scrutiny of their often radical demands.	Again, negotiating with terrorists gives them a legitimacy that they do not deserve. Those who use peaceful means to achieve their goals should be respected; those who murder and terrorize innocent civilians must be treated not as political leaders but as criminals.

Sample Motions:
This House would talk to terrorists.
This House believes that force cannot eliminate ideology.
This House would bomb their beliefs out of existence.

Web Links:
• Federation of American Scientists. <http://www.fas.org/irp/threat/terror.htm>
Information on steps taken to combat terrorism after September 11.
• International Policy Institute for Counter-Terrorism. <http://www.ict.org.il/>
Maintained by an Israeli institute, the site offers general information on state-sponsored terrorism, terrorism and the law, and international and national counterterrorism activities.
• U.S. State Department Counterterrorism Office. <http://www.state.gov/s/ct/>
Provides current information on terrorism as well as a statement of US counterterrorism policy.
• Terrorist Group Profiles. <http://web.nps.navy.mil/~library/tgp/tgpmain.htm>
Maintained by the Dudley Knox Library of the Naval Postgraduate School, this site links to hundreds of reports and Web sites on terrorism.
• The Terrorism Research Center. <http://www.terrorism.com/index.shtml>
Offers essays on current issues as well a link to documents, research, and resources devoted to counterterrorism.

Further Reading:
Hoffman, Bruce. *Inside Terrorism.* Columbia University Press, 1999.
Lesser, Ian O., Bruce Hoffman, James Arquilla, et al. *Countering the New Terrorism.* Rand Corporation, 1999.
Reich, Walter, ed. *Origins of Terrorism: Psychologies, Ideologies, Theologies, States of Mind.* Woodrow Wilson Center, 1998.

CREO

TOBACCO REGULATION: ADDICTIVE DRUG?

Historically, the production and sale of tobacco products were not regulated by the federal Food and Drug Administration (FDA). Early in the 1990s, the new director of the FDA, Dr. David Kessler, wanted to bring tobacco products under the control of the FDA. He reasoned that the nicotine in tobacco qualifies as a drug under the FDA definition. After investigation, he concluded that tobacco companies themselves knew that nicotine was an addictive drug and that they deliberately manipulated the nicotine content of their products. Accordingly, he ruled that cigarettes and smokeless tobacco should be seen as "drug delivery systems," under the jurisdiction of the FDA, and he introduced rules forbidding their sale to minors and restricting their promotion through advertising. He was supported by an executive order from President Bill Clinton in 1995. His ruling was challenged in court in 1997; the court concluded that the FDA had jurisdiction to control sales, but not advertising. On appeal, a higher court ruled that the FDA had no jurisdiction at all over tobacco. This ruling was reaffirmed by the Supreme Court in 2000. In some ways, the question has been answered by history, but it is not closed because Congress has the power to give the FDA appropriate jurisdiction should it so choose.

PROS

The Food and Drug Administration is responsible for regulating drugs, which are defined as "substances (other than food) that are intended to affect the structure and function of the body." Since the nicotine in tobacco has this effect, it should be classified as a drug, and its sale, distribution, and promotion should be controlled by the government.

Restricting the sale of nicotine is especially important because it is harmful and addictive. Most people who smoke are unable to quit, even though they want to.

The addictive power of nicotine is recognized by the tobacco industry. Internal industry documents show that tobacco companies recognize that nicotine is the element in cigarettes that smokers crave most. They have taken care to ensure that even low-tar cigarettes remain high in nicotine, and one tobacco company actively tried to develop tobacco plants with higher nicotine content. Clearly, the tobacco industry intended this drug to have an effect on the function of the body.

Given that nicotine is addictive, discouraging young people from smoking is vital. Surveys show that very few people start smoking after the age of 18. Therefore, we must ban the sale of cigarettes to minors and outlaw advertising directed to them.

CONS

When Congress delineated the role of the FDA in the Food, Drug & Cosmetics Act of 1938, it did not stipulate that the FDA should regulate tobacco. Given the existence of another agency that had tobacco in its purview—the Bureau of Alcohol, Tobacco and Firearms—it is clear that Congress had no such intent. Moreover, as Congress clearly regards tobacco as a completely legal substance, the FDA has no business restricting it.

Yes, the FDA has regulatory power over drugs; the FDA is also responsible for ensuring that drugs are "safe and effective" before allowing them to be marketed. Given earlier FDA statements, clearly the agency does not intend to rule that tobacco is safe. Rather, the FDA plans to rule that tobacco is unsafe and dangerous, and ban it from the market completely. Remember: Congress never intended to ban tobacco from the market.

The FDA has taken advantage of a very vague definition of "drug" in order to classify nicotine as such. In addition, labeling nicotine an "addictive drug," which makes it sound like heroin, is patently unfair (and untrue). Millions of people have quit smoking, usually without outside help, and former smokers outnumber current smokers in the adult population.

The dangers of smoking have been known for more than 30 years, and every cigarette package acknowledges them. But the individual has a right to assess those dangers personally and make a decision about whether to smoke. The government has no right to interfere with that right or to make the decision for the individual.

PROS	CONS
Unquestionably smoking creates health problems; indeed, tobacco has caused a major public health crisis. The FDA has a responsibility to the citizens of the United States to do what it can to improve public health, including implementing regulations to reduce the use of tobacco in the country.	The decision to classify tobacco as a drug is an example of government by fiat. The representatives of the people, members of Congress, did not make the decision; it was made unilaterally by a government agency, one that was far exceeding its designated powers, and seconded by an executive branch that had no regard for due legislative process.

Sample Motions:

This House would petition Congress to designate tobacco as a drug.

This House believes that the Food and Drug Administration should label tobacco as a drug.

Web Links:

• American Cancer Society. <http://www.cancer.org/eprise/main/docroot/PED/ped_10?sitearea=PED>
National organization's Web site supplies cancer information and statistics.

• American Lung Association. <http://www.lunguse.org/tobacco/index.html>
National organization Web site offering information on the relationship between smoking and lung disease.

• Brown University's Smoking From All Sides. <http://www.cs.brown.edu/people/lsh/smoking.html>
Web site includes several documents discussing both sides of the debate.

• Society for Research on Nicotine and Tobacco. <http://www.srnt.org>
Symposia of abstracts on tobacco and nicotine addiction.

Further Reading:

Gately, Iain. *Tobacco: A Cultural History of How an Exotic Plant Seduced Civilization.* Grove Press, 2002.
Lemieux, Pierre. *Smoking and Liberty: Government as a Public Health Problem.* Varia Press, 1997.
Rain, Robert L., and Stephen D. Sugarman. *Regulating Tobacco.* Oxford University Press, 2001.

CRITICAL

UN SECURITY COUNCIL VETO, ABOLITION OF

The United Nations Charter gives the UN Security Council the primary responsibility for maintaining international peace and security. It is the only UN body that has enforcement power, and, as such, it can approve diplomatic and economic sanctions or vote military action. The Council includes five permanent (P5) members: the United States, the United Kingdom, China, France, and Russia. In addition, 10 seats on the Security Council are held by member nations that are elected for two-year terms. Although the Council makes decisions by the affirmative vote of nine of the 15 members, any member of the P5 can veto any decision. When a P5 member registers an unpopular veto, reformers often call for the restriction or abolition of the veto power.

PROS

The veto power is an anachronism. The P5 got this privilege for two reasons that have no application in the post-Cold War world. First, to protect national interests, the Big Three (the US, Britain, and the Soviet Union) made the veto a prerequisite for establishing the United Nations following World War II. Second, the P5 held unrivaled strategic might through their nuclear weapons technology or nuclear capacity. The P5 will

CONS

The P5 has wielded veto power with increasing success both during and after the Cold War. Between 1945 and 1990, members of the P5 vetoed 240 resolutions. Yet between 1990 and 1999 they utilized the veto on only seven occasions while mandating more than 20 peacekeeping operations. This figure exceeds the total number of operations undertaken in the preceding 45 years. The use of the veto during the Cold War may

not abandon the UN or the cause of global peace if they lose the veto power. Moreover, the global power balance has shifted dramatically since 1945. Nuclear weapons have spread in the past decades: Pakistan, North Korea, Egypt, Iraq, and Iran have or are developing nuclear weapons.

Statistics do not reveal the true defect of the institutional arrangement. The Security Council consistently fails to consider issues that might be vetoed. For example, NATO initiated military action against Yugoslavia without Security Council authorization because it had become evident that Russia and China would veto UN military involvement.

In the rare recent circumstances in which the veto has been exercised, it has been hijacked by ideological demands and petty national interests. China prevented peacekeeping operations in Guatemala and Macedonia because these countries had ties to Taiwan. The veto is no longer applied for the maintenance of collective security.

The issue of abolishing the veto is worthy of discussion. A debate will clarify the nature of the veto and its application and educate the public on the Charter's aims. The public could then pressure members to act in accordance with the Charter.

The veto power operates to the detriment of international arms control agreements. The Security Council directly or indirectly enforces the web of treaties dealing with weapons of mass destruction either because treaties make the Council the enforcing agent or because members of the P5 are prominent signatories. The veto prevents the Council from fulfilling its most vital function. Iraq, for example, has breached every Council measure pertaining to arms limitation to the extent that UN inspectors were withdrawn from Baghdad. The absence of an effective response can be attributed to Russian support of Iraq.

have saved the world from nuclear war. Now, increasing proliferation of nuclear weapons is a reason for maintaining the unity of the P5 by means of the veto. If the P5 is split on a matter of international security, any of its members could become a rogue state. In addition, the logic of divide-and-rule applies in the international arena.

We must expect that nations will circumvent the Security Council. Following the Yugoslav conflict, the Security Council endorsed NATO's campaign. The Council then authorized the deployment of a peacekeeping force. The Security Council thus proved to be a unifying force.

Collective security is often indistinguishable from the national interests of the P5. The military might of P5 members is such that they must avoid disagreement to preserve international peace. The P5 may occasionally cast the veto for selfish reasons. Maintaining unity is more important (and more critical than ever) in today's multipolar world.

Abolishing the veto is impossible. The P5 will not willingly cede its preeminent position in international politics. And remember, each member of P5 would have the power of veto over any proposal to remove the veto.

You cannot glibly attribute the failure to create an effective system for arms limitation to P5 veto power. Veto or no veto, what should constitute the appropriate Security Council response to a breach of a nonproliferation treaty? Under the Charter, the Council could authorize economic sanctions or direct military intervention. Would either overtly hostile approach encourage disarmament? Diplomacy is often best conducted without the big stick of the Security Council. Sympathy for Iraq is not limited to Russia. France, also a P5 member, has objected to the Council's sanctions against that country. Nonproliferation is precarious because nations have different interests. These interests would likely be inflamed without the crucial safety valve the veto provides for power politics.

Sample Motions:
 This House would abolish the Security Council veto.
 This House would say no to the veto.
 This House would veto every veto.

Web Links:
- Commission on Global Governance. <http://www.cgg.ch/unreform2.htm>
Presents proposals for reforming the United Nations.
- Global Policy Organization. <http://www.globalpolicy.org/security/docs>
Offers documents on the Security Council as well as proposals to reform it.
- The United Nations: Security Council. <http://www.un.org/Overview/Organs/sc.html>
Provides information on the Council's members, structure, powers, and functions as well as links to recent Council documents.

Further Reading:
Roberts, Adam, and Benedict Kingsbury. *United Nations, Divided World: The United Nation's Role in International Relations.* Oxford University Press, 1994.
Russett, Bruce, and Ian Hurd. *The Once and Future Security Council.* Palgrave, 1997.

CRSO

UN STANDING ARMY

A standing army is a permanent military force that is entirely under the command of a single authority. This is almost always a national government, although in the past European colonial companies sometimes maintained their own private military forces, as did feudal barons and warlords (for example, in China in the 1920s). At present the UN has no military force of its own to send on peacekeeping or peacemaking missions; instead it must gather together troops and equipment volunteered by member states on an ad hoc basis for each individual crisis.

PROS

The UN must reform the way it raises military missions. Under the present system, months pass before troops are in the field; these forces are often inadequate to the assigned mission because member states have pledged fewer troops than requested. Thus, the UN has often acted too late, with too little force, and, as a result, has failed to avert humanitarian disasters in Somalia, Bosnia, and Sierra Leone. A UN standing army would be able to rapidly contain crises before they turn into wars and humanitarian disasters.

Because a UN standing army would be independent of the great powers, it would be respected as a neutral peacemaker and peacekeeper. It would also be free of accusations of meddling and self-interest that accompany the troops from neighboring states in UN interventions.

A UN standing army would be more effective than the troops currently staffing many missions. Most UN operations are supplied by developing nations whose troops are underequipped and badly trained. A UN standing army would be better prepared, and its soldiers would be more highly motivated because they would

CONS

A UN standing army is unnecessary. In many cases UN missions are very successful; some problems arise from lengthy and difficult Security Council deliberations, inadequate mandates, etc., rather than the speed at which the UN gathered a peacekeeping force. If the UN had a standing army it would be more likely to use inappropriate force. A very rapid response may also worsen problems. The time it now takes to gather and insert a UN force may provide a period in which the warring groups feel compelled to negotiate before outside intervention becomes a reality.

Only governments have standing armies. This plan would inevitably make the UN a world government, one that is not democratic and where a totalitarian state has veto power over key decision making. A standing army may be counter-productive, undermining current perceptions of the UN's neutrality and weakening its moral authority and ability to broker peace agreements.

Differences in language, culture, etc., will seriously mar operational effectiveness, especially in combat situations. In addition, in a multinational force the suspicion always arises that a great many individual soldiers may be taking sides in a particular conflict. Are such soldiers to be pulled out from a particular mission,

be enlistees rather than conscripts. A single UN force would also have better command and control than is currently the case: Often, different national forces and their commanders fail to work effectively together. Successful forces like the French Foreign Legion show that differences in language and culture need not be problems in combat situations.

A UN standing army would benefit the world economy by preventing refugee crises and other humanitarian disasters. These costs are both direct (through aid) and indirect (as developed nations often become the destination of illegal immigrants fleeing conflicts at home). War also disrupts trade and thus damages the global economy. Greater confidence that war can be avoided will encourage long-term investment and contribute to greater prosperity. The UN pays member states for providing troops, so a UN standing army would not be much more expensive than the present system.

Without the creation of a standing army other UN reforms will not address the central problems of peacekeeping. A rapid reaction force drawn from member states might speed up the arrival of troops slightly, but the UN would still be dependent upon the goodwill of its members.

thereby weakening the whole force? A UN army might also be very poorly equipped; if the advanced military powers see the UN as a potential adversary, they will refuse to sell it their best arms and munitions.

The cost of such an army would be very high; the UN would have to train, transport, and equip the force for every possible type of combat situation. At present the UN can draw on the equipment and skills of member states to deal with various situations.

The UN can improve response without resorting to a standing army. A Rapid Reaction Force with elite military capability, pledged in advance for UN operations, would build on the best features of the current system. Removing the veto power of the Permanent Five in the Security Council would avoid deadlocks and the compromises that produce weak mission mandates. Better intelligence and analysis, as well as central logistical planning, would permit the UN to assemble forces and draft mandates before problems became full-blown crises. Rules could be changed so that the Security Council could not pass resolutions requiring force until members have pledged troops.

Sample Motions:
   This House would create a UN standing army.
   This House would give the watchdog some teeth.

Web Links:
   • UN: Peacekeeping. <http://www.un.org/Depts/dpko/dpko/home_bottom.htm>
   Extensive UN site providing an overview of philosophy and goals behind peacekeeping missions as well as historical information on missions since 1948.
   • UN: Report on the Panel on United Nations Peace Operations. <http://www.un.org/peace/reports/peace_operations>
   Text of the 2000 panel report on peacekeeping operations as well as information about ongoing peacekeeping, political, and peace building missions.

Further Reading:
   Biermann, Wolfgang, and Martin Vadset, eds. *UN Peacekeeping in Trouble: Lessons Learned from the Former Yugoslavia*. Ashgate, 1999.
   Gordon, D. S., and F. H. Toase, eds. *Aspects of Peacekeeping*. Frank Cass, 2001.
   Sarooshi, Danesh. *The United Nations and the Development of Collective Security*. Oxford University Press, 2000.
   Shawcross, William. Deliver *Us from Evil: Peacekeepers, Warlords and a World of Endless Conflict*. Simon and Schuster, 2000.
   Whitman, Jim. *Peacekeeping and UN Agencies*. Frank Cass, 1999.

VEGETARIANISM

Very few human societies have forsworn eating meat, fowl, and fish, although in some parts of the world grains constitute almost the whole of the diet, with meat, fowl, or fish rare additions. These diets often have been the result of poverty, not choice. In modern Western societies, however, voluntary vegetarianism is on the increase. Many believe it is immoral for human beings to eat other animals. Some take an even more absolute line, refusing to eat dairy products or eggs as well because of the conditions in which the animals that produce them are raised.

PROS

The main reason to be a vegetarian is to reduce animal suffering. Farm animals are sentient, living beings like humans, and, like us, they can feel pleasure and pain. Farming and killing these animals for food is wrong. The methods of farming and slaughter are often barbaric and cruel, even on "free range" farms. Also, in most countries, animal welfare laws do not cover animals farmed for food.

To suggest that farm factories are "natural" is absurd; they are unnatural and cruel. To eat meat is to perpetuate animal suffering on a huge scale, a larger, crueler, and more systematic scale than anything found in the wild. Humanity's "superiority" over other animals means humans have the reasoning power and moral instinct to stop exploiting other species. If aliens from another planet, much more intelligent and powerful than humans, farmed (and force-fed) human beings in factory farm conditions, we would think it was morally abhorrent. If this would be wrong, then is it not wrong for "superior" humans to farm "lower" species simply because of our ability to do so?

Human beings are omnivores and are rational agents with free will, thus they can choose whether to eat meat, vegetables, or both. It might be "natural" for humans to be violent toward one another but that does not mean that it is right. Some natural traits are immoral and should be restrained. In any case, our closest animal cousins, the apes, eat an all-vegetable diet.

Becoming a vegetarian is an environmentally friendly thing to do. Modern farming is one of the main sources of pollution. Beef farming is one of the main causes of deforestation, and as long as people continue to buy fast food, financial incentives will be in place to continue cutting down trees to make room for cattle. Because of our desire to eat fish, our rivers and seas are being emptied and many species face extinction. Meat farmers use up far more energy resources than those

CONS

Eating meat does not need to mean cruelty to animals. A growing number of organic and free range farms can provide meat without cruelty. We can extend animal welfare laws to protect farm animals, but that does not mean that it is wrong in principle to eat meat.

It is natural for human beings to farm, kill, and eat other species. The wild offers only a brutal struggle for existence. That humans have succeeded in that struggle by exploiting our natural advantages means that we have the right to use lower species. In fact, farming animals is much less brutal than the pain and hardship animals inflict on each other in the wild.

Human beings have evolved to eat meat. They have sharp canine teeth for tearing animal flesh and digestive systems adapted to eating meat and fish as well as vegetables. Modern squeamishness about eating animals is an affectation of a decadent society that flies in the face of our natural instincts and physiology. We were made to eat both meat and vegetables. Cutting out half of this diet will inevitably mean we lose this natural balance.

All of these problems would exist without meat farming and fishing. Deforestation has occurred for centuries as human civilizations expand, but planting sustainable forests can now counteract it. Meat farmers contribute little to pollution, and many worse sources of pollution exist. Vegetable and grain farmers also pollute through use of nitrates, pesticides, and fertilizers. Finally, the energy crisis is one of global proportions in which meat farmers play a minute role. Finding alternative sources

growing vegetables and grains. Eating meat, fowl, and fish causes not only cruelty to animals, but also harm to the environment.

"Going veggie" offers significant health benefits. A vegetarian diet contains high quantities of fiber, vitamins, and minerals, and is low in fat. A vegan diet (which eliminates animal products) is even better because eggs and dairy products are high in cholesterol. Eating meat increases the risk of developing many forms of cancer. In 1996 the American Cancer Society recommended that red meat be excluded from the diet entirely. Eating meat also increases the risk of heart disease. A vegetarian diet reduces the risk of serious diseases and, because it is low in fat, also helps to prevent obesity. Plenty of vegetarian sources of protein, such as beans and bean curd, are available.

Going vegetarian or vegan reduces the risk of contracting food-borne diseases. The inclusion of animal brains in animal feed led to outbreaks of bovine spongiform encephalitis ("mad cow disease") and its human equivalent, Creutzfeldt-Jakob Disease. Meat and poultry transmit almost all of the potentially fatal forms of food poisoning.

of energy, not limiting meat farming, will solve this problem.

The key to good health is a balanced diet, not a meat-and fish-free diet. Meat and fish are good sources of protein, iron, and other vitamins and minerals. Most of the health benefits of a vegetarian diet derive from its being high in fiber and low in fat and cholesterol. We can achieve these benefits by avoiding fatty and fried foods, eating only lean grilled meat and fish, and including a large amount of fruit and vegetables in our diet. A meat- and fish-free diet is unbalanced and can result in protein and iron deficiencies. Also, in the West a vegetarian diet is a more expensive option, a luxury for the middle classes. Fresh fruit and vegetables are extremely expensive compared to processed meats, bacon, burgers, sausages, etc.

Of course we should enforce the highest standards of hygiene and food safety. But this does not mean that we should stop eating meat, which, in itself, is a natural and healthy thing to do.

Sample Motions:
This House believes that if you love animals you shouldn't eat them.
This House would go veggie.

Web Links:
• BritishMeat.Com. <http://www.britishmeat.com/49.htm>
Despite its name, the site offers 49 reasons for becoming a vegetarian categorized by general area-health, economy, environment, ethics.
• Earthsave.Org. <http://www.earthsave.org/index.htm>
Provides information in opposition to factory farming and in support of a grain-based diet.
• People for the Ethical Treatment of Animals. <http://www.peta.org>
Radical animal rights organization offers arguments in favor of vegetarianism and information on how to become a vegetarian.
• The VivaVegie Society. <http://www.vivavegie.org/vv101/101reas98.html>
Essay offering 101 arguments for vegetarianism.

Further Reading:
Eisnitz, Gail. *Slaughterhouse: The Shocking Story of Greed, Neglect, and Inhumane Treatment Inside the U.S. Meat Industry.* Prometheus, 1997.
Marcus, Erik. *Vegan: The New Ethics of Eating.* McBooks, 1997.
Walters, Kerry, and Lisa Portmess, eds. *Ethical Vegetarianism: From Pythagoras to Peter Singer.* State University of New York Press, 1999.

CR8O

VOTING, COMPULSORY

Voter turnout in US elections has decreased dramatically in recent decades. In the 2000 presidential election, only 55% of adult American citizens voted, one of the lowest percentages in a national election of any developed country. There are many reasons for the decline, including complicated registration procedures and voter apathy. To reinvigorate the electorate some have suggested making voting compulsory as it is in Australia, Switzerland, and Singapore. Some nations with compulsory voting levy fines against those who do not participate. To accommodate those voters who do not wish to vote for any of the candidates, they make available a no-vote option on the ballot. For many Americans the issue of compulsory voting is intertwined with the issue of individual rights vs. civic duties.

PROS

In all democracies voter apathy is highest among the poorest and most excluded sectors of society. Because poor and marginalized people do not vote, governments do not create policies addressing their needs. This leads to a vicious cycle of increasing isolation. When the most disenfranchised are required to vote, then local, state, and national governments will take notice of them.

A high turnout is important for a proper democratic mandate and the functioning of democracy. In this sense voting is a civic duty comparable to jury duty. We've made jury duty compulsory to ensure that the courts function properly. This is a strong precedent for making voting compulsory.

Soldiers in numerous wars and the suffragettes of many countries fought and died for the right to vote. We should respect their sacrifice by voting.

People who know they will have to vote will take politics more seriously and start to take a more active role.

CONS

This idea is nonsense. Political parties do try to capture the votes of the poor. Low turnout is best cured by more education. In addition, the forced inclusion of these less-interested voters will increase the influence of political "spin" because presentation will become more important than clear argument. This will further trivialize politics and bury the issues under a pile of hype.

In a democracy, the right not to vote is as fundamental as the right to vote. Individuals should be able to choose whether they want to vote. Some people are just not interested in politics, and they should have the right to abstain from the political process. We could also argue that those who care enough about key issues to vote deserve to be heard above those who do not. Any given election will function without a 100% turnout; a much smaller turnout will suffice. The same is not true of juries, which do require a 100% turnout all of the time. Even in healthy democracies people don't want to perform jury duty; therefore it has been made compulsory. However, in a healthy democracy people should want to vote. If they are not voting, it indicates there is a fundamental problem with that democracy. Forcing people to vote cannot solve such a problem; it merely causes resentment.

Those who fought for democracy fought for the right to vote, not the compulsion to vote. The failure to vote is a powerful statement because it decreases turnout, which decreases a government's mandate. By forcing unwilling voters to the ballot box, a government can make its mandate much larger than the people actually wish it to be.

People who are forced to vote will not make a properly considered decision. At best they will vote randomly, at worst they will vote for extreme parties as happened in

Australia recently.

Compulsory voting is effective. In Australia turnouts are as high as 98%!	The idea is not feasible. If a large proportion of the population decided not to vote it would be impossible to make every nonvoter pay the fine. The government would have to chase down millions of people and take action against millions who would not pay. Ironically, this measure would hurt most those who are supposedly being enfranchised because they are least able to pay.
In nations with compulsory voting, postal and proxy voting is available for those who are otherwise busy. In addition, when Internet voting becomes available in a few years, those with computers will be able to vote from their own homes.	Many people don't vote because they are busy and cannot take the time off. Making voting compulsory will not get these people to the ballot box if they are actually unable to do so.

Sample Motions:
    This House would make voting compulsory.
    This House believes that a democracy is no place for apathy.
    This House believes that voting is a duty, not a right.

Web Links:
    • The Great Voting Hoax. <http://www.mind-trek.com/writ-dtf/votehoax/index.htm>
    One individual's response to compulsory voting.

Further Reading:
    Smith, Lindsay. *Compulsory Voting: A Comparative Approach.* Mitchell College, 1980.

CREO

WAR CRIMES TRIBUNALS

Always controversial and shrouded in the solemn aftermath of terrible crimes, war crimes tribunals are the international community's response to national wrongdoings. They raise serious questions about sovereignty and international law. Whether held after World War II, Rwanda, Bosnia, or Kosovo, they never fail to provoke outrage from one corner and vindictiveness from the other. Would such matters better be left alone? The trial of Slobodan Milosevic in The Hague in the opening years of this century is an example of how complicated issues of international justice and power come to the fore in such tribunals.

PROS	CONS
Wrongdoing and wrongdoers must be punished. When a crime has consumed an entire nation, only a foreign trial can supply disinterested due process.	Of course wrongdoing should be punished. But the trial should be held in the country where the crime was committed. Any outside intervention in matters of sovereign states is high-handed and imperialistic.
Countries can explicitly cede jurisdiction for such crimes to international tribunals. These bodies are trying to achieve justice and closure that will benefit the entire nation.	Closure is the last thing tribunals bring. These trials alienate large portions of the nation and turn people against the new government, which is seen as collaborating with foreign imperialists. Such trials increase tension.

PROS	CONS
The world community must send a clear message that it will act against appalling war crimes. This must be done on an international stage through international courts.	No one can dispute the enormity of such crimes. But these trials damage a nation by reopening old wounds. Spain, for example, did not embark on witch-hunts following the bloody and repressive regime of Francisco Franco. Instead, it turned the page on those years and moved on collectively with no recrimination. Between justice and security there is always a trade-off. Where possible, peace should be secured by reconciliation rather than recrimination.
The issue of sovereignty is increasingly less important in a globalizing world. The pooling of sovereignty occurs with increasing frequency, and any step toward an internationalization of legal systems, such as the use of international tribunals, is welcome.	Whatever the truth about globalization and sovereignty, war crimes tribunals do not standardize justice. They are nothing more than victors' arbitrary justice. This type of justice undermines international law.
We have to uphold the principle that if you commit serious crimes, you will be punished. If we do not take action against war criminals, we will encourage future crimes.	The threat of possible legal action has not stopped countless heinous crimes in the past, so why should it now? These people are not rational and have no respect for international law.

Sample Motions:

This House would have war crimes tribunals.

This House believes war crimes must be punished.

Web Links:

• American University: Research Office for War Crimes Tribunals. <http://www.wcl.american.edu/pub/humright/wcrimes/research.html>

Detailed site on actual tribunals.

• Issues and Controversies on File: War Crimes Tribunals. <http://www.facts.com/icof/warintro.htm>

Clear and comprehensive introduction offering historical background as well as arguments for and against tribunals.

• War Crimes Tribunals. <http://www.globalpolicy.org/intljustice/tribindx.htm>

Provides information on UN war crimes tribunals in Rwanda and Yugoslavia as well as efforts to establish tribunals in East Timor, Cambodia, and Sierra Leone.

Further Reading:

Askin, Kelly Dawn. *War Crimes Against Women: Prosecution in International War Crimes Tribunals.* Martinus Nijhoff, 1997.

Bass, Gary Jonathan. *Stay the Hand of Vengeance: The Politics of War Crimes Tribunals.* Princeton University Press, 2000.

Harris, Marshall Freeman, R. Bruce Hitchner, et al. *Making Justice Work: The Report of the Century Foundation/Twentieth Century Fund Task Force on Apprehending Indicted War Criminals.* Twentieth Century Fund, 1998.

Hitchens, Christopher. *The Trial of Henry Kissinger.* Verso, 2001.

CRSO

WATER RESOURCES: A COMMODITY?

With increasing population and growing water usage, water shortages have become a source of potential and ongoing conflicts. One of the main issues is the competing claims of upstream and downstream nations. As downstream nations attempt to win more water rights, upstream nations try to keep control of the water resources in their territories. While current resources are insufficient in many regions, water will become even scarcer in the future, producing tension among nations sharing rivers.

PROS

Water occurs randomly, just like oil and gas, which are treated as commodities that can be bought and sold. If countries can take advantage of their geographic location to sell oil and gas, they are justified in using water resources to support their economies. Failure to view water as a precious, marketable commodity makes it far less valued and leads to unrestricted water use by environmentally unconscious societies.

Control and management of water—the maintenance of dams, reservoirs, and irrigation systems—costs millions of dollars and is a burden on upstream states' budgets. All of these expenses, including the opportunity cost of fertile lands allocated for reservoirs and dams, should be covered by downstream states, which are the primary consumers of water. For example, that an upstream state cannot use the water flowing through it to produce electricity to offset the costs of water management is unfair.

Water resources are distributed unequally. Uneven distribution and wasteful consumption warrant the introduction of the "pay-for-water" approach. Is it fair to prefer to use water to irrigate infertile semi-deserts downstream rather than using water more efficiently upstream?

CONS

Water is the most vital of Earth's randomly occurring resources; it is essential for survival. Consequently, water-rich countries have no moral right to profit from this resource. Every inhabitant of the planet has an equal right to water, and flowing water has no political boundaries.

It is immoral to charge for water beyond the cost of water systems' maintenance. Water is a commodity only up to a certain point. Once water exceeds a reservoir's capacity, it is not a commodity because it will flow free over the dam. Dams may also create dangerous conditions because downstream states may be flooded if a dam breaks.

Faced with scarcity and drought, states may resort to force to gain control of water resources. Therefore, making water a commodity is a potential cause of many conflicts and should be avoided.

Sample Motions:
This House agrees that water flows can be an article of trade.
This House should endorse international commerce in water resources.
This House does not support legislation for trading of water resources.

Web Links:
- The Transboundary Freshwater Dispute Database. <http://terra.geo.orst.edu/users/tfdd/>
A comprehensive resource on water treaties.
- Water Conflicts. <www.waterconflicts.com>
A site promoting understanding of water rights and water conflicts.
- World Water Council. <www.worldwatercouncil.org>
Site maintained by an international organization dedicated to improving world management of water; offers articles and resources on water issues.
- The World's Water. <www.worldwater.org>
Up-to-date information on global freshwater resources.

Further Reading:
Amery, Hussein A., ed. *Water in the Middle East: A Geography of Peace.* University of Texas, 2000.
De Villiers, Marq. *Water: The Fate of Our Most Precious Resource.* Island Press, 2000.
Postel, Sandra. *Last Oasis: Facing Water Scarcity.* Norton, 1997.

CRSO

WHALING, LIFTING THE BAN ON

Whaling became an important industry in the nineteenth century because of the increased demand for whale oil used in the lamps of that time. The industry declined in the late nineteenth century when petroleum began to replace whale oil. Nevertheless, whales were still hunted for meat and other products, and modern technology made hunters more efficient. The increasing scarcity of many whale species, together with growing recognition of the intelligence and social nature of whales, led to the creation of the International Whaling Commission (IWC), which instituted a ban on whale hunting effective in 1986. In the 16 years since, whale stocks appear to have recovered, although the extent of the recovery is a matter of debate. Some whaling continues for research purposes, mostly by Japan, which has been widely criticized for taking hundreds more whales than can be justified by the needs of scientific inquiry. Recently Japan and Norway have demanded that whaling be allowed to resume under regulation. Most other members of the IWC and conservation groups are opposed.

PROS

Whales should be treated in the same way as other animals, as a resource to be used for food and other products. Whales should not be hunted to extinction, but if their numbers are healthy, then hunting them should be permitted. Scientists have conducted studies of intelligence on dolphins, not whales; these studies, however, cannot measure intelligence in any useful way. Although people in some Western nations view whales as special and therefore in particular need of protection, this view is not widely shared by other countries. To impose it upon others is a form of cultural imperialism.

Whale populations are healthy, particularly those of minke whales, which now number over a million. A resumption of hunting under regulation will not adversely affect their survival. The IWC did not impose the ban on whaling for moral reasons but to prevent extinction. Numbers have now greatly increased. The ban has served its original purpose, and it is time to lift it.

Whale hunting is an important aspect of some cultures. For some groups the hunting of a small number of whales is an important feature in the local subsistence economy, a way of reconnecting themselves with the traditions of their ancestors and affirming their group identity against the onslaught of globalization.

CONS

Killing whales for human use is morally wrong. Many people believe that no animal should suffer and die for the benefit of humans, but even if you do not hold such views, whales should be treated as a special case. Whales are exceptionally intelligent and social beings, able to communicate fluently with each other. The hunting and the killing of animals that appear to share many social and intellectual abilities with humans are immoral.

We should adhere to a precautionary principle. Actual whale populations are not truly known, but they appear to be nowhere near as great as pro-whalers suggest. Until the international ban several species were close to extinction. This could easily happen again if the ban were lifted, especially because regulation is difficult. Even if hunting were restricted to the more numerous species of whales, other, less common species may be killed by mistake.

Traditional hunting methods are often cruel; they involve driving whales to beach themselves and then killing them slowly with long knives, or singling out vulnerable nursing mothers with calves. Because only small numbers are taken with relatively primitive equipment, the hunters do not develop enough skill or possess the technology to achieve the clean and quick kills necessary to prevent suffering. Also, what if the whales these groups wish to hunt are from the most endangered species? Should these groups be permitted to kill them because of their "cultural heritage"? In any case, many traditional practices (e.g., slavery, female genital mutilation) have been outlawed as abhorrent in modern society.

Economic factors argue for a resumption of whaling. In both Japan and Norway remote coastal communities depend on whaling for their livelihood. Both countries have an investment in ships, research, processing centers, etc., that would be wasted if the temporary whaling ban were extended indefinitely.

Whale-watching now generates a billion dollars a year, more income worldwide than the whaling industry brought in prior to the hunting ban. This industry and the jobs it creates in remote coastal areas would be jeopardized if whale numbers fell or if these intelligent animals became much more wary around human activity.

Modern whaling is humane, especially compared to the factory farming of chickens, cows, and pigs. Most whales die instantly or very quickly, and Japanese researchers have developed new, more powerful harpoons that will make kills even more certain.

Whaling is inherently cruel. Before the whale is harpooned, it is usually exhausted by a long and stressful chase. Because whales are moving targets, a marksman can achieve a direct hit only with great difficulty. The explosive-tipped harpoon wounds many whales, who often survive for some time before finally being killed by rifle shots or by additional harpoons. Even when a direct hit is scored, the explosive often fails to detonate. Japanese whaling ships report that only 70% of whales are killed instantly.

Whales damage the fish stocks on which many people depend for their food and livelihood. Culling whales will reduce the decline in fish stocks.

The decline in fish stocks is caused by overfishing, not whale predation. Many whales eat only plankton. The oceans had plenty of fish before large-scale whaling began. Indeed some whales eat the larger fish that prey on commercially important species. A whale cull might have the perverse effect of further reducing valuable fish stocks.

A policy of limited hunting could prevent the potential collapse of the International Whaling Commission. The IWC ban was intended to allow numbers to recover; this temporary measure has served its purpose. If prohibition continues and the IWC becomes more concerned with moral positions than whaling management, Japan and Norway may leave the organization. Nothing in international law prevents them from resuming whaling outside the IWC. Thus, whaling will again be unregulated, with more whales dying and perhaps greater cruelty.

Any system that allows whaling will be open to cheating, given the demand for whale meat in Japan. DNA tests reveal that Japan's "scientific whaling" has resulted in scarce species being taken and consumed. Japan and Norway could leave the IWC but this would provoke an international outcry and possibly sanctions, so it is not in their best interests to do so.

Sample Motions:
    This House would allow whaling to resume.
    This House would harvest the bounty of the sea.
    This House would save the whale.

Web Links:
- The International Whaling Commission. <http://www.iwcoffice.org>
Links to information on the organization as well as to information on conservation efforts and scientific research on whales, dolphins, and porpoises.
- Japan Whaling Organization. <http://www.jp-whaling-assn.com/>
Pro-whaling site offering information on the importance of whaling in Japanese culture and the history of whaling in Japan.
- Makah Whaling: Questions and Answers. <http://www.makah.com/whales.htm>
Native American site explaining plans to resume traditional whaling.
- ODIN. <http://odin.dep.no/odin/engelsk/norway/environment/032001-990108/>
Norwegian Foreign Ministry site with information on that country's decision to resume some whaling.
- Whale and Dolphin Conservation Society. <http://www.wdcs.org/>
Provides information on the status of whales, dolphins, and porpoises as well as efforts to protect them.

Further Reading:
Stoett, Peter J. *The International Politics of Whaling.* University of British Columbia, 1997.

CRBO

WORKFARE

Traditionally people on welfare were not required to work for their benefits. In fact, if they did work, their benefits were cut off. Critics claimed that this approach led to a cycle of poverty, and in the mid-1990s the United States adopted workfare—programs in which welfare recipients had to work for their benefits. This approach, too, has had its critics. Many claim that workfare does not give people the training and opportunities necessary to move out of poverty.

PROS

Making people work for their welfare benefits breaks the dependency culture. Receiving benefits for doing nothing makes individuals too reliant on the state and encourages apathy and laziness. Tying welfare payments to productive work challenges the something-for-nothing assumptions of some welfare recipients and shows that the state has a right to ask for something in return for the generosity of its taxpayers.

Workfare offers a route out of poverty by giving participants the skills needed to find and keep jobs. Productive work increases self-respect and provides the poor with more confidence in their abilities. Individuals who are currently working are also more attractive to potential employers than those who are unemployed.

Making the unemployed work for their welfare benefits calls the bluff of those claiming benefits but not really looking for jobs. Moving from a traditional something-for-nothing welfare policy to a workfare system stops individuals from being a burden on the state. It cuts

CONS

Workfare programs are demeaning to the poor, who are treated as slave labor. No one voluntarily seeks to live on the very low income provided by welfare benefits. Workfare ignores the talents and ambitions of those involved, typically using them for menial tasks and manual labor that teach them no useful skills.

Workfare programs are of little use if no jobs are available. Often programs do not teach people necessary skills, such as literacy, facility with math, and familiarity with modern information technology. Instead workfare recipients are given menial tasks unlikely to make them more employable. Government should invest in education and training programs instead of workfare. Finally, if people on workfare are forced into real jobs that need doing, they should be employed through normal channels.

Putting the unemployed into workfare programs limits their opportunities to look for real work. Some may turn to crime rather than be forced into workfare projects.

welfare rolls very rapidly and allows the government to concentrate upon assisting the truly needy.

Spending money on workfare programs is an investment in people, who gain the opportunity to lift themselves out of poverty. Workfare also benefits the economy, by providing a better supply of labor and by increasing consumer spending. Although workfare programs might cost more per person than just handing out welfare checks, their ability to deter fraudulent claims makes them cheaper in the long run.

Society also benefits from the work done by those in workfare programs that improve the economy or help the elderly and disabled. In many cases the labor they provide would not have been available in any other way.

Workfare projects can be designed so that they do not displace low-paid workers. In any case, many of those in minimum wage jobs do such work for a relatively short time before finding better positions. Consequently workfare will not jeopardize those at the low end of the job market.

Workfare is actually more expensive than traditional welfare programs because the state also has to pay the costs of setting up the programs and supervising them.

Individuals forced into workfare lack incentives to work to a high standard and may be actively disaffected. The work they do is therefore unlikely to benefit anyone and raises a number of issues: Would you drive across a bridge built by workfare labor? Would you trust your aged parent or preschool child to someone on workfare?

Those on workfare will be competing with those who are already employed, particularly workers in menial jobs. Why should local government pay people to pick up litter if workfare teams can be made to do it for much less? If low-paid workers are displaced, the ultimate result may be higher unemployment.

Sample Motions:
This House would introduce workfare.
This House would end welfare.
This House believes in the dignity of labor.

Web Links:
• Is Workfare Working? <http://www.lincproject.org/Newsletters/WRI/TheWord/issuesfolder/barraises.html>
Short article summarizing the opinions of six experts on workfare.
• Workfare: Boom or Bust? <http://www.poetic-justice.com/essays/workfare.htm>
Summary of Canada's experience with workfare.
• Workfare Research and Advocacy Project. <http://www.welfarelaw.org/wrap_progress.html>
Site provides information designed to empower those on workfare.
• Workfare to Wages. <http://www.arc.org/gripp/researchPublications/publications/POWER/powerPg02.html>
Report on the problems of workfare in San Francisco.

Further Reading:
Mink, Gwendolyn. *Welfare's End.* Cornell University Press, 1998.
Peck, Jamie, Frances Fox Piven, and Richard Cloward. *Workfare States.* Guilford Press, 2001.
Shagge, Eric. *Workfare: Ideology for a New Underclass.* Garamond Press, 1997.

ZERO TOLERANCE POLICING

Zero tolerance policing aims at stopping serious crime by clamping down on all types of disorder, including minor misdemeanors such as spray painting graffiti. It mandates set responses by the police to particular crimes, although the courts still maintain discretion in sentencing criminals. Adherents of this policy believe in the "broken windows" theory, which postulates that quality-of-life crimes, like littering or graffiti writing, prompt "respectable" citizens to leave communities, which then fall into decline. They also emphasize that most serious criminals begin their careers with minor crimes. By punishing minor crimes, zero tolerance policing prevents future crimes and, in the process, stops neighborhood decline.

PROS

Zero tolerance policing provides a powerful deterrent to criminals for three reasons. First, it is accompanied by a greater police presence. Research shows a direct link between the perceived chance of detection and crime rates. Second, strict and certain punishment deters criminals. Third, it provides the "short, sharp shock" that stops petty criminals from escalating their criminal behavior. It gives a clear message that crime is not tolerated.

Zero tolerance policing is extremely effective against small-scale drug pushers whose presence in a neighborhood creates an atmosphere in which crime flourishes. Drug use is a major cause of crime because addicts usually steal to support their habit.

Zero tolerance also allows for rehabilitation. A prison sentence, particularly for juveniles, takes them away from the environment that encouraged criminality. Rehabilitation is a central tenet of most penal codes. The large number of police on the streets also increases the supervision of released prisoners, preventing repeat offenses.

Zero tolerance improves the standard of policing. It reduces corruption and racist treatment because individual officers are not given the scope to decide their actions on a case-by-case basis. Their response is set. In addition, zero tolerance policing takes officers out of their cars and puts them into the community where they have contact with individuals. Chases and shootouts actually are less common under zero tolerance.

Zero tolerance is vital for rebuilding inner cities. Zero tolerance reduces the amount of dead ground used for

CONS

Minor offenders, gang members, and the poor are very unlikely to be aware of the punishments for their crimes, so the threat of punishment has little effect on them. Many crimes are a result of poverty and drugs and can be reduced only by structural changes to the society, not by threatening punishment. The idea of a "short, sharp shock" is unconvincing. Labeling people criminals at an early age causes them to perceive themselves as such. This leads petty criminals to commit more serious offenses.

Arresting small-scale pushers and users targets the victims to stop the crime. As well as being unfair, it is ineffective. As long as there is a demand for drugs, there will be drug dealing. Demand can be stopped only by rehabilitation.

Prison sentences contribute to repeat offenses. Prisons should have a rehabilitative role, but they don't. Juveniles with criminal records have difficulty finding jobs, and so are likely to resort to crime. In prison they meet established criminals who both encourage the lifestyle and teach the skills needed to be a successful criminal. Prison often fosters resentment of the police. The harassment that juveniles associate with zero tolerance also creates an extremely antagonistic relationship with the police.

Zero tolerance gives the police almost limitless power in poor communities. They are able to stop and search and harass individuals constantly. Usually ethnic minorities are targeted. New York City saw a tremendous growth in complaints about police racism and harassment after zero tolerance was instituted.

Rebuilding inner city neighborhoods is one of the most powerful ways of targeting crime, and it occurs inde-

drug dealing and so returns parks and open spaces to the community. By offering protection against petty crime, it encourages small businesses (vital for neighborhood rehabilitation) to return to an area.

pendent of zero tolerance. For every city where urban renewal and zero tolerance have together been associated with a falling crime rate (New York City), there is an area where renewal has worked on its own (Hong Kong). Most important for urban renewal is individuals taking pride in their area. This is far more likely to happen when people don't feel persecuted by the police. No police presence is sufficient to defend a business that has not fostered good relations with the community.

We can afford zero tolerance. Protecting businesses and developing a reputation for low crime attracts both people and investment. Deterrence reduces crime and thus the cost of policing; although prisons are expensive, the reduction in recidivism should empty them in time. The most important question is whether we believe spending our tax dollars to guarantee our safety is a good use of that revenue. Most voters say yes.

The enormous expense of zero tolerance in money, manpower, and prisons limits policing. It leaves little money for addressing serious crime. So, although total crime rates may drop, serious crimes may still be a problem.

Sample Motions:
This House believes in zero tolerance policing.
This House would clamp down.
This House believes in strict punishment.

Web Links:
• What Is Zero Tolerance? < http://news.bbc.co.uk/1/hi/uk/182553.stm>
BBC site offering general information on the subject.

Further Reading:
Ayers, Rick, et al., eds. *Zero Tolerance, Resisting the Drive for Punishment.* New Press, 2001.
Dennis, Norman, and Norman Davis, eds. *Zero Tolerance, Policing a Free Society.* Coronet, 1998.
Downes, David M., and Paul E. Rock. *Understanding Deviance: A Guide to the Sociology of Crime and Rule Breaking.* Clarendon, 1988.

CRSO

UNITED NATIONS

UNITED STATES IN THE WORLD

DATE DUE

HIGHSMITH #45115